**Centre for Business, Arts
&Technology**
444 Camden Road
London N7 0SP
020 7700 8642
batlib@candi.ac.uk

CITY AND ISLINGTON
COLLEGE

This book is due for return on or before the date stamped below. You may renew
by telephone. Please quote the barcode number or your student number.
This item may not be renewed if required by another user.

Fine : 5p per day

ONE WEEK LOAN

New American Design
Products and graphics for a post-industrial age

Hugh Aldersey-Williams
Preface by Ralph Caplan
Introduction by Michael and Katherine McCoy

RIZZOLI
NEW YORK

First published in the United States of America in
1988 by
RIZZOLI INTERNATIONAL PUBLICATIONS, INC.
300 Park Avenue South, New York, NY 10010

Reprinted in 1989

Library of Congress Cataloging-in-Publication Data

Aldersey-Williams, Hugh.
   New American Design.

   Bibliography: p.
   Includes index.
   1. Commercial art—United States—History—
20th century. 2. Graphic arts—United States—
History—20th century. 3. Design—United States—
History—20th century. I. Title.
NC998.5.A1A43 1988   745.4′4973   88-42698
ISBN 0-8478-0992-7

Designed by Richelle J. Huff
Set in type by Rainsford Type, Danbury, CT and
David E. Seham Associates Inc., Metuchen, NJ
Printed and bound in Japan

Contents

Photographic, client and design credits

18 Instrumentation Laboratory
18 frogdesign
19 Cousins Design
20 Ford Motor Company
21 Smart Design/Ken Skalski
21 Henry Dreyfuss Associates
22 Ford Motor Company
24 I.D. Two
25 Henry Dreyfuss Associates
25 AT&T Company
25 IBM Corp.
25 Swid-Powell
29 Technology Design/Wood Photography
29 frogdesign
29 Design Logic/Tom Wedell
31 Seymour Chwast/The Push Pin Group
32 Vignelli Associates
32 Department of Health and Human Services
32 Paper Publishing Company
33 Art Spiegelman, Gary Panter/
Raw Books
33 Milton Glaser
33 Koppel and Scher
34 Skolos Wedell and Raynor
35 Sussman/Prejza
35 Émigré Graphics
35 April Greiman
36 Marks Communications/Pacific Data Images
36 Massachusetts Institute of Technology/David Small
37 Vignelli Associates
37 M & Co.
37 Ilona Granet/Fred Krughoff

Chapter 1
40–47 M&Co. Portrait: © Chris Callis (left to right, back row: Eric Pryor, Marion McLusky, Bethany Johns, Sharon Briggs, Ruth Kysileskyj; middle row: Alexander Brebner, Tibor Kalman; front row: David Mann, Susi Cahn, Maira Kalman, Douglas Riccardi, Emily Oberman).
Clients: 1. Florent restaurant; 2. China Grill restaurant; 3. American Institute of Graphic Arts; 4. Sire Record Company; 5. A&M Records; 6–10. Own projects; 11, 12. *Artforum* magazine.
Art direction: All pieces. Tibor Kalman.
Design: 1. Timothy Horn; 2. Riccardi; 3, 5, 6, 10. Alexander Isley; 4. Chris Frantz, Tina Weymouth, Carol Bokuniewicz; 7. Maira Kalman; 8. Tibor Kalman; 9. Maira Kalman, Oberman; 11, 12. Oberman.

48–53 Smart Design Portrait: Philip Sayer, © *Blueprint* (left to right: Tom Dair, Jeanni Gerth, Tucker Viemeister, Annie Breckenfeld, Dan Formosa).
Clients: 1, 2. Sanyei; 3–5, 9, 10. Copco; 6–8. Corning Optics.
Design: 1, 2. Viemeister, Davin Stowell, Dair, John Lonczak; 3–5. Breckenfeld, Dair, Cindy Gerow, Lonczak, Stowell; 6. Viemeister; 7. Dair; 8. Viemeister; 9. Viemeister, Linda Celentano, Brent Markee; 10. Breckenfeld.
Photographs: 1, 2. Ken Skalski; 3. Stowell; 4–6, 8, 9. Viemeister; 7. Dair; 10. Breckenfeld/Viemeister.

54–59 Design Logic Portrait: François Robert (left to right: James Ludwig, David Gresham, Martin Thaler).
Clients: 1–5. View-Master Ideal Group; 6, 7. RC Computer; 8, 9. Own projects; 10–14. Dictaphone Corp.
Design: 8. Gresham; All other pieces. Gresham, Ludwig, Thaler.
Photographs: 1–3, 5, 8–14. Tom Wedell; 4, 6, 7. Robert.

60–67 Drenttel Doyle Partners Portrait: Karen Kuehn (left to right: Bill Drenttel, Debbie Morris-Adams, Leslie Ginway, Stephen Doyle, Lynn Saravis, Rosemarie Sohmer, Katy Delehanty, Tom Kluepfel).
Clients: 1–5. *Spy* magazine; 6. Icon Records; 7, 12–14. Own projects; 8, 9. *New Republic* magazine; 10. *Industrial Design* magazine (adapted from *Catcher in the Rye* by J. D. Salinger, Little, Brown/Bantam); 11. Caroline's at the Seaport restaurant.
Art direction: 1–5, 8, 9. Doyle.
Design: 1–5, 8, 9, 11, 14. Sohmer; 6, 7. Doyle; 10, 12, 13. Kluepfel.
Photographs: 7. George Hein; 10. McGovern and Pivoda.

68–73 Zebra Design Portrait: Wolfgang Kaiser (left: Jörg Ratzlaff, right: Thomas Bley).
Clients: 1. Zelco Industries; 2–4, 9–11. Own projects; 5. Ortopedia; 6. Famus Corp.; 7, 8. AquaSciences.
Design: 1. Zebra Design and Steven Holt; All other pieces. Zebra Design.
Photographs: 11. Kaiser; All others. Zebra Design.

Chapter 2
76–81 Design Continuum Portraits: Dana Sigall (left to right: David Chastain, Gianfranco Zaccai, Bruce Fifield, Jerrold Zindler, John Carl Costello, Jules Pieri, Arthur Rousmaniere, Luis Pedraza, Eric Cohen, Michel Arney, Stephen Guerrera, Christopher Chiodo).
Clients: 1, 2. Instrumentation Laboratory; 3. C and C Metal Products; 4. Photest Diagnostics; 5, 12. Own projects; 6. By Design; 7–9. Symbolics; 10. Au Bon Pain; 11. Ronald Schaich.
Design: 1, 2. Zaccai, Barbara Trezinski, Richard Holtz; 3, 6. Andrew Jones; 4. Arney, Zaccai; 5. Zaccai, Greg Walker; 7–9. Costello; 10, 12. Arney; 11. Zaccai, Costello.
Photographs: 1, 2. Instrumentation Laboratory; 7–9. Symbolics; All others. Design Continuum.

82–89 Doublespace Portrait: Marcus Leatherdale (Jane Kosstrin, David Sterling).
Clients: 1–4, 10–13. Brooklyn Academy of Music; 5–7. Own projects; 8. Modern Mode; 9. Calck Hook Dance Theater.
Art direction and design: 8. David Harrison, designer; All other pieces. Kosstrin, Sterling.
Photographs: 5. Rik Sferra (*Fetish* cover); 8. Elliott Kaufman.

90–95 frogdesign Portraits: frogdesign (clockwise from left: Dan Sturges, Hartmut Esslinger, Herbert Pfeifer, Marek Sekowski, Patricia Roller, Felix Abarca, Jeannette Schwarz, Gert Teschner, Jacinda Madrid, Daniel Aschbacher, Jim Abendroth, Fred Polito, Howell Hsaio, Bettina Teschner, Yvan Tynel, Lorie McDonald, John VanDam, Paul Montgomery, Michael Pizzuti, Ray Gradwohl).
Clients: 1–3. Apple Computer; 4, 5. Worlds of Wonder; 6. König and Neurath; 7. Kaltenbach and Voigt; 8. Helen Hamlyn Foundation; 9. Indusco.
Design: All pieces. frogdesign.
Photographs: 1, 9. Ditmar Henneka; 8. Victor Goico; All others. frogdesign.

96–103 Tom Bonauro Portrait: Jeffery Newbury (Tom Bonauro).
Clients: 1. DNA Lounge; 2–7. Business cards, see names; 8. Sundance Institute; 9–12. Own projects; 13. Prototype Project; 14, 15. San Francisco Art Directors' Club and Advertising Club; 16. Ralph Records; 17. Scharffenberger Cellars; 18. Gary Hutton Interior Design.
Art direction and design: All pieces. Bonauro.
Photograph: 18. Newbury.

104–109 Lunar Design Portrait: Rick English (left to right, back row: Marieke Van Wijnen, Gil Wong, Stacy Neranchi; middle row: Braxton Lathrop, Jeff Hoefer, Ken Wood; front row: Robert Brunner, Jeffrey Smith, Gerard Furbershaw).
Clients: 1. Amtel Systems; 2–4. Esprit Systems; 5. Droidworks; 6. Morrow Designs; 7. EMU Systems; 8. Molecular Dynamics; 9, 10. Own project.
Design: 1. Smith; 2–4, 6, 7, 9, 10. Brunner; 5. Brunner, Smith, Furbershaw, Wood; 8. Smith, Brunner, Lathrop.
Photographs: 2, 8, 10. English; All others. John Long.

Chapter 3
112–117 Design Central Portrait: Larry Friar (left to right, individuals: Gregg Davis, Brenda Tice, Sabina Mueller; group: Rainer Teufel, Drew Holland, Sarah Stibbe, Lois Kolada, Diana Woehnl, Deborah Davis-Livaich, Paul Kolada).
Clients: 1, 6–11. Own projects; 2. Jenn-Air Company; 3–5. Sterling Plumbing Group.
Design: All pieces. Teufel, Davis, Woehnl, Kolada.
Photographs: Friar.

118–125 Tenazas Design Portrait: Richard Barnes (Lucille Tenazas).
Clients: 1. American Institute of Graphic Arts; 2. *Photometro* magazine; 3–6. Business cards, see names; 7, 10, 11. International Paper Company; 8. Artspace; 9. California College of Arts and Crafts; 12–18. Own project.
Art direction and design: 7, 10, 11. Marshall Harmon, art director; All other pieces. Tenazas.
Photographs: 12–18. Barnes.

126–131 Technology Design Portrait: Herb Franklin (left to right: Loyd Moore, Jim Fowler, Nick Barker, Valerie Milliman, Steve Kaneko).
Clients: 1–4, 7. Own projects; 5. Data I/O; 6. Output Technology Corp.
Design: 1–3. Moore, John Cordell, Kaneko; 4. Barker; 5. Moore; 6. Moore, Barker; 7. Moore, David Gilpin.
Photographs: 1, 3, 7. Jeff Curtis; 2, 4–6. Wood Photography.

132–139 Koppel and Scher Portrait: Caroline Greyshock (Terry Koppel, Paula Scher).
Clients: 1–4. Own project; 5. Swatch Watch USA; 6. Blue Note Records; 7. Columbia Records; 8. Prentice-Hall Press; 9–11. EMI Manhattan Records; 12–14. *European Travel and Life* magazine; 15. Harry N. Abrams; 16. School of Visual Arts.
Art direction and design: 1, 2, 5–11, 15, 16. Scher; 3, 4, 12–14. Koppel.

140–145 Polivka Logan Designers Portrait: Stan Waldhauser (left to right: Dan Cunagin, Gene Reshanov, Lars Runquist).
Clients: 1, 2. Synergy III Industries; 3. Maico Hearing Instruments; 4, 5. Minnesota Laser Corp.; 6, 7. Innovex.
Design: 1, 2. Michael Krol, Reshanov; 3. Reshanov, Runquist; 4–7. Reshanov; 1–5. Cunagin, mechanical engineer.
Photographs: Waldhauser.

146–153 Skolos Wedell and Raynor Portrait: Skolos Wedell and Raynor (left to right: Tom Wedell, Nancy Skolos, Kenneth Raynor).
Clients: 1. Symmes, Maini and McKee Associates; 2. Own project; 3. Delphax Systems; 4, 5. Berkeley Typographers; 6. Reynolds-Dewalt; 7. SBK Entertainment; 8–12. Weymouth Design; 13. Kloss Video Corp.
Art direction and design: 1, 2, 4, 6, 7, 13. Skolos; 3, 5. Skolos, Wedell; 8–12. Wedell.
Photographs: Skolos Wedell and Raynor.

Chapter 4
156–161 Tanaka Kapec Design Group Portrait: Roy Gumple (Jeffrey Kapec, Kazuna Tanaka).
Clients: 1. De Puy; 2. Johnson and Johnson Dental; 3, 4. Brother Industries; 5–7. Kliegl Brothers Stage Lighting; 8, 9. Melnor Industries.
Design: 2. Tanaka, Kapec, George Robinson; All other pieces. Tanaka, Kapec.
Photographs: 1, 2, 8, 9. Kenro Izu; 3, 4. Mitsuya Okumura; 5–7. Gumple.

162–169 Émigré Graphics Portrait: Ed Kashi (Rudy VanderLans, Zuzana Licko).
Clients: 1–11. *Emigre* magazine; 12–16. Own projects; 17, 18. *Glashaus* magazine.
Art direction and design: 1–11, 17, 18. VanderLans; 12–16. Licko. (3. John Hersey, illustrator; 6, 11. Tom Bonauro, design; 8. Stefano Massei, photographer; 9. Carlos Llerena Aguirre, Scott Williams, illustrators; 18. Mary C. Podgurski, photographs).

170–175 ID Two Portrait: Mikkel Aaland (left to right: Anne Silckerodt, Daniele De Iuliis, Bob Yuan, Bruce Browne, Bonnie Whalen, Nicholas Dormon, Robin Chu, Bill Verplank, Jane Fulton, Bill Moggridge).
Clients: 1–3. Grid; 4–6. Lynk Corp.; 7–9. Simline; 10–13. Joe; 14–16. Own projects; 17, 18. Newex.
Design: 1, 4–6. Winfried Scheuer; 2, 3. Moggridge; 7–9. De Iuliis; 10–13. Scheuer, Moggridge, De Iuliis; 14–16. Brian Stewart; 17, 18. Chu.
Mechanical engineering: 2, 3. Steve Hobson; 7–9. Dennis Boyle, David Kelley Design; 17, 18. Yuan.
Photographs: 14–16. Michal Venera; All others. Don Fogg.

176–181 Matrix Product Design Portrait: Rick English (Mike Nuttall).
Clients: 1, 2. Metaphor Computer Systems; 3. Own project; 4. Presentation Technologies; 5. Innovative Devices; 6. Microsoft; 7. Convergent Technologies.
Design: 1–3, 5, 7. Nuttall; 4. Nelson Au; 6. Paul Bradley.
Mechanical engineering: 1, 2, 6. Jim Yurchenko, David Kelley Design; 4. Dennis Boyle, David Kelley Design.
Photographs: 1, 5–7. English; 2. Carter Dow; 3. Geoffrey Nelson; 4. John Long.

180–189 April Greiman Portrait: April Greiman (April Greiman).
Clients: 1, 2, 8. Walker Art Center, © MIT Press; 3, 13. Fortuny Museum; 4. Sassons, Copains d'Abord; 5. Pearlsoft; 6. Vertigo Shops; 7. *Main* magazine; 9. China Club restaurant; 10. Great Design Company; 11. Preston Cinema Systems; 12. *Luxe* magazine; 14. Workspace. 15. Los Angeles Olympic Organizing Committee; 16. Pacific Design Center; 17, 18. Sebastian International.
Art direction and design: All pieces. Greiman.
Photograph: 3. Paolo Utimtergher.

Author's note

It is customary in books of this sort to begin with an apologia for the inevitably subjective criteria used to determine who is included and who is not. *New American Design* did not set out with such a selection: no strict guidelines were used to select the designers included here. Rather, certain common characteristics emerged as the list grew that painted a picture of the practices that are responsible for what amounts to a renaissance in American design.

The great majority of the designers in this book are in their thirties. They are in independent practice; their firms typically employ around a dozen people. The single one-man operation and the few firms with more than twenty staff represent the extremes of their size. They have been in business in most cases no less than three and no more than a dozen or so years. They have, in other words, been around long enough to indicate staying power in the ability to win and retain clients, but not so long as to have become ossified into a formula approach to the solution of clients' problems.

No in-house corporate design departments are represented: this is not to criticize the work these groups do, but it is indicative of where clients, sometimes even those with their own full-time designers, increasingly look for good design.

Graphic designers and industrial (product) designers are the subject of this book. Other equally active design fields, such as furniture, interiors, and architecture, have been excluded as fields that in comparison, garner a disproportionate amount of media attention. My purpose is to show that the people who design the products and graphics that all of us use and see every day are doing work that is every bit as creative, and sometimes more valuable, than that by "designer" superstars in these other fields. It is my hope also to give American design a platform that will encourage a fair comparison with design from Europe and Japan, regions whose design has been far better documented in recent years.

The projects illustrated have been chosen partly from work done for clients, in order to show what the market judges acceptable at this time, and partly from non-commercial work—competition entries, design studies, and self-promotional work—in order to give an idea of what is possible. The range of clients is purposely broad, from large corporations to avant-garde arts organizations among graphic design clients, and from manufacturers of everything from cheap toys to sophisticated electronic instruments among industrial design clients.

Graphic designers and industrial designers have not been segregated in order to emphasize their shared influences and esthetics. Instead, chapter headings are deliberately vague and cross-disciplinary. They are to be read as signposts for the directions in which design is going, rather than as labels for mutually exclusive movements or professional activities. The inclusion of any design firm in one chapter does not exclude that firm from the themes expressed in other chapters. April Greiman, for instance, is one of the few designers using computers to good effect, and earns her place in the chapter on technology for that reason. But this is not to imply that her work lacks occasional touches of humor, emotional charge, or historical reference, the topics of the other three chapters. Loyd Moore of Technology Design is in the chapter on allusion, but he uses his referential design language to generate humorous or otherwise emotional responses to largely technology-based products.

Designers are not only accept of a broader set of design philosophies, they also increasingly ignore the boundaries that have traditionally defined their professions. Perhaps it is the example of European designers, whose work often mixes formal and functional projects in a variety of fields, or perhaps it is the fact that American architects are once again designing artifacts as well as buildings, but there is a new entrepreneurial spirit abroad in American design. Graphic designers are turning their hands to sculpture and textiles and even licensing their own product manufacture; industrial designers are doing interiors and graphics as well as their own lamps and furniture. These esthetic flights of fancy are something that the older generation of industrial designers could never have permitted themselves, but are to be welcomed now for the effect they will have in enriching their more conventional design.

The portfolio pages for each design group show a critical selection of recent work. Detailed captions have been omitted from these pages in order to let the design speak better for itself. Client and design credit listings are given on page 6.

My thanks are due to the design groups included here for their tolerance of my deadlines and production demands for the supply of illustrations; to designer Richelle J. Huff for her design of the book; to Ralph Caplan and to Michael and Katherine McCoy for honoring this book with their particular expert insights; to Jay Doblin and Larry Keeley, Mildred Friedman, Milton Glaser, Steven Heller, Deborah Karasov, Ellen Lupton, Deane Richardson, RitaSue Siegel, John Thackara, and James Woudhuysen for their observations; and especially to Tibor Kalman, Lisa Krohn, Dean Morris, and Tucker Viemeister for their encouragement and critical commentary. Finally, Jeremy Myerson, editor of *DesignWeek*, and Annetta Hanna and Chee Pearlman, editors of *Industrial Design*, provided the opportunities that began and sustained this sequence of interviews. I am indebted to them for their support.

Hugh Aldersey-Williams
New York, January, 1988

Sometime in the 1960s Gerald Gulotta designed some drinking glasses that were a delight not just to behold but to hold. At the bottom there was a sort of plinth around which the drinker's finger pleasurably and naturally curled. It functioned gloriously as the digital equivalent of a bar rail, and you didn't have to leave home to enjoy it. Now Lisa Krohn, a 24-year old student at Cranbrook, has designed into a prize-winning telephone-answering machine a bookish tactility that promises to provide a comparable feeling of rightness in use. She is the youngest of the young and fairly young designers included in this interpretive survey of new American design by the Anglo-American design writer Hugh Aldersey-Williams, who now lives in London after several years in New York.

We Americans have been surveyed and interpreted by the English before. In 1832 Anthony Trollope's mother returned to London from Cincinnati and published *Domestic Manners of the Americans*. Americans didn't like what Mrs. Trollope said, and her book was not popular here until it was revived in the 1950s, by which time there were very few Americans left who had any domestic manners to speak of. Not to worry. Our theatre, politics, music and literature have endured English critics and profited from them.

But when American *design* was new they left it pretty much alone. Postwar England had industrial problems of its own to address, and the energies of people who might have examined our national design tendencies went into the kind of government sponsored design evangelism that has never quite caught on here, although not for lack of trying. Scholars like Nikolaus Pevsner, J. Bronowski, and Siegfried Giedion illuminated the design process for all of us, but without any special attention to the colonies. Not until Reyner Banham identified the New Brutalism did we sense anyone across the Atlantic looking over our shoulders. Banham's opinions came thundering across the sea through the medium of design journals. Banham himself came soon after. His scholarship and his assessing wit were intact and his periodic residence in the United States never militated against his objectivity.

The British are still coming. And still staying for dinner. Like Banham, Hugh Aldersey-Williams fuses a journalist's instinct for what is current with a critic's concern for where it fits into some larger picture. He is, however, more journalist than critic. As a journalist he has written an enlightening survey of what younger American designers are doing right now, and of what they are saying about it. And as a journalist he sometimes records the opinions of designers as if they necessarily represent original, or even clear, thinking, as indeed some of them do. At times I wish he would cast a colder eye on our designs and listen to our designers with a more skeptical ear.

This is particularly true in regard to such trends in conversational design as "product semantics." Kingsley Amis's most memorable character is Jim Dixon, protagonist of *Lucky Jim*, a college professor who happened not to know what *scholasticism* was, although he "read, heard, and even used the word a dozen times a day without knowing, though he seemed to." Similarly, we know designers who speak a dozen times a day of *metaphors* and *semantics* without knowing what they mean, or even that they mean anything.

Is that important? Only if it confuses us or them, or the issues. We cannot, in any case, hold Aldersey-Williams responsible for the way his characters talk—he is not a novelist—and his book reflects the important fact that some of our most talented young designers have an interest in expressive design that goes beyond the trendy. Although what designers say may sound depressingly like the discovery of the old, Aldersey-Williams is enough of both journalist and critic to sense that if our most talented designers keep on talking about something, this in itself gives it a certain importance, however transitory. In respect to "product semantics," various designers are trying to deal with a phenomenon that design critics have also been noticing for decades. As Victor Papanek points out in *Design for Human*

Scale, designers, design critics and end users had agreed more than 200 years ago that "design should show how a tool was used and what it was used for," but this became harder to do as tools became more complex. There is a corollary: the same technology that made tools more complex vastly increased the number of options in determining how they looked.

At the same time that technology—microminiaturization in particular—was making it stylistically unnecessary to do anything, it was making it possible to do everything. If an answering machine, a word processor and a burglar alarm were all essentially contained in a chip, they could be housed in the same kind of box. But they could also be housed in almost any shape a designer responsibly (or irresponsibly) chose. Conventional industrial design wisdom held that an object ought to look like what it is and does. But now we have objects that are no longer tied to what they do. Functional Modernism emphasized the revelation of a product's working parts. But now there are likely to be no working parts visible to the naked eye. This was initially true of specialized instruments in particular, but today it applies to calculators, lighters, alarm clocks, VCRs and other equipment of daily living—an activity which relies on the same specialized instrumentation once reserved for advanced laboratory research.

In a 1964 article in the British magazine *Design*, I described an American electronic device as having "the restrained curves, the chromed bezel of everything else." The designer exploded with a letter protesting that it was impossible for a product to look like everything else, since everything else didn't look alike (he was right, if distressingly literal) and that I obviously had not understood the parameters of the problem. That was at a time when American designers talked about parameters as much as they now do about metaphors, and with about as much fidelity to meaning. It was, however, appropriate, for my point had been that, although many of the constraints that governed form were disappearing, we often failed to face the design implications of their absence.

The elimination of constraints always appears to be liberating, but the experienced designer will not rush to shout "Free at last!" In design, as in life generally, if we have no constraints, we have to invent them. Ascetics know how to do this, but not many of them practice design professionally. The new technology simultaneously frees designers and places a burden on them that design schools have never taught anyone to carry.

The new American designers that Aldersey-Williams reports on here are either product designers or graphic designers. Gianfranco Zaccai is the kind of industrial designer that industrial designers of an earlier generation might have dreamed of becoming when they and their profession grew up. He carries projects through the entire range of design-related services. But no one in an earlier generation would have dreamed of Tibor Kalman, who brings to both graphics and products a quality that the late Arthur Drexler once described as unique for industrial designers—a sense of humor. Actually, many industrial designers have a sense of humor. What is unique is the ability to express it in work that serves clients. The idea that products can be fun, and that many have to be fun in order to serve their purposes well, is also manifest here in the work of Tucker Viemeister of Smart Design.

Some of the design here is new only because the designers are, or because it is recent, or because technically it could not have been done in an earlier period. The designs of April Greiman, on the other hand, almost always *are* new. With new technologies shrewdly and enthusiastically integrated into them, they represent a running departure from the work of earlier designers and from her own work as well.

Does newness matter? "I'd rather be good than original," Mies said, and who wouldn't? In the end, What's new? is a reportorial question, always subordinate to the critical question: What's good? Here is a selection of designers who are new and good. That matters.

Ralph Caplan
Author of *By Design*, design columnist and consultant.

American design is facing a new complexity of its role at the confluence of the cultures of art and science. It is the profession between: between people and their technology, between the Apollonian and the Dionysian, between the rational and the emotional, between *mythos* and *logos*, between the production system and the consumer, between the sensual and the cerebral. But the challenge and the excitement of design is in the reconciliation and synthesis of opposites, and the particular aura of American design emanates from the oppositions found within the culture. By turns romantic and pragmatic, the new American design reflects not the America of isolationism and simplistic values, but the America of pluralism and experimentation, engaging in the international speculation about the nature of design in the information age.

American design has found its unique voice in the world before, in the 1930s when industrial and graphic design formulated an exuberant style that mythologized industry, and in the 1940s and 50s when people like Charles Eames and Paul Rand interpreted post-war culture with an optimistic design vocabulary for a new way of living. American design at its best has always been inclusive, open to influences from Europe and elsewhere, but always transforming them by the energy of its expansive cultural landscape.

In the twentieth century, it has been difficult to assign the exclusive origin of particular design ideas to one country or another. Designers around the world share the common history of early twentieth-century European Modernism, which criss-crossed national boundaries from the start. It was the conscious intention of the seminal Modern thinkers to establish an international movement, spreading their new ideas with missionary fervor. The upheavals of the 1930s dispersed the Modernist prophets around the world, and the United States was a major recipient of this wealth of new ideas. Philip Johnson and Henry-Russell Hitchcock correctly labeled twentieth-century Modernism as the International Style.

Although there are distinct characteristics of national design movements, they all draw from the international core of Modernism. What is clear is that design ideas, whatever their origin, take on the distinctive flavor or coloration of the host culture. Mies van der Rohe found in Chicago a set of influences and opportunities entirely different from those in Berlin. The new American design exhibits many qualities that are inescapably American, even as it shares roots and current concerns with our international colleagues. An international dialog should not result in a synthetic universal language devoid of regional character. It should be possible for a regional design language to have universal human appeal while retaining the flavor of its cultural origins.

What is the new American design? Some of it celebrates technology, some of it critiques technology. Some reveals process, some conceals it. Some is an homage to history, some denies history. Most is humanist in its intent if not in its result. All is non-ideological, reflective of the pragmatic roots of the culture. In fact, it is difficult to talk about *an* American design because of its breadth and heterogeneity.

The diversity of current design is in a way a reaction to the homogeneous design of the preceding decades. The 1960s and 1970s were a period of systematizing and rationalizing for both industrial design and graphic design. Multinational corporations responded to the idea of a universal minimalist design language in everything from computer systems to corporate identity to unify their product lines and public communications around the world. Designers embraced this consistent design language as a way of visibly demonstrating that they were professionals subscribing to generally recognized professional practices, and not to the erratic individualism of the previous decades of design.

But once this process of unification had succeeded, by the mid to late 1970s, designers were beginning to question the need and desirability for such an artificially limited design language. The influences that began to work to liberate design expression came from several disparate sources. Some were philosophical, some were cultural and some were technological.

The philosophical insight provided by structuralism and later, post-structuralism, was to realize the importance of verbal and visual language to our perception of the world. The philosophical chain of events leading to the present awareness of object as cultural sign, starting with Ferdinand de Saussure's definition of the sign as the union of signifier and signified, and broadening into the structuralist notion that we experience the world and form our cultural concepts through language, led designers to realize that they were the sign makers, the interpreters of the artifact culture. Robert Venturi and the Pop artists, in particular, opened the doors for designers to look at the vernacular as raw material to be transformed into a design language that acknowledged its sources in the popular culture even as it *became* the popular culture.

These ideas formed the basis for one of the most common characteristics of the new American design: the analytical and ironic use of images from popular culture and from history. First, there is the use of images that because of their innocence, their nostalgia and their naivete create a sense of irony seen as they are from our present, and more cynical, perspective. Then there is the analytical, virtually anthropological, dissection and reassembly through the processes of collage and assemblage. It may be that the fascination with fragmentation and the juxtaposition of seemingly unrelated images may stem from the fragmented nature of our lives today, a kind of endless channel switching.

The use of images from design history reflects our recognition that there is a genealogy of design, a family tree that we are part of and that we should acknowledge through reference and *homage* as do architects, painters, film-makers and writers. There is a richness to much of the work containing historical reference that derives from the sense of the passage of time, and also from the different meaning that the earlier ideas take on in this new time and cultural context. There is in many of these design *homages* a genuine affection for, and appreciation of, the earlier work. The use of historic reference is particularly important in that it represents a turning away from the Modernist idea that designers are bound to use only a "new" language to solve contemporary problems. This is a dictum that has been hanging over designers' heads since the early Modernists decried historicism as bourgeois sentimentality. All historicist design must, however, recognize the new meaning that the passage of time bestows and not merely re-present its images untransformed. It is crucial to assess intentions behind this work. Designers' understanding and viewpoint toward their reworking of these twentieth-century design themes makes the essential difference between reference, critique, appropriation, parody, pastiche and cannibalism.

We are a self-aware, self-analytical culture that is becoming accustomed to *reading* its object and events, so it is no surprise that design as a profession has become more self-referential as well. This is another aspect of the new American design. It is self-referential. There is a great deal of design about design. Much current design is about the process of design and the production of the results, the materials and their transformation. There is also the aspect of enigma, the unknowable and the ambiguous which exists in some of the current work, which gives it an intriguing depth. There is the feeling that you can never quite get to the bottom of it. Ambiguity is sometimes conveyed through minimalism, with a zen-like reduction of form: less information, implying more meaning. More often it is conveyed through layering of images and information. The viewer is perhaps easily able to understand the first layers and then must work through deeper layers to grasp the more profound meaning. Much design work challenges its audience actively to decode its meaning or to propose new meanings.

One thing is clear: innocence is gone. The naiveté of much of the design of previous decades has been replaced by very *knowing* work. The design scene has reached a mature stage of codification and intellectualized self-knowledge reminiscent of Mannerism, symptomatic of the late stages of a movement's development. While early Modernism was often raw, powerful and full of eccentricity, the postwar classic Modernists reached a clarified purity of concept. Recent work, while rooted in Modernism, elaborates on various segments of its historical phases with skillfully complex reiterations.

While some of the current design uses vestiges of the utopian design languages of the 1920s, none of it proposes utopian themes. At best, all deal with the smaller-scale issues of the experience of daily life and commentary on our culture. This comes from the conviction that design affects our lives as the cumulative effect of many small, civilized experiences rather than as one grand utopian scheme.

Changes in technology have profoundly affected the role of design in the culture and our view of ourselves as designers. As microelectronics have dematerialized technology and given it an intelligent presence it never had before, designers are forced to confront *meaning* rather than simply to package machinery in the most efficient way. Software writers and designers alike now recognize that it is the character of the machine that affects how we respond to it and what role it plays in our lives. The form of the product and the quality of its software language interact to determine the quality of the experience that we have in dealing with everything from automatic teller machines to computers. In this we find the concerns of industrial design and graphic design converging. Like graphic design, product and environmental design are increasingly defining their function as communication. Content and meaning are now shared concerns of all the design disciplines. Technology is becoming amorphous. The availability of extraordinarily versatile plastics and flexible control and display technologies now raises the question: If it can be anything, what should it be? The designer is now more than ever the interpreter of the meaning of the object to the user, the mediator between people and their object/information environment.

What American designers are saying through their design reveals much about their vision of the relationship of technology to people. Some are rendering machines as serious and cerebral. They feel that, as an extension of our intelligence, the form of the machine should be an intellectually rigorous composition designed to invite contemplation and respect as well as to reveal its operation. Others are attempting to humanize design by making it playful or casual, rather than formal in nature. If technology engenders uneasiness, why not make it friendlier and have it reach out to the user? The object as companion is an extension of this idea, a presence that you can relate to. Some are concerned with revealing the inner nature of the machine, the invisible processes within, with the intent of demystification. If technology is threatening because of its inscrutability, why not clarify how it works? Other current work deals with the place of an object in your daily life ritual, maintaining that those objects that are important to you, be it your coffee machine or your personal computer, should celebrate their role through their design. This is requiring the designer to be much more aware of the meaning of the formal gesture of the machine and how it relates to the user.

The designers published here do not believe in impersonal or "value-free" design. Each gives evidence of a personal vision or hand in his or her work. Gone is the invisible designer, the unseen hand. As a result, the work is far more biased than in the past, taking stronger positions conceptually and formally. The onrushing technologies of artificial intelligence and computer-aided design, rather than posing a threat to designers, are serving simply to clarify that which is most important about design. Designers who design like machines will be replaced by machines. It is not the digital but the intuitive, not the measurable but the poetic, and not the mechanical but the sensual, which provide the essential humanization of design.

Michael and Katherine McCoy
Co-Chairmen, Design Department
Cranbrook Academy of Art

Towards a designed American product

Toward the end of 1987 there appeared near the front of *Time* magazine a double-page advertisement for a new personal terminal from Apple Computer. It said a lot about the way we are now being encouraged to think of products and their design. Against a backdrop of glass brick, it showed what amounted to a still-life composition. The computer was joined by such design icons as Richard Sapper's Tizio lamp and the Mont Blanc fountain pen. It was "new product" as "cult object."

1987 was a good year for American design. Something happened that had never happened before. American designers won two of Europe's most prestigious awards for industrial design excellence. A Boston consultancy, Design Continuum, won a *Compasso d'Oro*, the Milan award that is the nearest thing industrial design has to a Nobel prize. Its design of a complex piece of medical equipment for an Italian client could have been an antiseptic white box. Instead it employs color highlights and appealing sensuous paths for the operator to follow as he works that bring a degree of fun to his job. And Lisa Krohn, a 24-year-old industrial design student at the Cranbrook Academy of Art, won the $70,000 first prize in Forma Finlandia, a competition run by a Finnish petrochemical company, Neste, for design in plastics. She beat entries from West Germany, Britain, and Scandinavia. Her design for a telephone-answering machine avoids the characterless shape that such products often assume by using a metaphor from everyday life to make it both easier to use and more attractive and familiar. Called Phonebook by its co-designer, Tucker Viemeister of Smart Design in New York, the machine looks like an open book. Its shape is powerfully expressive of the cultural continuity of communicated information, from yesterday's medium of print to today's electronic form. But Phonebook's particular cleverness is that it also works like a book, with "pages" that turn over to switch between electronic functions.

These products exemplify two things about the best of current Amer-

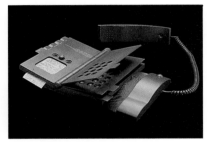

"Phonebook," a telephone-answering machine designed by Lisa Krohn, winner of the 1987 Forma Finlandia competition for design with plastics.

The Space-Tel telephone by Cousins Design is a polished example of a European style of design used in America. It is in the collection of the Museum of Modern Art and other museums.

ican industrial design. The first is that it can meet the highest criteria for form that have come to characterize European design, seen, for example, in the products of Philips, Krups, and Braun. The second is a more particularly American quality that tempers this highly formal esthetic, the result of 50 years' refinement of the Bauhaus and Ulm school's teaching of design, with a natural exuberance. American design now has a sense of fun, a spirit, that is sometimes lacking in the museum elegance of much European design.

Indeed, the museums, led by the example of the Museum of Modern Art, have encouraged the perception among the public and among designers that such elegance is what makes good design.[1] With a few notable exceptions[2], American designers after the Second World War largely rejected their own unique heritage in design from the 1920s and 1930s and set to emulate this "museum" style—what one designer says has now become a "Euclidean vernacular." For many reasons, often relating to cost of manufacture, the American "European" design was generally a poor imitation of the real thing. Meanwhile, genuinely American design, using more pragmatic determinants of form and adopting such populist aspects as woodgrain and gilt, did not make it into the museum collections, received little discussion or critical analysis, and have been largely forgotten today.[3]

There are signs now of a change, paradoxically more noted abroad than at home. "Today's economic environment is likely to force American design to break out of its anonymity and neglect . . . [it] is likely to have a bigger impact, over the closing years of this century, than many Europeans might suspect."[4] At the end of 1985, in the wake of Worlddesign in Washington DC, the first major international industrial design conference held on American soil, it was noted that design was back in fashion and that the search was on for a new American esthetic.[5] The conference stimulated a brief surge in general press coverage for industrial design, but now the subject is once again mostly ignored from day to day.[6] Even the novelty of two Americans

2. The furniture of Charles and Ray Eames, for example, is in the American tradition of technical innovation, and has a pragmatic rather than a purist approach to form. Loewy *et al* continued to develop their own design languages and did not adopt European Modernism.

4. British design critic James Woudhuysen of Fitch and Company, at the Design in Furniture exhibition, London, October, 1987.

5. "America the beautiful?" *Economist,* 14 December, 1985.

Notes
(Complete references to authors mentioned in the notes are given in the Bibliography on page 192)

1. Arthur Drexler largely excluded mechanical products from the MOMA collection, concentrating on craft products in furniture, textiles, and ceramics, because "too often their design is determined by commercial factors irrelevant, or even harmful, to aesthetic quality." Drexler, 1959, quoted in Sparke, 1986. The museum instead collected "mostly Italian and German products . . . and tended to be associated with the more European-oriented aspects of US design in this century." Sparke, ibid.

3. *In Good Shape: Style in Industrial Products 1900–1960* virtually omits American products from the 1940s and 1950s. Bayley, 1979.

6. *Time* and *Newsweek* have occasional design columns, but these concentrate on design celebrities and on architecture. Among business publications only the *Wall Street Journal* has any regular commitment to the subject, where Stephen MacDonald's perceptive and knowledgeable writing does much to make up for the dearth of coverage elsewhere.

Ford Taurus, designed by Jack Telnack and Ford design team.

winning European awards escaped much press attention.

Many manufacturers with insulated home markets remain unconvinced of the value of design.[7] Its acceptance is understandably higher where companies are competing in global markets. The new Ford Taurus, for example, won acclaim for a design that responds to Japanese and European car styling without merely imitating it. Its so-called "jellybean" aerodynamic shape is at once acceptable to a broad range of markets, yet still expressive of an American esthetic.[8] Ford not only realized the value of design in the product itself; it also uses it as a marketing tool in its advertisements.

The Taurus represents a rare exception. American designers report part of their work often involves convincing clients that they can do what they say they can. Designers with European clients note that this time-consuming struggle is not so much part of business life there. Research by the National Endowment for the Arts traces the ignorance of design back to most businessmen's training. Only one business school—Boston University's School of Management—offers regular courses on design.[9]

Government bodies such as the NEA and the Department of Commerce are looking more closely at the cultural and economic role for design in American industry. Design protection legislation was discussed as a rider to the 1987 trade bill.[10] These are small steps in the right direction. Some commentators predict, and many designers hope for, more comprehensive government intervention on their behalf. Many countries, among them Japan, Canada, and Britain, have government bodies to promote local industry's appreciation of design. But this form of support seems unlikely to gain ground here where businesses have learned to survive, or have perished, without such mothering. Thomas Watson, Jr., chairman emeritus of IBM Corporation, who was key to implementing the company's design policy 30 years ago, expresses the attitude well: "If I used my imagination and creativity and funds to develop a good design, I would hate to feel that some government

7. J.C. Penney, for example, disbanded its widely respected in-house design department in 1986.

8. For an appraisal of the Ford Taurus, see Earl Powell, "On the Road Again," *Industrial Design*, November/ December, 1987.

9. Deborah Karasov of the NEA Design Arts Program, private communication citing, among others, Stephen MacDonald, *Wall Street Journal*, 27 April, 1987.

10. The Industrial Innovation and Technology Act, 1987, sponsored by Sen. Dennis DeConcini, seeks to amend the copyright law to protect works of design, a provision that already exists in a number of other countries. It is now back in committee and unlikely to pass into law in the near future, due to lobbying from auto insurance companies who wanted to protect their access to cheaper Far-East-made replacement car parts and from typographers who wanted to be able to use new typeface designs without penalty. Conversations with Cooper Woodring, former IDSA president, and Rita Kassel, chairman of an industrial designers' coalition lobbying for the bill, July, 1987 and February, 1988.

11. Conversation with the author, November, 1985.

body would be urging on one of my competitors. If he was stupid enough not to design his products well, then in our free-enterprise system he deserves to slip back, just as IBM would if we began to neglect that area."[11]

There are parallels between the 1980s and the Depression period that saw emergence of the industrial design profession. Despite the very different economic and political philosophies prevailing in these two periods, their problems are both ones that can be addressed by design. "The search for a more emotive, daring aesthetics unites the contemporary era with that of 50 years ago. So, very importantly, does the non-price nature of commercial competition."[12] In the 1920s and 1930s, competition was stimulated not by imports but by the shrinking spending power of the home market. Design then was used to stimulate demand through rapid styling changes, a process ominously referred to as consumer engineering.[13] Today, design serves to stimulate consumption in a similar manner, differentiating products that use nearly identical technology.

12. Woudhuysen, ibid.

13. There are other parallels too in these two periods of relative techno-logical stasis. The context of 1920s and 1930s design patronage is well covered in Meikle, 1979.

The American heritage

It is perhaps ironic that one of the events signifying the birth of the American industrial design profession during the 1930s was when an Englishman, Sigmund Gestetner, owner of the duplicating machine company that bears his name, asked Raymond Loewy, a Frenchman by birth, to see what he could do to improve one of his products. Loewy took Gestetner's old machine and wrought great things with it. The event is well documented, not least by Loewy himself.[14]

14. Loewy, 1951.

The special American contribution to the emergence of a culture of the mass-manufactured product dates back rather further. Arthur Pulos places the origin of the ubiquitous design dictum, "form follows function," to an American around 1770[15], although it is more commonly ascribed to the Chicago architect Louis Sullivan, speaking more than a century later.[16] Early on, the functionalism of American design was matched by technological in-

15. Pulos, 1983.

16. See, for example, Heskett, 1980.

In some cases, the daring esthetics of the past are directly evoked. "SteamShip" travel iron for Sanyei by Smart Design echoes Henry Dreyfuss's 1938 "Twentieth Century Limited" steam locomotive for the New York Central System, with a bulbous streamlined shape common to both.

The first mass-production auto, the Model T Ford, used innovative manufacturing technology rather than esthetic embellishment to win customers.

17. American patents out-stripped British by more than 50 percent as early as 1820, for example. Pulos, ibid.

novation and engineering inventiveness.[17] This "yankee ingenuity" in a way is American design's substitute for European craftsmanship. Whereas an artisanal tradition formed the basis of design in Europe, in America it was the engineer who held this position in society. The engineer is still more highly regarded in the United States than in many countries, and the engineer's influence on design is correspondingly stronger. Tocqueville observed that an artisan in an aristocracy (a forerunner of the designer in Europe) was happy to sell his work at a high price to the few who could afford it. But in the American democracy it made more sense to sell at a low price to all, the reduction in price being dependent on the designer's technical ingenuity in increasing production without losing too much quality.[18] Tocqueville also saw the deficiencies of this expedient approach, writing that: "the democratic principle not only tends to direct the human mind to the useful arts, but it induces the artisan to produce with great rapidity many imperfect commodities, and the consumer to content himself with these commodities. . . . The handicraftsmen of democratic ages endeavor not only to bring their useful productions within the reach of the whole community, but they strive to give all their commodities attractive qualities which they do not in reality possess."[19] Nevertheless, in this attitude is the principle of American design that exists today. Here is its strength in its readiness to adapt to new production technologies, and its weakness in too readily conceding quality to quantity, and in substituting styling for design.

Innovative American manufacturing methods came to European attention by the time of the Great Exhibition in London in 1851.[20] But the American market also retained a fondness for craft-made products from Europe, and the view that "good design" came from abroad gained ground despite attempts by American designers to organize and state their case. "The American manufacturers and merchandisers were not moved by all these attempts to establish a viable basis for American design in the industrial

18. Tocqueville, 1835.

20. Heskett, ibid.

19. Tocqueville, ibid.

arts. No sooner had the [First World War] armistice been signed than advertisements began to appear from merchandisers promoting the fact that their stock of imported products had been replenished. Industry ignored the exhibitions being held to show what American designers could do."[21]

American innovation in areas other than manufacturing technology were also to have a great impact on design. The time-and-motion studies of F.W. Taylor[22] around the turn of the century led to the overhaul of American factory environments and was one of the foundations for the modern science of ergonomics or human-factors engineering. Later, human-factors studies by the American military for its own ends had broader applications in the civil environment. Although the United States soon lost its lead in civil ergonomics to Germany and Scandinavia, a few corporations, such as Xerox and Texas Instruments, continue to do research that will play a large role in determining the ease of use of future "intelligent" electronic products.

Form, function and styling

Visually, American products of the first two decades of the century left much to be desired. American representatives attended the 1925 Paris Exposition des Arts Decoratifs "but the USA had refused to exhibit because it lagged so far behind Europe."[23] Such national design esthetic as did emerge was a product of the industrial functionalism that historically underpinned American manufacture.[24]

Manufacturers began to realize the need for "styling," and the new industrial designers were happy to oblige. Loewy, who had come to America after the First World War, in particular shaped or reshaped several products that became the very icons of America.[25] Meanwhile, Walter Dorwin Teague, Loewy's senior by a few years, designed the first plastic mass-produced camera for Kodak, and Henry Dreyfuss, a generation younger than Teague, created the standard Bell telephone. The seductive lines of the machine-age style, promoted most flamboyantly by Loewy and Norman Bel Geddes, man-

21. Pulos, ibid.

22. Taylor, 1961.

23. Sparke, ibid.

24. Compare, for example, locomotive and railroad car designs from the United States and Europe in the nineteenth century, shown in Heskett, ibid. Despite an apparently well defined function in each region, they adopted very different appearances. Their forms drew less from function than from different interpretations of function by the American designers working to a system of standardized parts assembly, and European designers with a tradition of craft-based manufacture. A century later, there are equally great differences in the even more functionally constrained designs for American and Soviet spacecraft, which are explained in cultural terms.

25. Loewy's oeuvre includes the Greyhound bus, the Airstream trailer, the Lucky Strike cigarette carton, and parts of the NASA Skylab. Loewy, 1979.

23

Grid Compass computer terminal designed by ID Two. This magnesium-cased flat-screen terminal takes minimalism to excess.

aged to convince people that this was the first time that form and function were fully integrated in design. In fact, very nearly the opposite was true. That an abstract geometric basis for form-giving, such as characterized their designs, should automatically be considered functional is credit more to the persuasiveness of these designers than to their honesty.[26] From here on, form and function are misleadingly considered as two separate entities whose union it is the designer's job to bring about. As the designers of the machine age became more self-conscious, design began to express supposed machine qualities more blatantly, and a literal interpretation of the form-function equation became increasingly ridiculous.[27]

After the Second World War, the design of quotidian consumer products diverged sharply from that of objects with powerful status associations. Automobiles grew tailfins and furniture adopted flowing, organic shapes. But more mundane items—telephones, typewriters, radios and televisions, and kitchen appliances—generally rejected expressionism in favor of the clean lines of the International Style. Designers accepted the Modern movement as a way to demonstrate to clients that their profession was maturing. Not everyone, after all, could be as charismatic or as persuasive as Raymond Loewy, and it was thought the growing profession would serve itself better by adopting a quieter image.

In Europe at this time, there was a willingness among some companies to invest in the design fees and the tooling costs required to make an elegant product. So while the same minimal style was in vogue around the world, products from Philips in the Netherlands, Braun in West Germany, and Olivetti in Italy, and later, Sony in Japan, often looked better than those from their American competitors. The more astute American companies reacted by making their products look more European. IBM, for example, took its cue from its rival Olivetti in the 1950s. It appointed Eliot Noyes, who had been working for Geddes, as design consultant with responsibility to

26. The myth of form following function in these designs was exposed in Reyner Banham's essay, "A Throwaway Aesthetic," reprinted in Banham, 1981.

27. Loewy's streamlined pencil-sharpener was the most famous embodiment of this contradiction. There are excellent accounts of the flight into self-absorbed frivolous excess of the machine esthetic and the streamlining that followed it in Meikle, ibid.

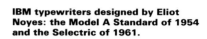

Opposing design philosophies in evidence at AT&T: post-Modern headquarters by Philip Johnson and John Burgee; Modernist logotype by Saul Bass; and the Modernist Merlin telephone by Henry Dreyfuss Associates.

IBM typewriters designed by Eliot Noyes: the Model A Standard of 1954 and the Selectric of 1961.

oversee not only product design but the whole visual aspect of the company, from its graphics to its architecture. Noyes's industrial design, while in the Modernist style, retained some vestige of the American machine esthetic, with gently expressive curves on typewriter bodies or colored electrical wiring visible behind glass in computer cabinets.[28]

The 1960s and 1970s saw the refinement of the European style to give a more depersonalized appearance that often expressed nothing specific to a product's function, only a vague sense of technological awe. Black-box industrial design parallels the rise of late-Modernism[29] in architecture.

The object culture

With the arrival of post-Modernism, the two divergent styles acted as a foil for each other, running in parallel, and enlivening architectural debate. But while businesses may have adopted post-Modernism for their permanent monuments, they have been reluctant to change their products' clothing so lightly. Thus, AT&T commissioned Philip Johnson to design its broken-pedimented skyscraper, but retained the late-Modernist firm of Henry Dreyfuss Associates to design its telephones and graphic designer Saul Bass to devise a new logotype. Post-Modern products have been slow to appear, in part due to client conservatism, but also because designers have been unsure what represents a suitable set of symbols with which to make the newly permitted references.[30]

Industrial designers have, however, absorbed the change of attitude that post-Modernism brought, and are beginning to accept a broader definition of their role. Just as architects are once again happy to turn their hand to a variety of design challenges,[31] so industrial designers are becoming more interested in formal, less "industrial," problems such as lamps and furniture.

All this is indicative of a new confidence. Now, industrial designers look to architects and to Europe where designers like Ettore Sottsass, Philippe Starck, and Mario Bellini successfully balance the demands of "serious"

30. When post-Modern sensibilities did begin to emerge in products, there were close parallels for the language of product design in its discussion of words, syntax, semantics, and metaphor as described in architectural design in Jencks, ibid.

28. Thomas Watson, Jr., "Good design is good business," in Schutte, 1975.

29. The definitions for late-Modernism and post-Modernism here follow Jencks, 1977. Among Americans, Bruce Graham of Skidmore Owings and Merrill would be a late-Modern architect, while Michael Graves is the leading post-Modern architect. Several architects, such as Cesar Pelli and Philip Johnson, work successfully in both styles and in hybrids of them, exposing the fragility of such labeling.

31. Architects are today designing an array of products, from furniture, to tableware, jewelry, rugs, and shopping bags, renewing a tradition of such interests from before the Modern movement.

This coffee-pot by Michael Graves for Swid-Powell shows that architects can design fine products. At best, their broader perspective on a design problem can lead designers into new expectations for form. This happened, for example, when Serge Chermayeff and Wells Coates designed radios for Britain's Ekco Radio Company that went beyond wooden cabinetry that had previously governed the form to evolve pure new shapes with modern materials. Often, however, architects are content just to apply patterns to existing forms.

industrial design with those of "design for art's sake."

The Apple II GS computer advertised in *Time* serves to symbolize the growing sophistication of American design and consumer culture. Pictured with its illustrious peers, it treads a thin line between being a designed product and a "designer" product. Usually, it takes a name associated with a product—Porsche sunglasses or Yves Saint Laurent cigarettes—to give it this status. But, used judiciously, good design can do it on its own. "Design has the capacity to cast myths into an enduring, solid and tangible form, so that they seem to be reality itself."[32] It is this elusive goal that tempts many American designers today. At one extreme, this pursuit promises to provide a much needed pluralism in what represents good product design in America; at another, it sometimes seems a conceited indulgence on the part of designers creating products that serve no real need, only meeting the demands of conspicuous consumption of the yuppie years. There is an awkward self-consciousness in product designers' striving to create "objects."

The notion of the mass-manufactured product as "object" has been given currency by the writings of the French semiologists. Roland Barthes' essays concern the quality of "myth" that can surround media events, personalities, and products.[33] His analysis goes beyond what consumer products *are* and tries to explain what they *signify*. George Nelson states with poetic clarity: "Objects are the fingerprints left by a culture on the walls of its particular cell in space and time. Anyone can learn how to read fingerprints. Part of the meaning of any object is exactly what the sponsoring culture says it is. That ornate gold cup over there may look to you or me like the Hepzibah M. Perkins Trophy, awarded last year to the Curling Club of Upper Hydrangea. But if the society which created it says that it is the Holy Grail, then that's what it is."[34] This can be said *by design* and, as in the cases of the Apple II GS and the Ford Taurus, it can be underlined in adspeak.

Jean Baudrillard places the genesis of the "object" with the Bauhaus.

32. Forty, 1986.

33. The essays on "Plastic" and "The New Citroen" in Barthes, 1957, are particularly relevant to product designers.

34. "The Future of the Object" in Nelson, 1979.

He argues that the separation of a product's utility from its esthetic was the result of a semantic accident, the existence of the words "form" and "function." Calling form something separate from function is the same, and he implies as invidious, as calling one type of worker different from another. Just as the division of labor permits more efficient operation of the means of production, but at the expense of individual expression and ability, so the artificial division of form and function stifles a variety of formal expression. "Functionalism is ascetic ... the functional liberation of the object has the effect of establishing an ethic of objects just as the emancipation of labor as a productive force has the consequence of establishing a work ethic."[35] Using terms from linguistic semiology, Baudrillard claims that in the Bauhaus ideal form *denotes* function and function only. In the messy real world, however, form denotes function, but it also *connotes* additional values.

Ornament and fashion, symbol and meaning

Function, in other words, is no longer enough. Technological means of production do not obviate the requirement to meet deeper needs. Bellini observes: "Today it is no longer acceptable to believe that the simple arrival of new methods of production is enough to substantially subvert the thousand-year-old flow of design of things such as ornaments and furnishings ... linked to the persistence and slow evolution of the culture of living."[36] Others suggest the search for added value marks a return to a norm after the aberration that was Modernism: "not only in many of the first, but also in the greatest cultural achievements of humanity, the practical problem-solving element is secondary or derivative ... in, say, ... Gothic crafts and architecture, the problem was aesthetic and symbolic *before* it was practical."[37]

A number of avenues are being explored in the attempt to restore symbolic value to today's products. The least welcome is the product as fashion accessory. Many products today do exactly the same things. In a nation where "choice" is virtually a Constitutional right, even sometimes

35. Baudrillard, 1981.

36. *Domus*, September, 1986.

37. Peter Fuller, "Ornamentation," *Design*, August, 1983.

38. Baudrillard, ibid.

39. Other critics echo this pessimistic sentiment. "At one end of the argument, the way technology is developing from mechanical objects towards electronic process appears to be rendering the designer obsolete: either he or she merges into the electrical engineer, or 'designs' yet another black or white case. Alternatively, the designer joins the novelty trade, and causes products to emit electronic messages, or to be castellated or polka-dotted." Fuller, ibid. For better or worse, all these trends are evident among the present generation of American designers, including those in this book.

40. Steve Braidwood, writing in *Design,* December, 1987, takes the standard view. On the structure of industry after the failure of globalism, he writes: "Take this approach to its logical conclusion and a future emerges in which companies like Ford stick to managing high-investment world centres, but sell their output to a lot of small companies, who in turn design and make products that are tuned to ever smaller segments of the car market. The danger is that industrial designers will be called upon to do more styling work." The argument is a general one; Philips and the consumer electronics industry are mentioned as another area where this danger exists.

coming ahead of "quality" in the purchaser's priorities, it is inevitable that fashion detailing should be used as a device to stimulate demand. Soon, flexible manufacturing systems will allow not only surface details, such as colors, imprinted patterns and textures to be changed regularly, as happens today in watches and electronic goods, but also non-functioning decorative plastic moldings or other components. For manufacturers, such advances herald a lucrative dream of allowing them to apply niche marketing techniques to global markets. The long-term benefit for design and the consumer is less clear. Baudrillard extends his thesis to deduce that ultimately the only function of a product becomes its "sign function." Thus, design plunges helplessly towards fashion, and the designer is left the powerless puppet of the capitalist machine.[38,39]

The return of "styling" is generally seen as a threat to the integrity, if not the very existence, of the industrial designer.[40] This need not be the case. The question is how to integrate meaningful decoration into products. Critic Peter Fuller warns against such phenomena as "the 'New Ornamentalism' [which] is no more than an instance of the way contemporary industrial capitalism betrays, suppresses, or distorts the human aesthetic impulse."[41]

A less superficial ornamentalism could emerge from the use of "product semantics" as a way to unite form and function and permit a degree of ornament that enhances, rather than detracts from, functionality. The underlying assumption of the proponents of product semantics is that every product carries a meaning or meanings to the person who uses it and to others who see it. "Even the use of things for utilitarian purposes operates within the symbolic province of culture . . . thus it is extremely difficult to disentangle the use-related function from the symbolic meanings in even the most practical objects."[42] The addition of these signs to products extends human-factors engineering from the physical and psychophysical into the cultural domain.

41. Fuller, ibid.

42. Csikszentmihalyi, 1981.

Technology Design's Elaine printer is a design that may be read semantically in a number of ways. It works as a simile, the paper-like base expressing the print medium. It also presents a functional contradiction wherein the base is rigid enough to support the unit, but is made to appear flexible like paper. The sexism implicit in the product name, however, diminishes the overall gestalt.

Technology Design's Elaine printer is a clear attempt to give a product symbolic value. It is a printer that says what it does through its design. That same design also suggests that it might be Nelson's Holy Grail among printers. Product semantics must also recognize that the right statement for some products is no statement at all. If the task the product performs is not especially important in its owner's eyes, then a design expressing great meaning is inappropriate. As Freud had it, sometimes a cigar is just a cigar.

Product semantics is not a style. It is not a design language, but a system within which design languages can express themselves clearly. Nonetheless, it risks becoming a style. Some designers fear that any product that involves water will soon be molded with wavy edges, that one that receives radio waves will sprout expressive antenna shapes. Such literal semantics adds little meaning. Less clear semantic design risks conveying the wrong meaning or no meaning at all.[43] Semantics used intelligently, however, can express a deeper sense of cultural place. One of the more promising investigations is in the use of elements from the vernacular. Design Logic's study for Dictaphone uses a mailbox as a simile for its operation. Lisa Krohn uses the Filofax as the icon for her answering machine.[44]

Product semantics concerns itself with information. Often applied in an attempt to humanize communications-technology products, it conveys information itself: how to use a product, how to regard it, where to put it, how it fits into your life and into your culture. When the first generation of American industrial designers attempted "to create a coherent environment for what they self-consciously referred to as 'the machine age,' "[45] the streamlined machine esthetic was the result. It is a style fondly remembered today as a zenith in American design, and one that spoke of its Americanness to the rest of the world. Handled with care, product semantics could be the designed expression of what we equally self-consciously refer to as our "information age."

44. Conversation with the author, September, 1987.

45. Meikle, ibid.

43. An amusing if unscientific street survey of people's reading of semantically intentioned product designs in the IDSA New York Chapter newsletter (September, 1987) produced mixed findings. Only three of fifty respondents incorrectly identified the Elaine printer, while no one correctly identified Paul Montgomery's design for a digital still camera.

Studies by Design Logic for Dictaphone celebrate vernacular forms (as on the answering-machine switch, left) and exploit their familiarity in making a product more readily understandable. Above, the US Mail box is the icon.

This digital camera design, by Paul Montgomery, while a student at Cranbrook, is elegant but enigmatic. In product-semantic terms, it is all but unreadable.

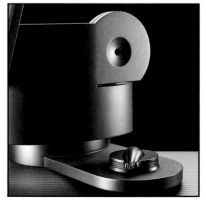

People judge products by whether they can afford them and by whether they are likely to do their job—a complex evaluation that depends not only on a visual appraisal of the product, but also on the price-tag, the advertising, the equity of the brand-name, and the nature of the selling environment. Few pieces of graphic design undergo such stringent tests. A book jacket, a poster, or a piece of packaging need only look attractive to do its job. Such work is easily judged by the general public on a simple criterion of esthetic preference. In this sense, a graphic designer's task is like that of an artist. On the other hand, graphic designers lag only behind architects in terms of the unavoidability of seeing their work. Like both artist and architect, in these celebrity-hungry days, the graphic designer has come to enjoy the prospect of a certain amount of media stardom.

Two New York designers, Milton Glaser and Massimo Vignelli, are well known names outside their immediate profession. Both have the versatility to turn their hands to tasks that lie outside the strict definition of the graphic designer's role. Vignelli has designed furniture, while Glaser has made a name as a restaurant critic. Both have made forays into interior design. Both also possess the sort of urbane charm that acts as a magnet for media attention. Two young San Francisco designers, Michael Vanderbyl and Michael Manwaring, recently won the rare honor of a feature in *Time* magazine. When Steve Jobs, the founder of Apple Computer, wanted to get his new company, Next, off to a flying start, he turned to the *eminence grise* of Modernist graphic design, Paul Rand for a logotype, not only for the near certitude that his design would be a good one, but also because the association of Rand, author of the IBM imprimatur, with the infant company would give it a credibility far in excess of its size or age.

Graphic design, then, has come to carry with it a modest share of the cult of personality. This situation has by and large been welcomed and encouraged by designers looking to overcome a long-held professional inferiority complex. The popular success of a few disguises a frustration felt by many. Graphic design practices are unlicensed, the profession officially unrecognized, and designers' names unaccompanied by a string of imposing initials.[1] Graphic design is experiencing growing pains. The American Institute of Graphic Arts, a body that has been in existence since 1914, has only recently begun organizing a national conference for its members. Steven Heller, editor of the *AIGA Journal*, speaking at the second of these conferences, stated the case for a body of serious, independent criticism, such as has long existed in architecture, as a necessary part of that growing-up,[2] something that might alleviate the field's damaging self-perception. Another critic notes that: "Because designers generally talk and write only about what they do themselves, design has come to be regarded as belonging entirely within their realm. This misunderstanding has . . . been taught in schools of design, where students are liable to acquire grandiose illusions about the nature of their skills, with the result that they become frustrated in their subsequent careers."[3]

Is design art?

Graphic designers have spent the postwar years trying to gain credibility with the business world by presenting their profession as an analytical process of diagnosis and cure that makes it something of a marketing specialty. Now, there is an understandable, if petulant, reaction among some designers who would have graphic design seen not as like architecture, advertising, or marketing, but as a branch of art that happens, fortuitously, to be salaried.[4] Proponents of graphic design as a quasi-artistic activity point out facetiously that bad graphic design never killed anybody. Indeed, the sort of graphic design currently thought the most desirable to work on—the books and magazine covers, records and posters—probably hasn't. But there are many areas where graphic design is not such a trivial pursuit. Milton Glaser foresaw the situation in 1975, when he wrote: "Often conspicuously absent is a sense of social responsibility that would inspire a communicator

2. AIGA National Conference, San Francisco, September, 1987.

4. For a discussion of this issue, see Lorraine Wild, "Art and Design: Lovers or Just Good Friends," *AIGA Journal*, Volume 5, Number 2, 1987.

1. Graphic designers are not regarded as professionals, like architects, doctors or lawyers, but neither are they subject to those professions' stringent professional liability legislation. There is discussion among several design groups about seeking licensed professional status from the states in which they practice. This is currently strongest among interior designers, but some graphic designers are also raising the issue.

3. The reference is to designers in general, but applies to graphic designers particularly well. Forty, 1986.

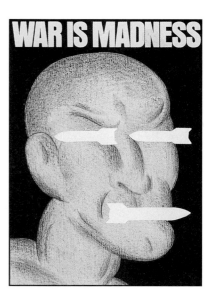

Social responsibility and political activism are neglected in marked contrast to 20 years ago when many designers used their medium to express their sentiments. This design is by Seymour Chwast.

Cover and an inside page from *Paper*, art director Richard Pandiscio.

New York subway signage, Vignelli Associates.

to take responsibility for the way he informs his public. The astonishing fact is that these scraps of printed ephemera have the capacity to be life-enhancing or life-reducing."[5]

Today, these fields are woefully overlooked. In part, this may be because America has always gotten along well without, for example, unified subway signage. The assumption that comes with this degree of organization that people need to be told what to do and where to go has seemed somehow unAmerican. The Vignellis, who designed the signage for the New York and Washington, D.C. subways, complain that both systems were wrecked by poor implementation and the introduction of extraneous signage. "Tremendous discipline is required to implement and protect a mass transportation sign system."[6] The situation is as bad in airports, post offices, and railroads. Such vital pieces as the Surgeon-General's AIDS mailing and the 1040 tax form could have used more thoughtful design, as could many labels on foods and medicines, instruction manuals, and an array of other material.

With few exceptions,[7] government and much of private industry seem to have little belief in the power of design to improve the environment or even, less altruistically, to increase their gains. Even in the retail area, where good graphics could have an immediate and demonstrable benefit, there is minimal patronage. "The saddest part," one design recruitment consultant noted recently, "is that too many designers are still only interested in producing nice-looking things. They aren't interested in content or the fact that many people can't read small type."[8]

There is instead an overriding passion for the single beautiful image.[9] In the attempt to create graphic "art," it is only natural that designers should look to the artists of the past. Today, there are two strains of post-Modernism[10] in graphic design. One is a conceptual form that accepts the idea of eclecticism in the use of elements and techniques from a number of periods to create a contemporary image.[11] The more prevalent, however, is

5. In *Images of an Era: the American Poster 1945–75*

6. Vignelli, 1981.

7. The National Park Service, run under the Federal design and graphics programs, and the Smithsonian Institution Traveling Exhibition Service are two rare cases of excellence.

8. RitaSue Siegel of RitaSue Siegel Agency, New York, at the AIGA National Conference, San Francisco, September 1987.

10. Post-Modernism in graphic design closely parallels that in architecture. Post-Modern architects have tried to develop a style that enriches the Modern movement or International Style with elements of past styles. See, for example, Jencks, 1977. Similarly, graphic designers are seeking to break out of the narrow confines of Swiss Modernism, more properly termed the International Typographic Style by Meggs, 1983.

11. Venturi, 1966, is the single work most often cited as the catalyst for post-Modern design of this sort.

9. Little spectacular work is seen where relationships or sequences of images are handled, not only in environmental graphics and signage, but also in magazines, on television and computer displays. Magazines with historically great art direction, such as *Esquire, Holiday,* and *Life,* have lapsed or foundered. Others' efforts at design are thwarted by the demands of advertisement placement that break up editorial continuity and graphics theme development. Some new magazines, such as *Raw, Paper,* and *Émigré,* are vehicles for graphic experimentation, but have tiny circulations. *Spy,* with its jokes at the expense of trends in magazine design, offers a welcome respite from banality, but is hardly a solution in itself. Not only magazines, but also posters and billboards have been largely superseded by television. Yet conventionally-trained graphic designers have shunned the medium.

The intimidatingly official design of the Surgeon-General's report on AIDS.

Poster by Paula Scher, 1987, uses Bauhaus themes.

13. Keynote address at the AIGA National Conference, Boston, September, 1985.

a referential form that often merely reproduces past styles regardless of their relevance to the design problem at hand, and ignorant, or ignoring, of the social and political circumstances that gave the work meaning in its day. Accepting the cyclical nature of fashion, it appears that the 1980s have brought the early decades of the twentieth century into focus. Just as some designers in the 1960s drew from the illustration techniques of the Art Nouveau artists, so some of today's graphic designers look to the artists of 1910s, 1920s and 1930s Europe for inspiration. This period was extraordinarily rich in artistic activity, seeing within a few years the rise of Constructivism, De Stijl, and the Bauhaus, among others. The appeal of these numerous abstract art movements for today's designers becomes almost irresistible when it is remembered that many of today's designers have come through schools that no longer teach their students how to draw.[12]

Tom Wolfe borrowed the term "The Big Closet" to describe the way history is being used as a source for styles. "There is a tendency today . . . to say, okay, let's rummage through the Big Closet. Let's do an A.M. Cassandre, or El Lissitzky, or Herbert Matter."[13] The truth is that the graphic designer's closet is not all that big. A more apt metaphor might be that history is a "narrow window" that offers at any one time only a restricted view (say, 1917 to 1930, at the moment) from which to draw references. Few designers are yet looking further afield for their found images.

The complex image

There is a better reason for looking back to the early Modern era, which leads to a conceptual post-Modernism rather than a trivial, referential one. Artists then were experimenting with techniques to create art and design that was something other than paint on canvas. Collage, photography, and typography were among their tools. These techniques form ideal starting points for the creation of images that designers wish to make more complex, rich and ambiguous, both in response to the demands of an increasingly visual

12. Milton Glaser points out that the power within art schools has historically resided with the fine-art faculties, providing a role model with an insidious influence on graphic design students. Without necessarily being able to draw, designers use geometric construction, collage, and found images, in the manner of the Modern artists. While designers control the hierarchy of image and text, the illustrator has become ancillary, whereas in the past the two activities were on an equal footing, if not actually indistinguishable. Conversation with the author, November 1987.

Covers of *Raw,* numbers one and three, by Art Spiegelman and Gary Panter, respectively.

1967 *Holiday* cover by Milton Glaser in the style of Beardsley. Much 1960s designed drew from the Art Nouveau period.

14. Two design schools (Kunstgewer-beschule), in Zurich and in Basel, were largely responsible for the Swiss modern style, through the work of teachers and designers such as Emil Ruder, Joseph Müller-Brockmann, and Armin Hoffman. Meggs, 1983.

17. The Basel school was early in challenging the tenets of Swiss Modernism under the teaching of Wolfgang Weingart. See Meggs, ibid.

culture, and to make a break from the approach of reductive synthesis promulgated by the Swiss school of designers in the 1950s.[14]

The design philosophy of the 1950s decreed that one image should be found to express the essence of an activity, whether it be a company's business, a festival, an exhibition, or a product for sale. This led to the minimalism of many corporations' logotypes and design programs that remains today.[15] Much of the business community still favors the Modernist design that did so much to establish the general image of the American corporation.

Other designers now prefer an additive approach, overlaying a variety of images, motifs, colors, and typefaces. Frequently, this approach is intuitive and spontaneous, more than rational and analytical. These designers look to the Bauhaus period, to Laszlo Moholy-Nagy, who experimented with photographic techniques, or to collagists such as Max Ernst and Herbert Matter, to find out how it was done rather than to imitate their personal styles.

Graphic design is not a profession that has collected -isms and experienced movements to quite the degree that art and architecture have in recent years (perhaps owing to the absence of that critical body whose job it seems to be to devise these terms). What has emerged to be a powerful national and international influence is "California New Wave." It is an inclusive style with such an absence of ideology that almost any designer in California risks being categorized under its heading. Some indeed take pains to disassociate their work from the trend.[16]

In its purist graphic form, California New Wave had its beginnings with April Greiman, who added to her influence by the teaching of Wolfgang Weingart[17] both in the United States and at the Basel school a vibrant new color palette that she credits to the climate and location.

For designers without the benefit of a training in the rigors of the Swiss school, New Wave is a more purely visual esthetic—a colorful, intuitive, what-the-hell style that expresses the carefree California lifestyle. This

15. It was frequently an impossible task, of course, to distill one strong visual idea from giant corporations that did many kinds of business, hence the inexpressive nature of so many logotypes from this period.

16. The work of many California designers is shown in the catalog of the Pacific Wave exhibition held at the Museo Fortuny, Venice, Italy, October 1987. Camuffo, 1987.

The techniques and esthetics of the European Modern artists are a popular source for reinterpretation, as in this reworking of a De Chirico painting by Skolos Wedell and Raynor.

The spirit of California New Wave was much in evidence in the graphics and building decoration for the 1984 Los Angeles Olympic Games by Sussman/Prejza and others.

Fonts designed on a computer by Émigré Graphics show the range of possibilities at high and low resolutions and with the use of computer smoothing techniques.

ABCDEF

ABCDEF

abcdef

approach is seen at its most dramatic in Deborah Sussman's graphics and environmental design for the 1984 Los Angeles Olympic Games. The fashion retail chain, Esprit, won the AIGA's 1987 award for design leadership with a graphic identity program based on the same basic style.

There have been other minor rebellions against the tenets of Modernism. The typefaces of Helvetica and Univers sanctioned by the Modernists have never enjoyed the popularity here that they did and do in Europe. Most Americans continue to work with a broader range of letterforms. This typographic eclecticism continues a distinctly American tradition stemming from the letterpress posters of Victorian times. Old typefaces such as Caslon, Baskerville, and Garamond are widely used, sometimes for their particular historical referential value, but more often for the simple pleasingness of their characters.

Byting the bullet

The nostalgia for these old fonts is in part due to the threat they face from the increasing use of computers in design, layout, and typography.[18] Attempts to design typefaces that make the most of the computer have been largely unsatisfactory. Graphic designers have generally not been attracted to the technology, and the exercise is in any case of limited usefulness, since computer technology will soon reach a point where it can provide high-quality typography using classic faces.[19]

Typeface design is not the only area where computer technology is making an impact. Largely through the advent of Apple Computer's Macintosh, a few designers have begun to create new design that does not always give away its computer origins. Some have found chance and accident to play a part in generating images—the computer working as a sort of electronic kaleidoscope. As the price of more powerful systems falls, graphic design methods and esthetics are sure to change. So far, however, enthusiasm for computers has been muted. Expense of hardware is undoubtedly one reason,

18. The majority of designers still feel the computer poses a pernicious threat to their professional practice, a feeling not entirely without justification given the liberties already taken in the name of new technologies in the redesign of classic typefaces by the Monotype and International Typeface Corporations.

19. The issue of computers and typography was a principal topic of the Type Directors' Club conference, New York, November, 1987. A special issue of *Print,* November-December, 1986, covers some of the general issues in the debate on typography.

The same technology was used by April Greiman to design sculpture for the Venice, Italy, Pacific Wave exhibition. The designer never worked in three dimensions, but merely sent drawings by facsimile transmission for on-site construction.

Network television has sought to impress viewers with graphics that show off its high-tech equipment more than a design sense, creating a banal glitz of "realistic" simulated chrome and glass, exaggerated perspective and tumbling captions.

but the poor esthetic quality of much existing computer graphics seems to have been a deterrent to professional designers.

More serious efforts to use contemporary technology are being made at the Media Laboratory of the Massachusetts Institute of Technology.[20] A veritable Bauhaus for the information age, the Media Lab is home to computer scientists, engineers, architects, psychologists and others who are tackling a wide variety of design problems without the inhibitions that come with narrow definitions of people's jobs. In graphic design, the Media Lab is able to work on technical aspects of, for example, the legibility of type fonts on video display terminals, but with valuable input on the esthetic and cultural values that are a part of any design.[21]

The development of a theory of graphic design concerns other educators. Thomas Ockerse at the Rhode Island School of Design has used semiotics in an attempt to analyze and assist the process of image creation. Ockerse notes the lack of a "language" that allows graphic designers to articulate the design process. Such a language should not bow to linguistic convention, an easy thing for it to do given that graphic design is frequently an alternative to writing or speaking, but should instead seek to work entirely visually.[22] A philosophy akin to Ockerse's forms a part of several other graphic-design-education programs, although more implicit in working methods and less expressed as theory. Ockerse feels the evolution of critical theory is another sign of professional maturity, allowing designers to use scientific methodology, but without rejecting the intuitive approach.

American graffiti

For the majority, however, turning their backs on either a technological or a deeply theoretical approach, the current backlash against Swiss Modernism has been neither very intellectually based nor always particularly heartfelt. Signs of rebellion against the blandly perfect mechanical have been seen in recent years in such mannerist shows of supposed spontaneity as

20. For broad design relevance of the Media Lab program, see Hugh Aldersey-Williams, "Social Science," *Industrial Design*, May/June, 1986.

21. These graphic design projects come under the aegis of the Visible Language Workshop run by Professor Muriel Cooper, whose aim is to give "soft copy the sophistication of hard copy." One area of interest concerns the use of color. Color is comparatively easy to provide on a computer screen, and this has led to gaudy and indiscriminate use to date. Cooper's program seeks to remind that color, because of its expense in traditional print, has historically been used sparingly, and with specific associations for its use in certain ways. Media Lab publicity material.

22. Ockerse uses the terms "design" and "super-sign" to describe the selection of information to be included in a graphic design and the sign system within which those elements operate to create a whole that is hoped to be somehow greater than the sum of its parts. Private communication, January 1988. Some critics think this whole has not been achieved with the complex layered images typical of post-Modern graphic design. "Whereas modernism provided a ready-made, often didactic, solution, post-modernism offers dissolutions that render individual meaning in the viewer's completion of the work. This is not a *Gestalt* but a schizophrenia." Sarah Bodine and Michael Dunas, "April Greiman: the 'New Wave' Revisited," *AIGA Journal,* Volume 4, Number 3, 1986

The Visible Language Workshop seeks to link computer graphic design with the traditions of print design. Here, images are manipulated and designs built up using prototype software for a knowledge-based design system.

Poster by Vignelli Associates expressing rebellion against Modernist perfection.

Poster by M & Co. celebrating the American graphic vernacular.

rough handwriting used instead of neat type, scribbles, or torn paper edges in the middle of an image. Perfection, in short, had become boring. The imperfect, the accidental, and the casual are their replacements.

Some designers have found less trivial ways to express the new freedom from the old constraints. Massimo Vignelli, for example, a Modernist at heart, had the last laugh on the torn-paper motif in a poster for a papermaking company in which each tear really was individually hand-torn for each poster. Designers like Tibor Kalman and Stephen Doyle have made related tongue-in-cheek *trompes l'oeil* more their stock-in-trade. At its best, this anti-art thinking parallels the work of the Dada artists in the 1910s protesting the intellectualized abstraction of the Cubist painters. Kalman and others wish to restore elements of humanistic intuition and creative immediacy to commercial graphic design, and like the original Dada artists, they are using shock tactics to make their point.

The search for a vernacular style and its appropriation into today's highly professional work marks another new direction. Amateur signage or imperfectly executed graphics from third-world printed matter that were never the subject of any corporate identity program are the inspirations. Away from the smart areas of America's big cities there is an abundance of individualistic handiwork. The sources are not just the supergraphics of Las Vegas and the urban strip,[23] but also the do-it-yourself design of the general store or local paper in any small town. The very spirit of chaotic individuality that dooms disciplined European-style graphics to failure can be the basis for a richer set of graphic languages. Such design has a fine pedigree that recalls an age when commercial art was uncomplicated by the pretensions it later took on, as European Modernism forever confused art and design.[24] Their reinterpretation today reflects a hope for an American graphic design style rooted in this country's considerable heritage, instead of in borrowed, outdated and irrelevant theories from European art and design.

23. *Learning from Las Vegas* has at least as much relevance to graphic designers as to the architects for whom it was written. Venturi, 1972.

24. "The popular graphics of the Victorian Era stemmed, not from a design philosophy or artistic conventions, but from the prevalent attitudes and sensibilities of the period." Meggs, ibid.

Ilona Granet, a New York artist, creates offbeat signage for display both in galleries and on the street. Although seen as art, the designs show an awareness of the American tradition of the individualistic and humorous in information graphics.

Back in the middle decades of this century, the new professions of graphic and industrial design were experiencing growing pains. If corporate America was to take them seriously, then they had to be seen to be serious. The priority was to communicate—to communicate a clear message, to sell a functional product. To extract from the new industries of mass-production and mass-reproduction a single, simple image or an attractive working product was the designer's humble goal. Modernism denied mockery. Functionality precluded frivolity.

Memphis changed all that. In the early 1980s, the anarchic Milanese design movement substituted fun for function. It was not an idea that could be applied directly to American business, reined in as it is by client wishes, market demands, and the practicalities of production. But Memphis was a catalyst for change. Now designers are going one better than the Memphis *méchants*.

Any product can now be ergonomic, affordable, reliable, comprehensible, should the client and designer so wish. Any graphic design can be clean, crisp, legible, and perfectly printed. Function now is basic, the designers are saying. Let's start having fun.

When Tibor Kalman addressed a New York design conference not so long ago, he startled the audience by speaking at length in his native Hungarian, and accompanied his talk with out-of-sync slides and mistranslated subtitles. It was his way of saying that ambiguous messages can be more fun and more informative than the slick, literal graphics of the corporate world.

The graphics produced by M&Co., Kalman's design group, often work the same way. They possess something that is rare in mainstream graphic design—wit. This is not the crass humorousness of an Eddie Murphy or the gentle gibes of a Johnny Carson, but the sophisticated, literate wit for which there is a whole lexicon of long Greek words. It surfaces sometimes as brazen satire, other times as hyperbole or meiosis.

Kalman the satirist is seen at work in a recent parody issue of *Print* magazine. There, M&Co.'s hypothetical commission to redesign the national identity program for Canada was an attack on the pseudoscientific methods used and the banal results obtained by identity consultants commissioned by large corporations. Canada, the putative brief explained, "had been losing the battle for prime shelf space" to the more popular brand, USA. M&Co. rejected "USA-Lite" and "New Canada Free" as possible new names, settling instead on a minor change to "Canada!" using the punctuation to breathe new life into a name that already had high market recognition. A typeface, "Canada Dry," was christened for the graphics program, along with its italic companion, "Sparkling Canada Dry." Among supposed competition entries for a new flag was one purporting to come from the California advertising agency, Chiat/Day, that was a lustrous color photograph of a polar bear frolicking in clear blue water with the word "Canada" run small in one corner. Prominent graphic designers such as Paul Rand and Massimo Vignelli came in for similar treatment. M&Co. even lampooned itself with a monochrome flag featuring that Canadian icon, the canoe, unmanned and adrift in a sea of white space, with the word CANADA inscribed above it with all the A's

inverted, all devices and ideas used rather more sensibly elsewhere in M&Co.'s "real" work.

Given the chance, Kalman spells out his frustration in bald terms: "There was a time before graphic designers were called graphic designers when the president of a company would call an artist, and the person would go home and take out paintbrushes and make paintings of things and say: 'What do you think of this?' That's how design decisions were made. Today, they do six months of study about people in shopping centers saying that they think the color red means this and the color blue means that and a triangle pointing up means this and a triangle pointing down means that. I think it's all a bloody waste of time. Good identities happen because a couple of people look at something and say: 'You know what? I like it!' "

Satire was an appropriate vehicle to get across this uncompromising message in *Print*, and M&Co. has the guts to make its satire cruel enough to be effective. But it's not the sort of thing generally appreciated by a paying client. Gentler forms of wit are called for. Two trendy New York restaurants give an idea of the range of funny ideas that can be appropriate. Uptown, for the China Grill, a restaurant serving what it describes as "*nouvelle chinoise*" food, the logo is a posh heraldic shield with a pair of chopsticks laid asymmetrically across it. The silly motif is repeated with deadpan seriousness on everything inside the restaurant. It's not only printed on the menus, but also stenciled onto plates and in gold on the doors. Rather different is Florent, a restored diner in Manhattan's earthy far West Village. M&Co. developed the authenticity on a menu with deliberately cheap-looking typesetting and a modest sprinkling of misspellings and typographical errors—not so many that everyone realizes, but just enough so that they wonder whether they are having their leg pulled or not. A postcard for Florent uses symbols and words to get the message across, but the match between them is not always straightforward. Against the phone number is shown a bell, but against the legend, "New York, New York," is a picture of a revolver.

Kalman puts his joking down to his early years in Hungary, which he fled at age seven shortly before the 1956 uprising. "The Hungarians always seem to be great pranksters, with a disdain for authority," he observes. To the prankishness was added a concern for words and their usage, the product of time spent at New York University's journalism school during the turbulent late 1960s. M&Co.'s literate zaniness in graphics is seen as some sort of parallel to Tom Wolfe's "New Journalism" from that period. Kalman does not think in terms of any visual esthetic, but rather in words that become graphic images at the hands of his staff of designers.

After M&Co.'s assaults on corporate graphic identities, it comes as a surprise to learn that giants such as IBM and Nynex number among its clients. More typical however is the band Talking Heads, for which M&Co. designed the title sequence of the movie *True Stories*, as well as a number of album covers. The *True Stories* graphics parodied the *National Enquirer*'s idea of news, while the cover of the *Remain in Light* album became a double-take by inverting the A's in TⱯLKING HEⱯDS to produce a graphic analogue of the unexpected verbal witticisms expressed in Talking Heads' lyrics.

The use, however well reasoned, of these devices opens M&Co.'s work to superficial imitation. M&Co. even hints at this in its self-parody with the Canadian flag design. The use of words juxtaposed against little icons (the canoe and the name "CANADA," or a coffee-cup or salt-shaker used on the Florent restaurant matchbooks) has been widely ripped off, as has the inversion of letters in a word. What is never imitated is the fact that these devices originally expressed an idea—the words said one thing, the image a slightly different thing, and the combination added a third, usually humorous, message. The copiers use the graphic motif as a literal expression of the written caption and thereby lose all humorous content. An unfortunate result is that the work of M&Co. and its imitators alike may date quickly.

The Florent work also shows a consistent influence of the earnest vernacular in M&Co.'s work, which is one reaction against the slickness in graphics that so offends Kalman. "Designers are taught that elegance is beautiful. I don't find that refreshing any more, partly because everyone's gotten to be so good. The fact is that you will be hard-pressed to find annual reports that are not elegant. Everything now is nice; it puts me to sleep." Kalman reacts with studied imperfection. The idea is to get the work just exactly not quite right. A party invitation is accidentally-on-purpose folded where the text is, making it hard to read. A poster for the American Institute of Graphic Arts "Humor Show" is mis-cut with the registration marks and color chips in the center, and the drawing of the banana skin intended for the center spot appears split down each border. All this despite the scribbled note to the printer to "watch the trim on this job—it's for the AIGA."

From studied imperfection it's a short step to look at graphics of the robust sort that never went near a design studio—what might be termed naturally occurring signage. This is to be celebrated on the 42nd Street Theater Row project where the architecture will be adorned with a rooftop sign "42. ST." in eighteen-foot characters. The word "THEATER" will be read vertically down the side of the building with each letter descending in size and mounted on brackets evoking the signage of the urban strip.

The studied imperfection and vernacular appropriations are clever, perhaps a little too clever, in the same way that Robert Venturi's architecture is often too clever for uneducated interpretation. Asked if his concern for the vernacular in any way parallels the work of Venturi, Kalman jokes: "That's a really adult question. I really feel I've arrived when someone asks me a question like that." He cites instead Bernard Rudofsky's *Architecture Without Architects*. But the anti-formal approach espoused by Rudofsky is not Kalman's. He is in fact much closer to Venturi in his concern for signs and what they signify and in his raising of the vernacular to high art. The risk both run is that such an approach will be taken as elitist. In M&Co.'s case, however, Kalman's need to puncture pretension and his ribald sense of humor should ensure that this pitfall is avoided.

2

69 Gansevoort Street → Open 24 hours → 989-5779

Restaurant Florent

1

M&Co.'s penchant for parody of different sorts is seen in restaurant graphics: a print advertisement for Florent (1), and the mock-serious logotype for the China Grill (2). The poster for the AIGA Humor show (3) is funny for its being mis-cut despite instructions to the printer, but it also carries a satirical message in that its intended central motif—a banana skin—is exactly the sort of design that many other graphic design firms might have come up with.

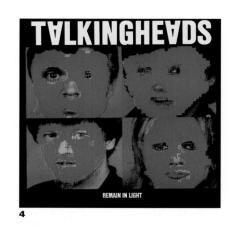

4

Lost in the Stars

MARIANNE
FAITHFULL
and
CHRIS SPEDDING

STING
and
DOMINIC MULDOWNEY

the
ARMADILLO
STRING
QUARTET

LOU
REED

the
FOWLER
BROTHERS
with
STANARD RIDGWAY

The Music of Kurt Weill

MARK
BINGHAM
with
JOHNNY ADAMS
and
AARON NEVILLE

TODD
RUNDGREN
with
GARY WINDO

TOM
WAITS

CHARLIE
HADEN
and
SHARON FREEMAN

CARLA
BLEY
with
PHIL WOODS

DAGMAR
KRAUSE

RALPH
SCHUCKETT
with
RICHARD BUTLER

JOHN
ZORN

VAN DYKE
PARKS

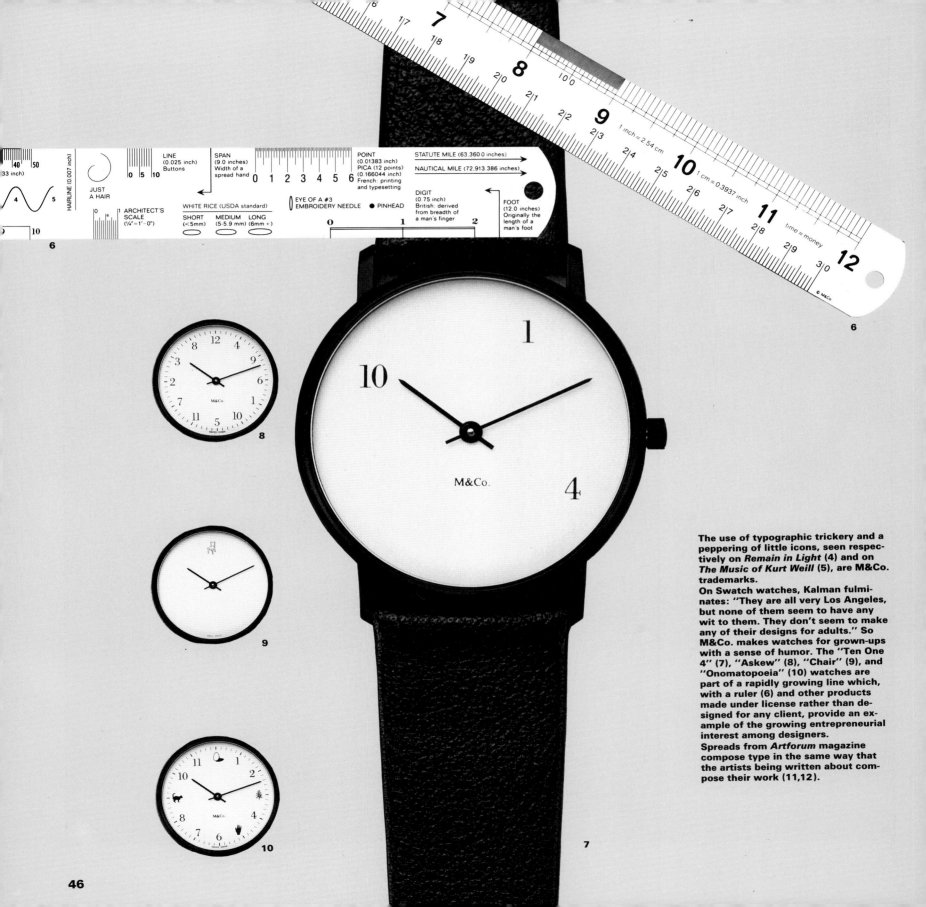

HAIRLINE (0.007 inch)

JUST
A HAIR

LINE
(0.025 inch)
Buttons

SPAN
(9.0 inches)
Width of a
spread hand

POINT
(0.01383 inch)
PICA (12 points)
(0.166044 inch)
French: printing
and typesetting

STATUTE MILE (63.360 0 inches)

NAUTICAL MILE (72.913.386 inches)

ARCHITECT'S
SCALE
(¼"=1'-0")

WHITE RICE (USDA standard)

SHORT   MEDIUM   LONG
(<5mm)   (5-5.9 mm) (6mm +)

EYE OF A #3
EMBROIDERY NEEDLE   ● PINHEAD

DIGIT
(0.75 inch)
British: derived
from breadth of
a man's finger

FOOT
(12.0 inches)
Originally the
length of a
man's foot

1 inch = 2.54 cm

1 cm = 0.3937 inch

time = money

© M&Co

6

8

9

10

7

M&Co.

The use of typographic trickery and a
peppering of little icons, seen respectively on *Remain in Light* (4) and on
The Music of Kurt Weill (5), are M&Co.
trademarks.
On Swatch watches, Kalman fulmi-
nates: "They are all very Los Angeles,
but none of them seem to have any
wit to them. They don't seem to make
any of their designs for adults." So
M&Co. makes watches for grown-ups
with a sense of humor. The "Ten One
4" (7), "Askew" (8), "Chair" (9), and
"Onomatopoeia" (10) watches are
part of a rapidly growing line which,
with a ruler (6) and other products
made under license rather than designed for any client, provide an example of the growing entrepreneurial
interest among designers.
Spreads from *Artforum* magazine
compose type in the same way that
the artists being written about compose their work (11,12).

46

Left: **Jan Vercruysse, A (Atopie), 1986**, mahogany and mirror. Installation view at the Palais des Beaux-Arts, Brussels, 1986. Below: **Jan Vercruysse, II, o.T., 1986**, painted wood. Installation view at the Galerie Joost Declercq, Gent, 1986.

By PIER LUIGI TAZZI

not utopia: *jan vercruysse*

What are Jan Vercruysse's works if not doors to nowhere, empty frames, blocked exits, views "through the looking glass"? As objects they hinge between the space we know (which includes what we know of art) and everything outside it, that unknown toward which art tends and on which life floats. When the works cover parts of walls (when they are panels, framed photographs, or mirrors, for example), they are not unlike the camouflage covers spread over the mouths of pits as traps. The cover makes what lies beyond seem full instead of empty; as a mirror reflection makes right into left, Vercruysse's work inverts the relations between the void and the solid. The work is rooted in contemporary poetics—especially in the heretical minimalism of Richard Artschwager, the impassioned rhetoric of Marcel Broodthaers, the sense of visual and cultural depth of European art in the '80s—and it has a contemporary field of view. One can approach it philosophically through Nietzsche's myth and psychoanalytically through Jacques Lacan's symbol (through their double reflections on origins, double in that they both analyze origins—the various ways we know the world—and provide reflections that, like a mirror, reflect the present in which the analysis is being done). Or one can quote Georg Simmel (the intrinsic confines of form, the limits of language), or perhaps Edmond Jabès (the undoing of the sign's interpretability, of its capacity for metaphor and symbol, when it presents itself as itself and not as a stand-in for something else). The frames, panels, fireplaces, and mirrors of Vercruysse's works fix fragments of space by their very occupation of it, but they also link us with infinity because of how they break from what they refer to, suggesting other possibilities in addition to their fixed meanings and an entrance into the limitless directions that spread out from the work, which lies precarious on several vertiginous edges at once. The works require dedicated attention if they are not to be lost in unmarked, undifferentiated space. Given that care, they are suddenly thrown truly open, and one feels an unexpected rush of pleasure—a heightened freedom and eroticism. (Here, where sensuality burns in a hidden state, Vercruysse's work shows its Nordic character.) Perhaps the works are not doors that mark the dangerous threshold between here and there, maybe they're windows open to the world—but windows that, when we look at them or through them, leave us faced with an enigma. Vercruysse makes sure its solution is indefinitely postponed. We can arrive at partial interpretations, but something tells us that their meaning is limited. And there is no guide to give the answers. If we are blinded by the vibrant glare of the unknown, the glimmer of nothingness, we can direct our timid, uncertain glance away from his art. Or we can experience being in front of it. Its elaboration of enigma, illusion, and deception is both more extreme and more ancient than those of Vercruysse's Belgian compatriots and predecessors René Magritte and Broodthaers. To explore Vercruysse's art the culture of the Enlightenment is a good background, the harbor from which his voyage departs. Yet that voyage leads through many other waters—the waters of Mannerism, the literary waves of the Spanish *conceptismo*,[1] the sea of the baroque, the medieval depths of hermetism and magic, the archetypes of the ancient world. If the bourgeois culture of the Age of Reason

---

THE WORLD IN A BOTTLE

by Maurizio Fagiolo Dell'Arco

It seems almost paradoxical to weave words around the silent art of Giorgio Morandi, the Italian painter known for his still lifes of bottles, jugs, bowls, and other table objects, as well as for his apprehensive Emilian landscapes. His is an art that amplifies rarefaction and concentration, analyzing not so much the object itself as the variations of light on the object-as-protagonist. It is a capturing of the sensation of the object, an esthetics of its quality; it is an art of silence and its double.

The writing about Morandi tends to gravitate around two poles. There's either the "we know everything there is to know about Morandi by now," closed-book approach that has pinpointed the importance of his art basically in the metaphysical dimension of his spare iconography and the tonal values of his painting, in conjunction with what his friends have said about his simple life and the places (two or three) where he worked. Or there's the "we really know nothing about Morandi" school of thought, this one influenced by the idea that his friends have repressed the disjunctive bits of

information that might embarrass, and that Morandi himself left little trace of his relations to the world, or, rather, to worldliness. He even—heresy—repudiated the market. A recollection of 1949, in the *Saturday Review* of November 4, 1958, by James Thrall Soby, the curator, art historian, and former director of the painting and sculpture section of the Museum of Modern Art, New York, is appropriate to this last point: "When I asked him the price of a painting he had agreed to sell me, he mentioned a figure so absurdly low that I told him it should be multiplied by at least by ten. 'No,' he replied, 'I set these prices twenty years ago, and it makes me nervous to think about changing them.'"

Neither of these views is foreign, but neither really place Morandi in his full depth. They are each picturesque in their own way, leaving the impression of a static facsimile of Morandi as a painter of bottles, a man detached from the world, a "pure" researcher. This picture is the one by which he is most recognizable in the history books. Yet if we scratch the surface of this removed image, we find that Morandi is in fact in many ways a model Italian artist of the new century, and dynamically so. I doubt that many moments exist in the development of the Italian art of Morandi's time in which the artist has no place, whether as restless soul or as secure protagonist. A look at his various alliances and affiliations quickly dispels history's image of him as an artist detached from his time. He is there in Futurism, in 1914, when the movement seems to get a new boost from Rome. He is among the first to sense the message about absence in Giorgio de Chirico's Metaphysics. He is also active in the decisive moment of the return to tradition after World War I, a shift widespread in Europe, and in Italy labeled *Valori Plastici*, from the magazine and artist's group of the same name. And he is a cantankerous actor in the early events of the Novecento, also involved in tradition, and in the "*Strapaese-Stracittà*" dispute over Italian art's national identity. After World War II, he even ends up among the inspirations

for a very different tendency in art, one involving spontaneity and improvisation, the *informel*. These involvements should suggest the sense of urgency, experimentation, and involvement in the role of art that lies beneath Morandi's work.

Morandi spent his student years at the Accademia di Belle Arti, Bologna, in the last years before World War I. Here he met other young artists, such as Osvaldo Licini and Severo Pozzati and, more important, was able to absorb the new ideas then blooming. "I listened with enthusiasm and interest to the ravaging words of the Futurists," he wrote in an autobiographical statement from 1928, and, "I too, like so many other well-intentioned young people, felt the need for a total renewal in the atmosphere of Italian art." Licini, in a later recollection, and long after launching himself into the skies of abstraction, remarked, "With Morandi, from the time we were boys, we drank deeply from early Cubism, and with Morandi we went to battle for Futurism, alongside Marinetti after the war." In April 1914 Morandi submitted three still

lifes and a drawing to the open Futurist exhibition organized in Rome by the young dealer Giuseppe Sprovieri. Yet the 24-year-old painter had already participated, in February of that year, in the "*Seconda esposizione della Secessione*" (Second exposition of the Secession); this avant-garde movement looked more toward the past than Futurism allowed, but Morandi's work was such that he could still find a place in it.

Morandi found security in certain elements of what had come before him, for example the work of Ardengo Soffici: "When I was 19 or 20, a most important age for our formation, [as a ground] for our culture we young people found the terrain that had already been ploughed by Soffici," he recalled fifty years later. (In 1932, in the magazine *L'Italiano*, Soffici would write, "Morandi is classical in the Italian style: that is, at the same time real and ideal, objective and subjective, and traditional. His style is modern, and at the same time legitimate and Italian.") And in the Roman "*Secessione*" exhibition Morandi saw a selection of Cézanne watercolors and a room of paintings by Henri Matisse, the two poles of construction, in other words, of a new space of color and the liberation of form in light. Yet another pole of influence can be discerned in the painting of the Douanier Rousseau, to which, at Soffici's instigation, a small volume published by La Voce

Giorgio Morandi, Natura morta (Still life), 1955, oil on canvas, ca. 10½ × 16". Collection of the Morat-Institut, Freiburg.

Smart Design

At first glance, the office of Smart Design in the area of Manhattan now known as the Flatiron district, shows its inhabitants to be design clowns, flouters of their profession's conventions. Post-Modern pastels mottle the cast-iron columns that characterize downtown converted spaces such as this. On a partition in the reception area is affixed a life-size cutout man adorned with his statistics from *Humanscale*, the volume of anthropometric data collected by the office of Henry Dreyfuss Associates and one of the standard references of all industrial designers. But the man is wearing jazzy Memphis-patterned boxer shorts.

This minor mark of apostasy is a model of Smart Design's approach to product design. For the firm in fact is a true inheritor of the tradition of New York's great machine-age industrial designers in the way that it tries to combine functional demands with more expressive concerns. Its synthesis is a rare one of competent ergonomics and designerly joking.

This double existence also shows in the roll-call of Smart designers. Some are quiet, responsible technicians; others are conspicuously young and lively, maintaining something of the atmosphere of a kibbutz in the office. Somewhere between these two extremes is co-principal Tucker Viemeister, too long in the business to be considered a youngster, yet obviously having too much fun to be one of the old guard. Ask about Smart Design's philosophy, and he'll tell you they're trying to think one up. More seriously, he observes: "Industrial designers have a really good sense of humor, but somehow they separate it from their work."

This has not been a problem for Smart Design, as its work for Copco, a manufacturer of inexpensive plastic tableware, shows. What came out of that long-running commission was a sharp riposte to the recent trend toward "designer" tableware. Here were plates and bowls and utensils for preparing and serving food that poked fun at Ettore Sottsass, Robert Venturi, Michael Graves and the legion of other architects and superstar designers who have discovered a lucrative sideline in creating similar, if rather more generously priced, goods through companies such as Swid-Powell in New York.

Smart Design's work for Copco is rather more thoroughgoing. It is not only the pattern printed onto the tableware that is designed, as is the case with much of the Swid-Powell crockery, but also the forms of the plates and bowls. With their subtle platonic curves and sharp beveled edges, the Copco designs capture some of the elegance of Japanese ceramics despite what some might see as a limitation of their Melamine construction.

Smart Design went further, satirizing these architects' use of vaguely architectural graphics on what were essentially standard plates. Says Viemeister: "Just like Michael Graves, we looked around for patterns in everyday objects and changed their scale and put them in odd places." One set of tableware adapts a motif close to the designer, blowing up a Letraset texture and showing it out of context to give a loud pattern that Viemeister dubs "power graphics." By the same token, an austere set of black salad-servers offers an inexplicable homage to Charles Rennie Mackintosh.

Original, if anonymous, design was achieved with cheap Melamine at approximately one-tenth the price of the architect-designed wares. From Copco, consumers get design that combines fun and function, and the design professions are left with some awkward questions about quality and originality and the meaning of celebrity. Innovation in both the treatment of the forms and their decoration was possible for Copco. For other clients, with more functionally specific needs, such a degree of innovation is not possible. What is needed is a refinement of a shape that is largely predetermined. "Refining and innovating can be the same thing," says Viemeister. "When you're designing something that's very specific, a major innovation there would be, to anyone else, a slight refinement."

Refinement was the order of the day for the Serengeti sunglasses, a series of minimal designs in high-tech materials such as carbon fiber, monel metal, and photochromic glass for Corning Optics. Smart Design owes this client to work inaugurated in the 1970s for Corning Glassworks cook-

ware by Davin Stowell, founder of the company that became Smart Design. With so many similar models of sunglasses already on the market, the first thought was that there was nothing new to say, and that all a new design could contribute would be some tiny decorative variation on previous glasses. As the designers set to work, however, they found that no one had ever developed the anthropometric database appropriate to the design project. So they took their own measurements on a number of subjects, correlated them with data in a NASA anthropometric source book to ensure their statistical significance, and incorporated their findings into the design process. The NASA data also allowed the designers to predict and then maximize the percentage of people that each style of glasses would fit. "Now we're experts on this," says Viemeister. "When we started we didn't know how big to make them. Before, everyone just designed sunglasses to fit on themselves. The problem with sunglasses is that they're sold on a stand—there's no one there to adjust them to fit you the way there would be in an ophthalmic store. So, if they fit more people, and make more people happy, more people will buy them. That's why we did this study: we knew that if they were made to these dimensions they would fit 70 percent of the people." The design of the Serengeti sunglasses is a classic case of what one might call supply-side ergonomics at work, in which the link between sound ergonomic design and the potential for increased sales could hardly be clearer.

Smart Design's best work mixes ergonomic design with an expressive or metaphorical content. A travel iron for Japanese manufacturer Sanyei provides an example. Its handle slides off the iron's body and then around its base for storage and transport, giving the design the necessary portability. This quality is invoked in the name, "PostCard," printed boldly on the side of the iron. A steam version of the iron, called, naturally, "SteamShip," conveys both steam and travel. Its water is contained in a clip-on capsule that looks like a steam turbine atop the sleek iron wedge shape. The metaphor and its careful emphasis in the name chosen for the product does not only

function at this basic level. There is a subtler historical reference in the forms of the "SteamShip" to the streamlined locomotives of the machine age. Promotional photographs of the iron with its steam jets in action bear a remarkable parallel to pictures of the Twentieth Century Limited engine designed by Henry Dreyfuss in 1938. Through allusions like this, Smart Design not only evokes an age when travel was more romantic, but also seeks to reappraise the reputations of the first great industrial designers and makes the case that their expressive charisma might once again be appropriate. "Systems designers and ergonomists shouldn't lead the profession. We need those people who have something to say, who can communicate with the general public, to elevate the public's expectations for design." A proselytizing body of design criticism, Viemeister suggests, could work as it does for architecture, both to show consumers what is possible and to raise professional standards.

A more real problem was confronted in a project to design an X-ray mammography unit for Lorad, now marketed by General Electric. The challenge was to reduce the implicit intimidatory qualities of the machine while preserving a certain dignity so not to offend the medical profession. Colors were chosen to be less clinical than the usual white—beige and pink-brown, with the brighter color on the vinyl padding where the patient comes into physical contact with the unit, signaling its friendliness. "There's no reason a mammography unit should be scary. The idea that medical equipment, because it is so serious, must have a 'serious' design is completely foolish." Smart Designers know that serious design need not be boring design, and that playful design need not crack "jokes" to work.

Success in this area could cement for Smart Design a reputation it wants, rather than the one that it is unwillingly having foisted upon it. "We're getting pigeonholed," Viemeister complains. "People think that we do fun, goofy consumer products, which is not true. The point is that the same kind of design can also be applied to serious equipment."

8

Unlike regular glasses, which are fitted by an optician, sunglasses are sold right off a stand in a store. In order to fit the greatest number of potential wearers, Smart Design had to carry out its own ergonomics research and data correlation before embarking on designs for these Serengeti sunglasses for Corning Optics (6–8). Allusions to Charles Rennie Mackintosh can be seen in salad servers for Copco (9,10). Molded in plastic, they cost only a few dollars a pair.

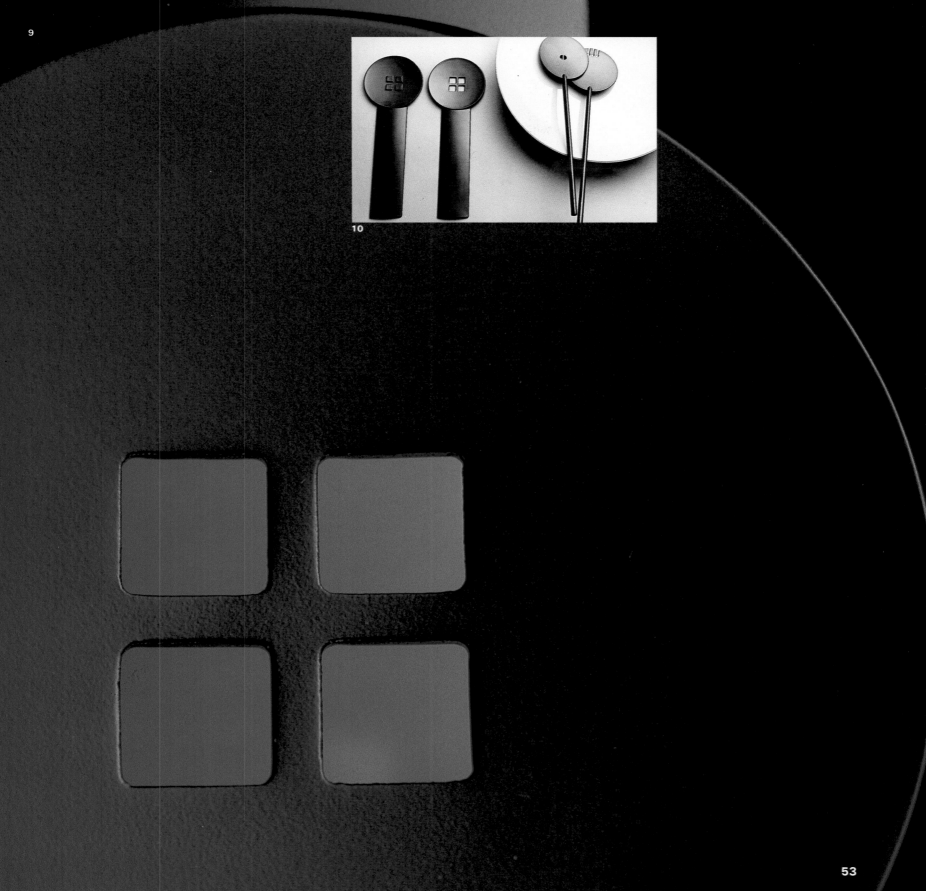

10

Looking out past the Barcelona chairs and chaise longue that adorn David Gresham's spartan Mies van der Rohe-designed Lake Shore Drive apartment to the Chicago skyline and Lake Michigan, it is hard to believe that his company, Design Logic, is not stuck in a Modernist rut, but is rather a hothouse for some of the most fertile and eclectic American product design.

Despite his love for Mies, Gresham's design has turned since the foundation with co-principal Martin Thaler of Design Logic in 1985 from a severe minimalism to a richer, more inclusive esthetic. He sees this as a logical reaction to the erosion by microelectronic miniaturization of the constraints that used to govern product form. Design Logic's manifesto explains: "the designer can no longer rely on physical requirements to dictate the boundaries of his/her decisions. From this position that 'technology is taking form away from the designer,' the designer must seek external inspiration.

"The wealth of imagery produced by the other visual arts can serve as a creative springboard." The use of the word "other" here gives away how Gresham and Thaler think about product design. To emphasize this brotherhood, Design Logic is drawing upon modern art movements for its new design vocabulary. Whereas the artist Marcel Duchamp made his name by raising everyday products to the level of high art simply by putting them in that context and thereby forcing people to think about what art meant, Design Logic is trying to do the reverse—to put art into products to make people think about the status of products in the home.

The symbolic role that products can play in people's lives is a central theme of the graduate industrial design program at Cranbrook Academy of Art, into which Gresham enrolled as a mature student, having been a practising designer for some time. His Cranbrook design study for a desktop computer shows the combination of his polished minimalist esthetic with a metaphoric approach. Instead of layering the computer's circuit boards, Gresham slots them together vertically to resemble books jumbled on a shelf.

Another student project, funded by RCA Corporation, accepts a more figurative semantic approach. Gresham's interest in the potential of fine art to inform product design began when he started looking around for appropriate metaphors that would enrich both the appearance and function of a video camera. Because the product was three-dimensional and related to facial features (both being held to the eye and ear in use and by acting as electronic surrogates to record sound and vision), Gresham looked at the paintings of the Cubists, such as Picasso and Léger, who sought to imply volume through the arrangement of surfaces. The form of the video camera became an extension of their interpretation of the face masks of African primitives. Gresham sees Cubism almost as "semantic painting." "I don't feel that we're just borrowing. I don't feel that we are ripping off details from paintings and putting them onto products. We're taking those ideas and extrapolating them into our time. We are taking that same idea of expression and trying to come up with technological analogue of the same idea." Just as Léger, for example, abstracted cogs and gears to symbolize the arrival of the machine age, so Design Logic has adopted a grid motif on a number of its products to express the digital electronic nature of their functioning.

Design Logic's output would be remarkable as student work, but what makes it truly exceptional is that it comes with full knowledge of the constraints and possibilities of the commercial world of manufacturers, mass-production, budgets and deadlines. Gresham and Thaler had previously held positions as staff industrial designers at the ITT Corporate Design Center, where they found their design solutions becoming formulaic. In addition, Thaler had come from the design methodological education of Bruce Archer at the Royal College of Art in London. Today, Design Logic vehemently opposes the process approach to design, taken by many large corporations, including ITT in Gresham and Thaler's day, and still high on the curriculum in many design schools, particularly at the nearby Institute of Design at the Illinois Institute of Technology. Gresham says scornfully: "If you make a big

enough bubble chart of all the impacting criteria, out of this distillation will drip the quintessential perfect solution—it's a fallacy. I don't believe that if you ask enough questions the form will determine itself. There is an infinite number of perfect solutions. I think the designer makes decisions along that process in terms of esthetics. So many designers in this country are trained that you can't make those decisions, that form follows function. Form follows function *sometimes*."

Design Logic sees itself more as a commercial test laboratory for Cranbrook's more intuitive and culturally attuned philosophy. Its first manufactured product, a redesign of the View-Master 3-D Viewer, shows that there is that commercially viable alternative, even if Design Logic did get the commission because Thaler's father is the president of View-Master Ideal Group. The success the product has enjoyed since has proven the design, by whatever route it came. One of *Time* magazine's best designs of 1986, the new 3-D Viewer has sales 20 percent greater than those of the old model.

The Cubists have inspired recent work, but Design Logic is aware that its design language must be broadened. Use of these fine art references exposes Design Logic's products to charges of elitism—many purchasers may not catch the references. New work extends the catalogue of references while sticking to the spirit of product semantics. Some allusions, for example to the abstract art of Malevich, Lissitzky and Nevelson, are no more accessible. Others are, however, harking back to America's great vernacular and expressive tradition in product design.

Three design studies for telephone-answering machines commissioned by Dictaphone show the range of sources. One is a low-lying flat unit with functions in low relief on its surface arranged as a highly formalized composition. A second version takes that icon of American communication, the mailbox, as its metaphor. The flag for mail is echoed by a screen to indicate the receipt of messages, and even the cheap corrugated metal construction of a real mailbox is not forgotten. The most successful of the three studies

is ostensibly a piece of art, a Cubist bust, that initially belies any function. In fact, the user speaks to record a message through its "ear," and it plays back calls through a loudspeaker that is its "mouth." The functional metaphor is rammed home by the message replay control on the base of the bust. By switching it, the user is giving the machine the electronic equivalent of a tap on the shoulder. The switch itself, intended to be manufactured in pressed aluminum, evokes the expressive knobs of 1950s electrical goods, but is rather at odds with the refined esthetic of the rest of the piece. The overload of imagery is an understandable reflection of Design Logic's unshackled creative powers, but it can lead to an unsatisfactory gestalt. Take Project 'n Sketch, a new View-Master toy that allows children to project the 3-D reel images onto paper and draw from them. The optics are hidden inside a circular vented molding that recalls Léger; light emerges from a mini Art Deco sconce; the tower that carries the mirror that reflects the light down onto the paper has streamlined motifs that pay homage to American machine-age design. Finally, the frame that surrounds the drawing paper is molded in plastic to resemble a traditional picture frame, a signal of the importance attached to children's pictures by their parents. Even the nameplate on the frame of a work of art is molded into the plastic as the natural place to put the manufacturer's logo. "Little tongue-in-cheek things like that, I think, are fun," says Gresham. "It's almost a dig [at product semantics] but it's also trying to get at a vernacular.

"By working on a definitely unique American vernacular," Gresham concludes, "we are doing something that is important to establish ourselves. We want to be a part of the world community, but we also want to find our own background. It's been my impression being there that what the European and Japanese consumers want to buy is something that is uniquely American—they want a Harley-Davidson, a Cadillac with tailfins. One of the ways for us to be competitive in the world community is for us to establish *ourselves* again. We're providing a way to end the trade deficit."

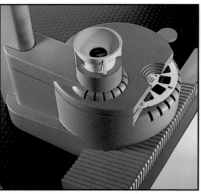

2

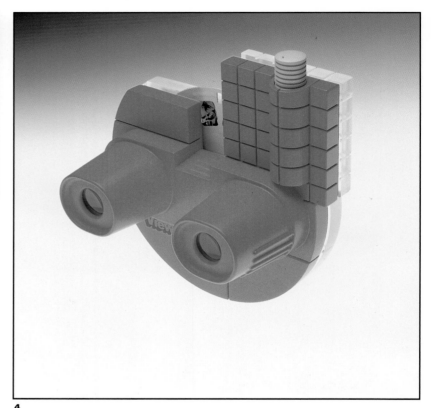

3

4

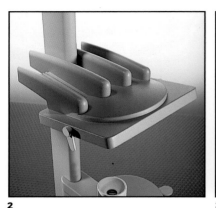

1

5

Toys for View-Master Ideal Group. "Project 'n Sketch" (1–3), which allows children to draw from slides, shows influences of Léger, Mendelsohn, the fascistic Art Deco, and the vernacular, to name a few. The redesign of the famous 3-D Viewer (4) and a talking "Book Reader" (5) use Cubist sources.

This terminal for Danish RC Computer (6,7) shows that American design can be prized abroad. Design Logic is also working for another Danish client, Bang and Olufsen, whose reputation for outstanding design is well known. Student projects for a computer (8) and video camera (9).

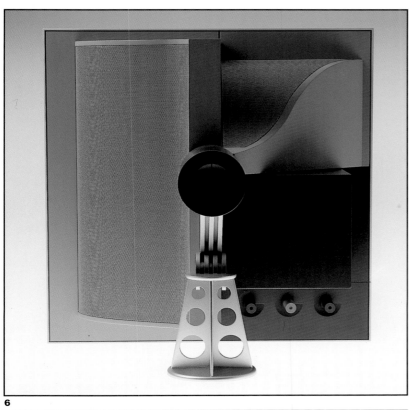

6

7

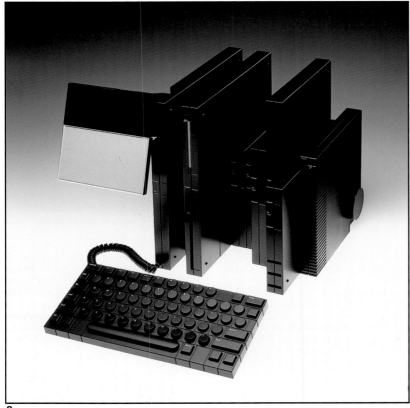

8

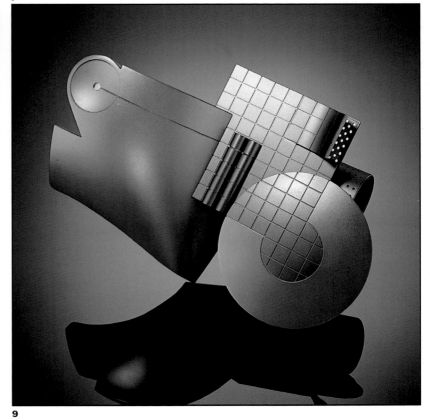

9

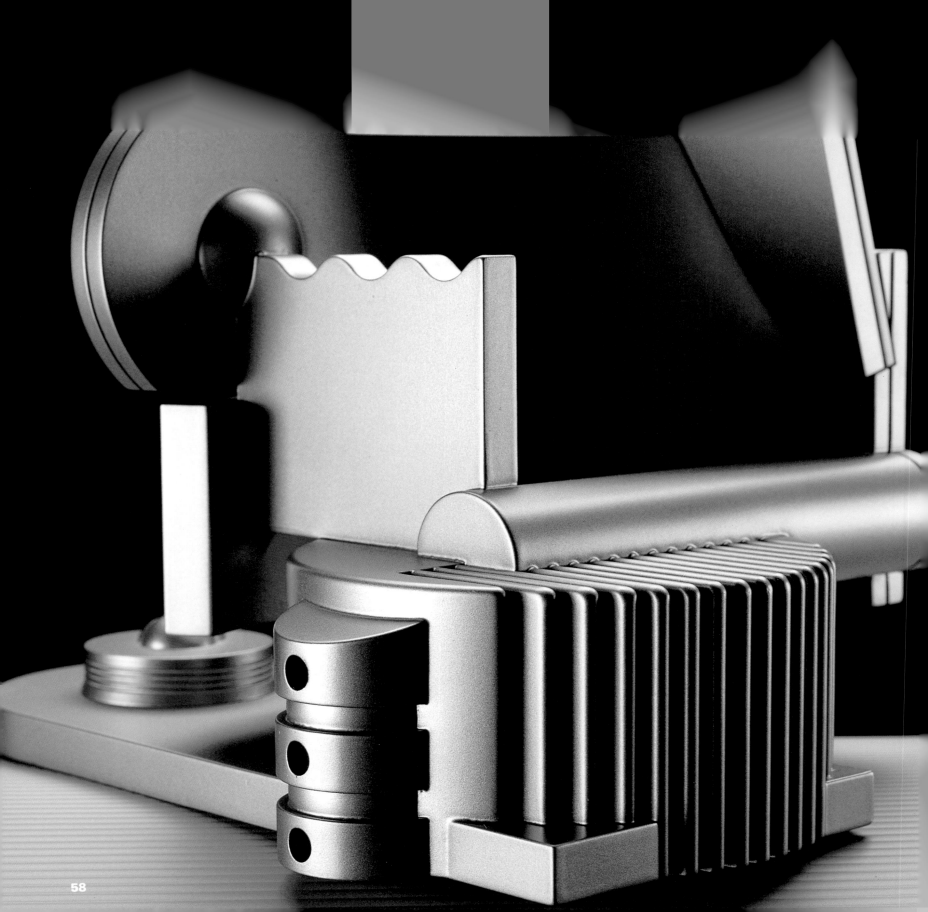

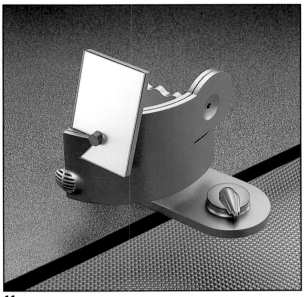

11

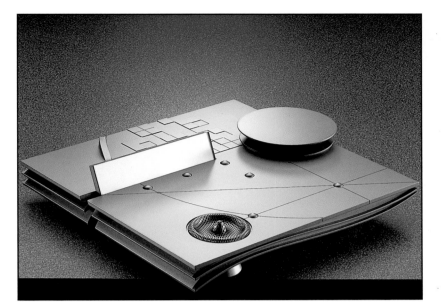

13

12

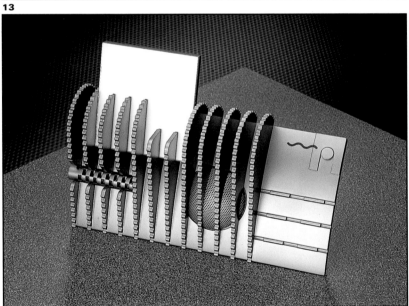

14

Three studies for telephone answering machines for Dictaphone. These designs take a variety of icons, from high art to the vernacular, as their starting points. One is a Cubist bust (10–12) with 1950s-style microphone and switch housings. Another is a sculpture garden (13) which combines the purist geometry of abstract art with references to the machine's digital functioning in the fragmented grid pattern across its surface, and to its human interaction with almost erotic forms for the microphone and loudspeaker. The third study (14) takes a traditional US mail box as its icon, even echoing the corrugated appearance of the original. The parallels are functional as well as visual, with the mail box flag recalled in the pop-up flat-screen message display facility.

Drenttel Doyle Partners

When the launch of a new magazine inspires its readers to write in, they usually talk about its articles. Not so with readers of *Spy*, an upmarket literary satirical magazine launched in New York in 1986. "*Spy*," wrote one, "is terrific. The graphics: absolute shit. So precious. So self-conscious. So challenging to one who wants to read without being *arted* to death." Another called the design "provocative and imaginative without being derivative and trendy." Well, there's no accounting for taste. More perspicaciously, a third remarked: "If your designer's aim was to produce a magazine that looks like the arrangement of messages, clippings and pictures on our refrigerator door, he or she has succeeded."

As it happens, that was more or less the aim of *Spy*'s designers. Stephen Doyle, formerly an art director at M&Co. and before that at *Rolling Stone* and *Esquire* magazines, was the creative force behind the dramatically different looking new publication. Four years ago, he and Bill Drenttel, who had worked his way up through the Saatchi and Saatchi advertising agency during eight years to the exalted position of senior vice-president, took their chances by setting up their own firm. It was, they insist, "the most irrational thing either of us had done."

Their success since then shows it may not have been such an irrational thing after all. *Spy* was one early client for the agency before it was even sure what services it was going to be offering. Initially, Drenttel Doyle was to be its advertising agency, but as meetings went by, there arose the opportunity to design the magazine as well.

Doyle's aim was to express the multilayered urban sensory experience in the two dimensions of print. "We wanted to make the magazine look the way all those guys sitting round the table sounded arguing with each other. We wanted to bring to life graphically their differences of opinion and their sense of humor and all the different voices and undertones. It's information at different volumes. This magazine is about the experience of New York, where there are so many layers of things going on at the same time."

Spy achieves this with a number of quirky devices. A variety of typefaces is used, but mainly distinguished old ones so not to sacrifice readability for novelty alone. Doyle says ingenuously that he doesn't know or care whether he is using the original or a redrawn version in these instances, however. A complex grid allows a range of column widths, and colored type and background tints add to the layered effect. Overall, it looks a nightmare to spec.

There are problems with the design, but they are a small price to pay for the fun and the innovation. Some of the type is painfully small (the subject of another complainant's letter), and some of the motifs (such as rat and roach silhouettes to codify closed restaurants), funny the first time, do not really bear repetition every issue. Even these irritations are deliberate, of course. Small type is the visual analogue of barely being able to eavesdrop on some exciting piece of gossip at a party. Huge clamoring headlines are used ironically, at the expense of less knowing publications. The list of contents pushes the title logo off the top of one page, an ironic comment on the need for magazines to trumpet all their material at the front of the book. A similar trick overlaying the logo on top of the masthead of staff and contributors to fit the column knocks the self-importance of publishing people. All this confusion produces an effect it at first seems set on preventing—to make people read. "You cannot browse *Spy*," say Drenttel. "It's too dense, too layered."

A more serious, though in other respects quite similar, project is for the redesign of the *New Republic*, again a lively, literate, political, opinionated publication, though rather more restrained than *Spy*. And again, the magazine does not condescend to its readers by using lavish color illustrations. "I don't think that one of the problems is that they don't have a lot of spot art or photographs running through it. It's nice that it's a journal." Given this, sophisticated and witty use of type again became Drenttel Doyle's tool. "The magazine was too pale; it had a washed-out look, kind of overall gray. If you read it, in fact it's got a lot more color and contrast than that in the words." The grayness was relieved with frequent changes of typeface and size. A prototype contents page is so much better spaced and weighted than the old one that editors doubted whether is contained all the information (it did). A section of short news items takes the refrigerator note concept from *Spy* and reworks it elegantly in black on white only, with three different body styles on a page where a less considered magazine might have used rules and boxes and tints to break the monotony. Main opinion sections have huge initial capital letters to their bold headlines and a little mark like an embossed seal, in fact the long-running boat motif of the *New Republic*, to balance the composition without fussing up the text of the essay.

The use of these little graphic icons and sophisticated typographic tricks has much in common with work that Doyle and his art director, Tom Kluepfel, were doing at M&Co. under the direction of Tibor Kalman. When they left M&Co., one aim was to bring that sort of clever humor to a wider audience. Drenttel Doyle's dual role as a designing advertising agency helps them achieve that end. The design involvement with *Spy* now over, there is the magazine's advertising—the original role intended—to be taken care of. Here, design has been used to subvert the traditional distinction between editorial and advertising material. A series of multi-page ads for J&B Scotch whisky is given a running head, not "ADVERTISEMENT," as it would be conventionally, but "A J&B PROMOTIONAL SUPPLEMENT DESIGNED TO LOOK LIKE A REAL STORY IN SPY." As the 1988 election neared, the supplement was replaced by "The J&B Scotch-*Spy* Route *88 Campaign Manual." Providing answers to everything you ever wanted to know about the election but were afraid to ask, it uses stark Franklin Gothic headlines set in several sizes across narrow columns. The *National Enquirer* is echoed here, but there is a more subtle recall of the handbills that might have been found at Victorian political hustings back when everyone was less cynical about the electoral process. The general tone is summed up on the back cover

of the Campaign supplement with the Seal of the President of the United States encircling a cooked goose.

A series of advertisements for Caroline's, a New York seafood restaurant, attacks a different set of clichés. Most ads show a picture and run a few words that tell you what the picture already showed. Most ads also assume that the bigger and bolder the type, the more it will be read. Drenttel Doyle lambasts this commonplace redundancy with an overbold typeface coughing out one giant monosyllable, "Cod," say, and accompanied by a picture not of the offending fish, but of some dill or a piece of lemon or some other sea creature on the menu.

The underlying concern is that the content and design of what we see in print advertising need not insult people's intelligence quite so much as it does, and that it can and should be more on a par with the quality of words and images on magazine pages or graphics posters.

While most advertising agencies give short shrift to such design niceties, most design firms hardly regard billboards or magazine space as the greatest opportunity to do their best work either. Coming from both jaundiced viewpoints, Drenttel Doyle can perhaps do something about it. Says Drenttel: "It is rather ironic that there are what the design world might think of as mundane categories where I think we're doing some pretty exciting design. It comes from running the place based on a client relationship where you can take Mr. Average Business Guy who has never even heard the word design, and have a basis for trust."

The thinking is that people can respond to greater subtleties than they are often given credit for. "The audience has reference and memories, they have read books, they have heard music in their lives," Doyle points out. They can make associations. There's no reason that the selling message should be the *only* message in an advertisement even if the client insists it is *one* message. "Wouldn't that be nice, if people selling soap decided to talk to people like they were *people*?"

THE NEW YORK MONTHLY · OCTOBER $2.50

SPY

JERKS
THE TEN MOST
EMBARRASSING
NEW YORKERS

A PENN & TELLER
TRICK TO PLAY

HAREM, SCARE 'EM
THE GORDON LISH STORY

ROY BLOUNT JR.'S CROSSWORD

SPY MAP: GANGLAND NEW YORK

PAUL RUDNICK ON MISSING MOMS

1

Kurt Andersen   E. Graydon Carter
EDITORS

Thomas L. Phillips Jr.
PUBLISHER

George Kalogerakis   Susan Morrison
DEPUTY EDITORS

Drenttel Doyle Partners
DESIGN DIRECTORS

Mark Michaelson
ART DIRECTOR

Santiago Cohen
ASSISTANT ART DIRECTOR

Karin Silverstein
PICTURE EDITOR

Joanne Gruber
COPY EDITOR

Nell Scovell
REPORTER

Joseph Mastrianni
EDITORIAL ASSISTANT

Eric Kaplan
CUB REPORTER

Kathleen Adams   Caroline Howard (photo)
Lisa Lampugnale   Anne Mortimer-Maddox
RESEARCH

**Roy Blount Jr., Holly Brubach,
Sarah Crichton, Tad Friend, Joey Green,
Tony Hendra, Ann Hodgman,
Howard Kaplan, Melik Kaylan, Mimi
Kramer, George Lange, Jamie Malanowski,
Guy Martin, Patty Marx, Ann C. Mathers,
David Michaelis, Lawrence F. O'Donnell Jr.,
Mark O'Donnell, David Owen,
James Pendergrast, Paul Rudnick, Taki,
Nicholas von Hoffman, Luc Sante,
Richard Stengel and Ellis Weiner,
among others**
CONTRIBUTING EDITORS

**Holly Barnett   Caldwell Davis   Emma Joels
Anne Shearman**
ADVERTISING SALES REPRESENTATIVES

John Norton
ADVERTISING CONSULTANT

David Lange
PRODUCTION CONSULTANT

Lisa Auslander
OFFICE MANAGER

Peter Lubell   Matthew Nelson
INTERNS

SPY (ISSN 0890-1759) is published monthly,
except February and August, by Spy Publishing
Partners, The Puck Building, 295 Lafayette Street,
New York, N.Y. 10012. © 1986 by Spy Publishing
Partners, L.P. Application to mail second-class
postage rates is pending at New York and
additional mailing offices. Subscription rate in the
United States, its possessions and Canada: $25 a
year. POSTMASTER: Send address changes to
SPY, P.O. Box 854, Farmingdale, N.Y. 11737-9954.

2

Party Poop

With everyone complaining about the mea___ restrooms at the Javits Center, Glenn Be___ baum has decided to rent Mortimer's out ___ trade events. When Wanamaker heiress Fernanda Ni___ launched her collection of familiar-looking chintzes (ins___ Glenn let her turn his restaurant into a ladies' boud___ Nancy Kissinger found somebody her own size to p___ on—she and Jamie Niven (below right) pillow-talked ___ the shadow of a giant chintzy canopy bed. The next we___ the Dallas Apparel Mart unhitched at Mortimer's to h___

3

NAKED CITY

f

THE *f*INE PRINT

(continued)

KEEP YOUR EYE ON THE TIP OF MANHATTAN
There have been nine cases of leprosy in New York City so far this year. In California,

t

___he ___
Harrim___
might b___
after al___
what bu___
could ac___

4

Inaugural issue cover (1), a masthead (2), details from the "Naked City" short items pages (3,4) and a spread (5) from *Spy,* a much needed satirical magazine for New York and beyond, started in 1986. Doyle, who was art director for the early issues, explains how it differs from other publications: "It's more of a vaudeville magazine. It's kind of a three-ring circus, rather than having the flatness of many magazines as they tell you exactly what is going on in a deadpan, put-you-to-sleep tone of voice . . . I think that in American magazines there's an awful flattening out going on. More and more magazines are less and less one man's or a group of people's viewpoint about something meant really to stimulate and inform and argue . . . magazines baby-talk to people . . . *Vanity Fair* sort of minces around. *Spy* does the same thing with a chip on its shoulder. Americans haven't seen anything like that before. . . . This magazine is much more about the experience of New York, where there are so many layers of things going on at the same time. That has to do with the size of the type . . . It's not afraid to be ugly once in a while."

CAN ANYONE BE AN ARTIST?

He was a regular guy, a writer. But then the German authorities decided he was a talented sculptor. And then, three months ago, he took Berlin by storm. A hoax? High culture gone wacko? GUY MARTIN *tells his amazing true story.*

Ich Bin Ein Artist

In Berlin, the mock artist   amid his mock work

As far as I've been able to understand it, the whole thing started because I owned a dog, a brilliant Irish setter bitch that I'd brought to New York from Alabama. Marlene and I used to walk through the Bowery, where I had a loft, and around Orchard Street. We communicated with each other telepathically as we strolled through the souk of junkies and whores on Delancey. Since life prevented the dog from using her omniscient nose to read for prey, she developed a remarkable ability to read the street: who was harmless, who was in trouble, who was bad.

We also had cats, given to us by people who thought we needed them. I built the cats a scratching post out of some scrap wood and an old piece of carpet turned jute side out. It was an ugly, khaki-colored object six feet tall or better. They used it as a sort of reconnaissance pole and emergency bailout tree when they weren't getting along with the dog. The tree bore a lot of traffic.

The cats shredded the carpet in very short order, great dun-colored chunks of it hanging this way and that. Because my loyalties lay with the dog, I was lazy about replacing it. I figured I'd just let them rip the whole thing off and then I'd tack on a new rug.

It was summertime. Summer is traditionally the season for Europeans to tour the city, and that year the hip ones had discovered the charms of the Lower East Side. When they got as far down the Bowery as our house, however, it usually meant that they were lost. The dog knew they were in trouble.

One afternoon at the corner of Bowery and Spring we saw a pleasant-looking fellow, dressed in white, puzzling over a map at the phone booth. His name was Norbert Stück; he was an artist from Berlin and he was looking for Clintonstrasse. I told him Clinton wasn't the sort of *Strasse* where one stood around with luggage. He said he would call to see if his friends were home. I used to live in Berlin, and my German was good enough to get the idea that Norbert's friends, one after another, were giving him the old brush-off on the phone. He badly needed help.

My wife has never been very good with social surprises, at least not with the ones I've presented her over the years, and so she was put out that I'd invited Norbert to park his bags in the loft. Somebody from the street? *Was I crazy?* She likes to hang about in her underwear in the summertime, and I think it irritated her to have to get dressed. But I'm convinced what upset her most was the language problem—that is, she'd never really heard me speak German. I won't say she imagined SS men jackbooting through her life, but I believe that for some time she and a large number of my friends had secretly felt that I was capable of a radical personality change, that my purchase on reality was just thin enough to let me jump ___

gument was not exactly how Norbert had imagined spending his first afternoon in America. He had good manners, and so he began to look around the loft in a heroic attempt to act invisible until the vibes settled down. Then he noticed the cat tree. He exclaimed at once that he must put this object in his next exhibition in Berlin. This seemed like a perfectly reasonable request to me, if a little sudden. But I had enough presence of mind to know it wouldn't look good if I translated it for my wife right then—"Great news, dear! Norbert here wants to take the cat tree back to an art show in Europe!" Instead, I asked Norbert, in German, "Don't you think it might be a little cumbersome on the plane?"

Norbert asked if I could send him the carpet. What seemed to move him most was that this object, once removed to a gallery, would be perceived as intentional. Norbert would be channeling the cats' obsession in a new direction, reducing the tool-ness of the object and replacing it with a nameless but awesome function. I didn't know it at the time, and didn't really care, but this was my first lesson in art. Then we went out for some beer.

I sent the cat tree to Berlin, where, I'm obliged to report, it was a huge success. Norbert exhibited the wrapping in which the thing arrived, including my exceedingly artistic customs declaration. What could they have made of all this? It wasn't important. The important thing for any budding artist, as I was to learn, is never to ask this question.

We couldn't stop there: for the next four years, Norbert peppered me with letters detailing his projects. His work grew to be admired for its rambunctious wit, and he had shows—or art actions, as he called them—in Berlin, Brussels and Lublin. In 1984 Norbert asked me to participate in an action called Projekt Kernseife—"Project Suet Soap," more or less. As part of a worldwide network of correspondents following his instructions, I was required to collect and send him pieces of used soap from restrooms in major museums.

Norbert's projects formed my outlook on postmodern art to a remarkable degree, naturally without my realizing it. At the time they simply fit my definition of pure fun: ludicrous but somehow meaningful errands, with no chance of a profit motive to creep in and spoil them. Plus, I enjoyed the conceit: I meet a guy on the street, I send him a piece of carpet, presto, now I must search for used soap in public bathrooms. What would he think of next? The key was to have no aspirations, none at all, and never to think of my jobs for Norbert as art.

But I'm getting ahead of myself. Looking back over the years, the determining factor in my development as an international artist was my arrest, at the hands of a gun-toting New York Sanitation Police officer, for walking my dog without a leash. It was again summer. The dog and I were apprehended in our usual lounging spot, a small

voracious heroin community and several dozen round-the-clock fellatio artists. The lieutenant said it was part of a citywide crackdown on unleashed dogs. Then he handed us a summons for $50.

To earn money to pay the fine, I wrote a portrait of our arrest, published under the title "Walking the Dog." When it came out, I sent it to Norbert, simply as an amusement. It galvanized him. He thought we should do some art based on it. He thought I should come to Berlin to walk the dog.

During 1985 there were strange bubblings out of Berlin about some sort of project. In the fall I received an urgent call—was I participating or not? *Participating?* In what? Norbert and some fellow artists had put together a group show, wherein each Berliner would work with a New Yorker to develop projects about the two cities. Norbert asked me to be his partner. It seemed baroque enough—no curator, huge art egos working on the buddy system—to be in no real danger of happening. I said yes.

But I had underestimated the power of art in Europe, and particularly in West Berlin. Somehow somebody persuaded a gallery, the Neue Gesellschaft für bildende Kunst (NGBK, "New Society for Visual Art"), to take on the show, and with that the Berlin senate coughed up DM 19,000, or about $9,500, for our catalog, our plane tickets and living expenses. *Catalog?* Suddenly things were serious. Then the senate gave us more money. People were calling me transatlantic to ask for "slides" of my "work." *Slides?* I had some slides from a trip to Africa. I did my best pretending to forget about it.

But my friendship with Norbert forced me to meet my casual commitment to art. We talked about walking the dog around Berlin. Norbert had in fact already committed us to this program by including it in the catalog. My "slide" in the

High concept, high charlatanry: the watchman's stool was swiped, the author's legs were stuck into the holes, the typewriter was in a cage. Voilà—*sculpture.*

5

Photographs: top, Enzo Eastel; center and bottom, collection of the artist

63

IDJAH HADIDJAH

JAIPONG

TONGGERET

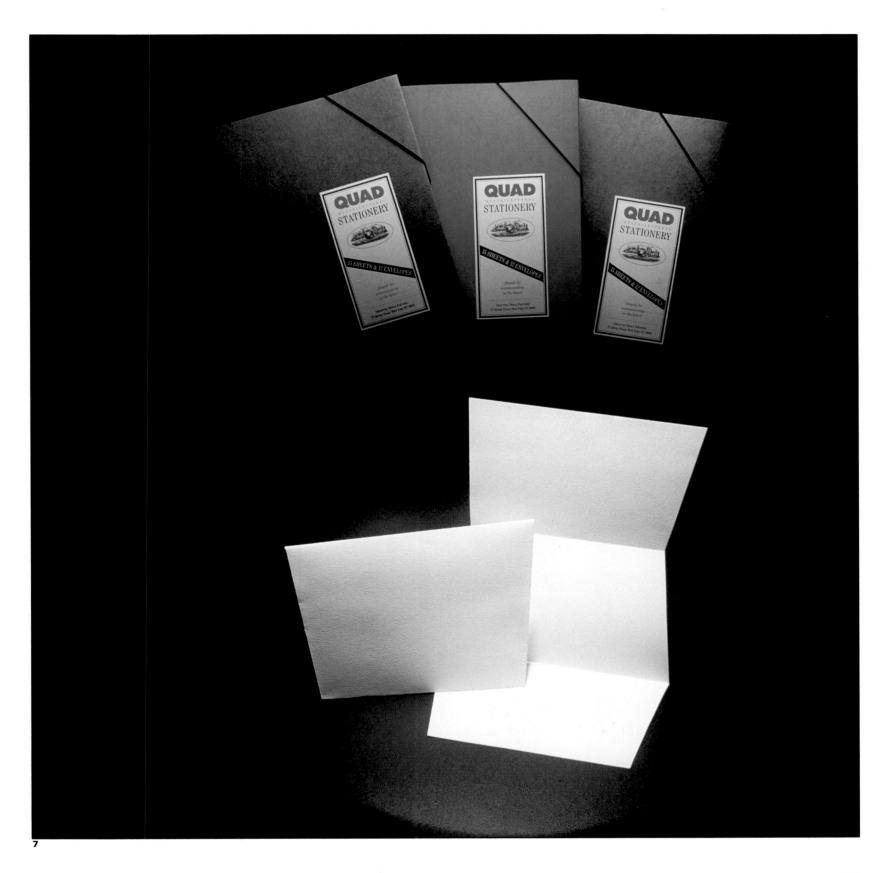

8

Eclectic combinations of typefaces, seen in album covers (6) and self-promotional pieces (12–14), mark Drenttel Doyle's work and continue an American tradition from the last century.

Irregularly shaped stationery (7) crosses the boundary between graphic and product design.

Page designs for the *New Republic* (8,9) taking themes first seen in *Spy*, work here in a rather more refined setting.

Drenttel Doyle's continuing flirtation with matters of literacy and literature is highlighted in a proposal, called KleenExLibris and published in *Industrial Design* magazine, for the redesign of the traditional book format (10). "KleenExLibris renders one's place in a book a complete mystery," the designers wrote. "Not 'til the last leaf do you know it's time to turn the television back on. Besides, you can also pocket your favorite passages for emergencies."

9

10

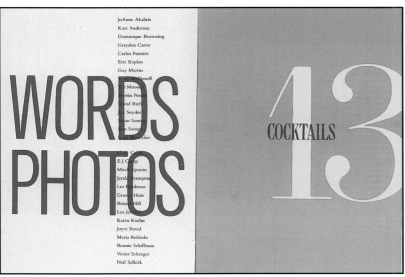

WORDS
PHOTOS

JoAnne Akalitis
Kurt Anderson
Dominique Browning
Graydon Carter
Carlos Fuentes
Eric Kaplan
Guy Martin
Terry McDonell
Jonathan Mooney
Martin Peretz
David Rieff
Joel Snyder
Susan Sontag
Sam Swope
Lois Wvethier

Chris Callis
E. J. Camp
Mitch Epstein
Jerald Frampton
Lee Friedman
George Hein
Brian Hill
Len Jenshel
Karen Kuehn
Joyce Ravid
Maria Robledo
Bonnie Schiffman
Victor Schrager
Neil Selkirk

COCKTAILS 43

12

13

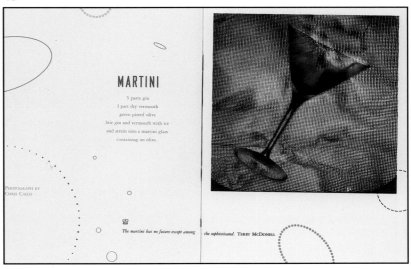

It's not something you'd belly up to order in a bar, because bourbon tastes better without the sugar, but the

MINT JULEP

is necessary, a sweet, heavy party-duty imposed on you by rooms of elderly people, by women you need to cultivate. The drink is baroque, theatrical, sad,

FEMININE.

And deceptive. The South lost the war of course (stop laughing, Yankee dogs, this is important), and so we have an unquenchable thirst for deception. We deceive ourselves so that we can afford to be

HONEST.

In this case, we camouflage our favorite poison from our palates.

How will a mint julep deceive you? Mint juleps are served at parties where everybody is drinking the same thing, namely, mint juleps. Thus the drink holds you captive. Served by waiters in mess jackets, drunk from a sterling Jefferson cup, the first mint julep will be

A SYRUPY KICK

that makes kissing the old biddies a lot easier. The second will get you through a conversation about dogs with a fascist mill owner, and the third will introduce you to his niece, somebody you'd actually like to meet. But by then—why in hell did you order it?—the fourth mint julep will have knocked you deceptively but firmly on your ass.

In a saucepan, bring the sugar and water to a boil, then stir over medium heat for five minutes. Let cool. In silver julep cups or highball glasses, add mint leaves (crushed once with the back of a spoon) and one tablespoon of

1 CUP SUGAR
2 CUPS WATER
3 FRESH MINT LEAVES
CRUSHED ICE
SPRIG OF MINT

sugar syrup from above. Mound crushed ice on top, pour in bourbon, stir, then add more ice to form mound slightly above rim. Freeze for thirty minutes, then add mint leaves tossed in powdered sugar as garnish.

GUY MARTIN · JOYCE RAVID

CAROLINE'S
At the Seaport

Pier 17

Shark

Catch of the day.
Grilled and served
with a choice
of tomato, spinach,
mustard, garlic
and Oriental sauces.
Hungry? Go fish!

11

MARTINI

5 parts gin
1 part dry vermouth
green pitted olive
Stir gin and vermouth with ice
and strain into a martini glass
containing an olive.

PHOTOGRAPH BY
CHRIS CALLIS

The martini has no future except among the sophisticated. TERRY McDONELL

14

Posters and print pieces for Caroline's at the Seaport restaurant (11) challenge some advertising conventions and mock others. The type is as bold and black as any client would want to see, but its meaning conflicts with the image part of the design in an oblique attack on the redundancy of many advertising messages.

"Right now," says Jörg Ratzlaff, "it's very fashionable to be European-trained. It's a good selling-point." Design firms don't come much more European-trained than Zebra Design, of which Ratzlaff is one principal. Ratzlaff was formerly at the prominent German-based frogdesign, and Thomas Bley, his partner, was the only German member of Memphis, the Milan-based international design group that revolutionized furniture and design in general at the beginning of the 1980s.

The two met as students at Hamburg's Academy of Fine Arts. Bley then won a graduate scholarship to Pratt Institute in New York, and Ratzlaff followed him two years later on a scholarship to New York University. The American courses complemented Bley and Ratzlaff's academic grounding from Hamburg with practical skills in business techniques and computer technology, and gave them what they needed to start their own business. Bley's wife, Bettina, will provide expertise in interior design once she has graduated from her architecture course at Pratt. Zebra's fourth limb is Hans Sommerhof, a retired Wall Street businessman who looks after the financial side of things.

Bley and Ratzlaff rejected the designer ghetto of downtown Manhattan when looking to establish an office, and opted instead for a spacious Brooklyn loft around the corner from Pratt. Lower rent and easy access to transportation both locally and back to Europe were the prime considerations.

Although Europeanness is a good self-promotion ploy, the Zebra designers are trying to create their own design vocabulary from their separate European roots. Says Bley: "While I was fooling around more with the avant-garde design, Jörg was interested in more straightforward industrial design. We have two different kinds of experience which we are now putting together." As Zebra Design, "we have done work on the fun side 'like Memphis' and more serious things 'like frogdesign,' whereas most designers here in America only do clean industrial design." Already, though, it is impossible to tell who designed what. A piece of furniture is as likely to be by the industrial designer Ratzlaff, and Bley contributes to the most functional product designs.

Levity is what Ratzlaff and Bley bring from their previous experience. A main aim of Memphis was to make design fun, while the approach that has made frogdesign successful has been the bringing of a lighter emotional content to a wide range of product types. Zebra has done some truly oddball products for Zelco Industries, manufacturer of the Itty-Bitty Book Light. These include a clock with twelve hour markers that are affixed to a wall separately from the central mechanism, and a Lapdesk product that incorporates the Book Light into a fold-out flat surface with a bean-bag-like base for it to sit comfortably on a user's lap. "There's a huge market in America for these kinds of whimsical items," notes Bley.

But it is with products that combine a certain degree of whimsy with clean industrial design that the company is really earning its stripes. The design is literally clean for a so-called "travel oral hygiene device" that won the 1986 Krups of North America design competition. One day the design will make an ideal gift for the executive on the go for whom the use of a mere toothbrush is just too proletarian.

The device is ingenious, unpacking to reveal an elastic loop that is adjustable to fit over most faucets and a toothbrush that snaps onto a length of plastic tube to give a fresh water rinse as you brush. When the device is stored away, its polished white plastic finish and subtle curves give it an uncanny resemblance to a human tooth. The designers did not set out with that intent, they say. As the design took form in sketches, a point came where it was realized the product could be made to look vaguely like a tooth. From there on, the form was preserved and the remaining details made to conform to the overall gestalt.

Semantics are equally strong in a water purifier designed for AquaSciences. Two irregularly-shaped water containers slot snugly into the purifier like parts of a puzzle. Each has a wavy motif along the outer edge

to signify the evaporation and condensation process by which the purifier works. These opaque containers hold the "dirty" water, while clean water collects, logically enough, in two transparent pots at the front of the unit.

Semantic expression can convey more than just the functional aspects of a product. The idea of technological change is what comes across in a digital audio tape-player that expresses the freedom that miniaturization brings. The body of the player is a wafer-thin substrate in the shape of a wave. The tape is left sitting visibly on top of the player, not encased within it, an indication that the tape itself is now the largest component of the audio unit. The fact that electronics goods of this type are getting ever smaller is further hinted at with one corner of the player seemingly nibbled away to leave an irregular edge. Day-Glo buttons on the metallic paint on the main body of the player complete the dramatic composition.

An altogether more serious project was the design of a wheelchair for a European client. Zebra's innovative solution was to be constructed almost entirely of injection-molded plastic parts, the potential advantage being a chair that was much lighter than most and thus more manoeuverable by disabled people. The drawback that helped dissuade the client from producing the chair was the high tooling cost required to fabricate all the plastic parts. Ratzlaff paints a cynical picture of design and marketing for such products: "The client said: 'We have these injured people, and they really need something new.' So we did it for them." Now, they haul the design around the trade shows and pick up awards for it. "They still use it for their shows to show the injured people, 'Oh, look, we have done something here, but right now we can't produce it.' That's all untrue. They could do it, but they don't want to do it. There's no need for them to." The cruel truth is that the rules of supply and demand do not apply where the need for a basic level of functionality is foremost. The client knows that the customers who will buy his wheelchairs need them badly enough to take what is offered. There is moral but little commercial incentive for improvement by design.

More formal furniture design is still important to Zebra Design, although this is no mere hangover from Memphis days. The hope is to bridge the gap between what is seen in America as "art furniture" and what can realistically be mass-produced. The manifest impracticality of Memphis furniture notwithstanding, this division is far less pronounced in Europe. In the United States, the problem is in the nature of the contract furniture business. The people who can afford "designer" furniture have a professional decorator to appoint their apartments with avant-garde items that never see a Main Street store. The rest of us fall prey to the dull conservatism of a retail industry that sees style as a choice between "colonial," "traditional," and "contemporary." American furniture designers, says Bley "have a lack of ability to design a chair that can be retailed for five or ten dollars. It's easier for them to do a chair for $5000 than for $5." While the five-dollar chair may be over-optimistic, any challenge to this area of design is to be welcomed.

Zebra's furniture design studies defy easy categorization. A display table for the Italian Driade company was a simple geometric prefabrication; a sofa designed to look comfortable only from the front (in reaction to plush sofas that look luxurious but are actually impossible to sit in) owes as much to the French designer Philippe Starck as to Memphis; simple, elegantly resolved chairs in aluminum, wood and fiberglass, or in spring-steel, rubber and laminated wood, recall the inventiveness with materials and techniques of Charles and Ray Eames.

In the European mold, Bley and Ratzlaff believe design is a multi-faceted discipline. It is already rare enough to be designing creditable furniture alongside competent products. Even in European countries, which never segmented design disciplines to quite the extent that America did in the postwar years, this degree of versatility is the exception rather than the rule. But when Zebra Design begins to fulfill its intention to do more graphics and interior design, it will be among the leaders in setting a new standard for the way design is seen in America.

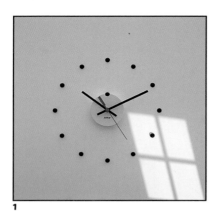

1

2

3

4

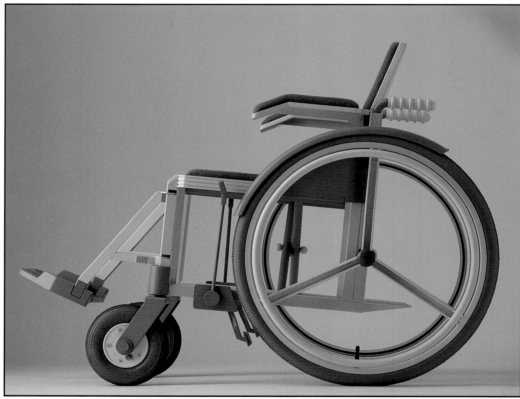

5

Apparently self-indulgent formal design can often shed light on more pressing problems. Zebra Design's interest in furniture design (1–4) gave it additional expertise when commissioned to design a lightweight wheelchair (5). The design won a Braun prize, but is not being manufactured. Designs for solar-powered model automobiles (6) show an opposing light-hearted trend in Zebra Design's work. The firm has designed toys and gadgets for clients in West Germany and in the United States. "There's a huge market in America for these kinds of whimsical items," says Bley.

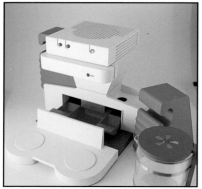

7

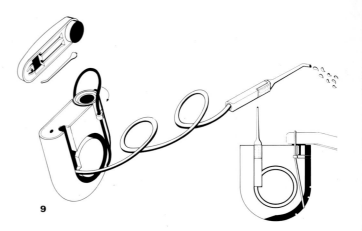

9

8

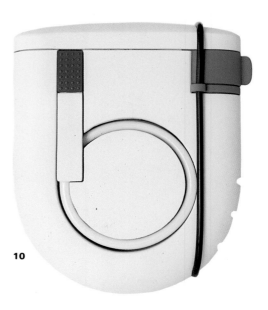

10

Water distiller for AquaSciences (7,8). The toothlike Travel Oral Hygeine Device (9,10) won the 1986 Krups of North America design award. Anticipating technological advance, Zebra Design's digital audio tape player (11) expresses the ever-shrinking nature of the recording medium by making the machine that plays the tape even smaller than the tape itself.

The great painters and sculptors have always strived to convey the power of human emotion in their work.

But,

over the years,

designers have found themselves less and less able to emulate them.

The technologies of printing and mass-production have carved a gulf between creator and respondent.

With the loss of the craft tradition of the cabinetmaker and the letterpress typographer,

the metalsmith and the illustrator,

it seems,

the prospect died that design could engender emotional response.

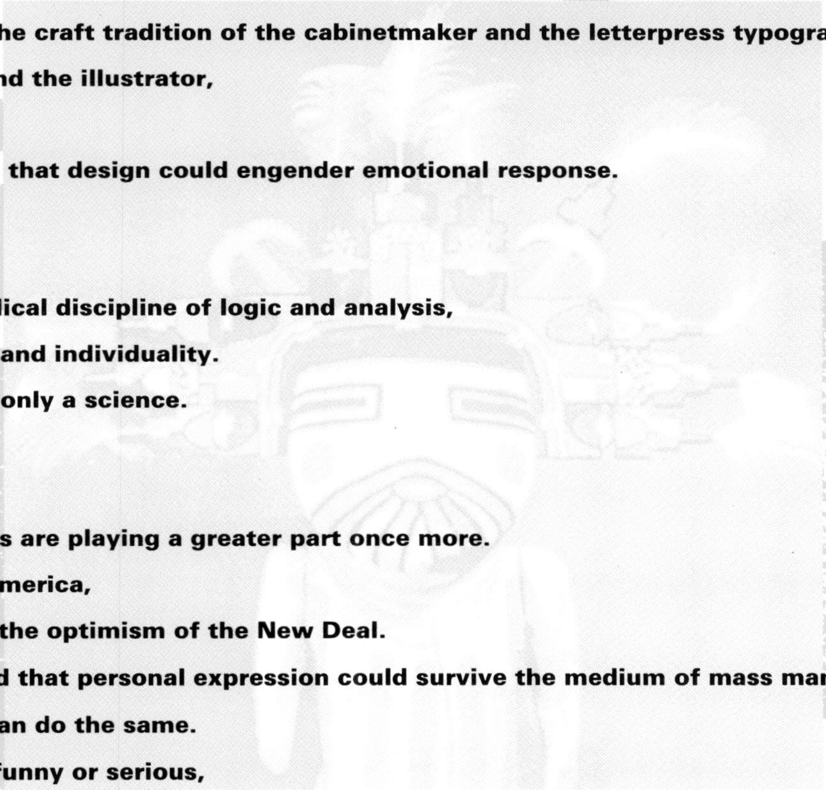

Design,

some say,

became a methodical discipline of logic and analysis,

devoid of feeling and individuality.

But design is not only a science.

Intuition,

expression,

and pure esthetics are playing a greater part once more.

In machine-age America,

design conveyed the optimism of the New Deal.

Designers showed that personal expression could survive the medium of mass manufacture.

Design this day can do the same.

Products can be funny or serious,

sexy or austere.

Graphics,

like art,

can express emotions running from agony to ecstasy.

With today's design expected to satisfy world markets,

an appeal to our basic shared human emotionality becomes one of few routes to appeal to all cultures.

Some say Boston is the most European city in the United States. So there is some logic in its being the home of Design Continuum, a versatile design practice set up five years ago by Gianfranco Zaccai, after 12 years as an industrial designer for a company with offices in the United States and Italy.

Zaccai commutes between Boston and Milan where Design Continuum maintains its other office and where, in 1987, it won a prestigious *Compasso d'Oro* award, Italy's highest industrial design honor, for its medical equipment design for Instrumentation Laboratory, the company where Zaccai first worked.

"The reason I'm in Boston wasn't a premeditated business decision," he confesses. "It was a nice place to live. I envision Boston to be a hybrid between Europe and America." Zaccai's move was well timed. It came as the phoenix of Boston's rise from incipient post-industrial slum to high-tech utopia was first stretching its wings. With Philadelphia and Montreal the other North America cities perceived as having the right qualities, hindsight allows that Zaccai probably made the right choice for his business as well as for himself.

His priorities in choosing his location were those, increasingly today, of any new design firm. A designer's modelmaking services, the client's manufacturing plant and tooling suppliers, and even the client itself can now be farflung. As it is no longer impractical to have clients across America, in Europe and in Japan, the location of an office becomes largely a personal choice, once the requirement for easy access to an airport is satisfied.

Zaccai left Italy at the age of ten, but got himself something that looks suspiciously like a typical Italian, broadly-based design education by first switching from architecture to industrial design at Syracuse University, and then adding a degree in architecture from the Boston Architectural Center. The result is that Design Continuum, if not quite a *salone*, is unusually open-minded about what it calls work.

Recent projects range from the industrial design of medical and laboratory instrumentation, to toys for Fisher-Price, to a series of street kiosks for Au Bon Pain, a local gourmet bakery, to an identity and promotional program to help the Massachusetts Department of Commerce promote the work of local craftspeople. One client retained Design Continuum to create a lecture hall interior for user-group demonstrations of its Continuum-designed laboratory equipment; another commissioned an apartment interior design.

Design Continuum has done well by being probably the best of the still surprisingly few design firms in Boston, one of America's stronger local economies. "We were able to benefit not so much from dealing with American companies as with European companies," Zaccai says paradoxically.

Starting with one Italian and one American client gave Design Continuum its edge. "European customers tend to be more demanding. They are less likely to part with their money on a device and see it as a disposable item. They will appreciate all aspects of the product characteristics that communicate value," says Zaccai. The consequence of this consumer outlook is that the companies serving them and their designers build in added value. "There is a cultural predisposition amongst European clients, certainly Italian clients, to incorporate good design even if they don't believe it will make the product sell better. There is still a greater view of a business activity being somewhat a cultural activity as well. There is a pride factor in making a product beyond something that merely generates income. It's an extension of the people who are making it." This has not been the case in the past in the United States "because there is an excessive amount of specialization on the part of business managers and not enough broad education background in things such as history and the arts—a broadness of cultural perspective."

Now, however, Zaccai detects a change. It seems fair that Boston, with its European affinity, its own cultural, historical and intellectual heritage, and its booming, free-spending new industry, should be among the first

areas to reflect such a change. "I think corporations are appreciating more a liberal arts background with specialization to follow. American products are much higher in quality than they were even a few years ago. It's happening because the United States is becoming less insular. It has to."

There are no prizes merely for pointing this out. What separates Zaccai from his competition is his company's approach to this shifting scene. "I was interested in providing planning, industrial design, engineering, and then graphic design and taking it all the way through to architectural design. It's not nearly so much fun always to be designing things in the same context and to the same scale. I enjoy one day designing something whose major function is to be decorative, and the next day something where decoration has almost no role and yet it's still a piece of design." By way of contrasting examples, Zaccai offers a cranial drill that will never be appreciated for its esthetics, and a seldom-occupied apartment for a workaholic that was designed to be appreciated almost solely for its superfluity of formal ideas as a therapeutic environment and an extension of the client's personality.

Somewhere between these two extremes comes the main body of Design Continuum's work. Here, the need is to suppress unnecessary manifestations of technological excess, and the design problem is knowing what to replace it with. The two extremes—the functional solution and the formalist solution—are most closely united in a current project to design a peritoneal dialysis machine. A functional design would suffice for use in a hospital environment, but because this dialysis unit is intended for home use there were new considerations. Zaccai's answer was to design it to be both a machine and a piece of furniture, giving it an active role within the home since it could not readily be disguised or hidden away. The project illustrates clearly how "formal" design can benefit practical design.

A similar problem was confronted in the design for an artificial-intelligence workstation for the Symbolics computer company. To what extent should such a workstation convey in its design its essential difference from previous workstations—its ability to "think"? Design Continuum's answer was that it shouldn't. The skilled scientist who will use the workstation is unimpressed with such gee-whizzery. The design solution was to make the machine disappear as much as possible, so that it became simply the contact between the operator and the machine.

A second medical example provides a different case study. Having hidden the essential complexities of a medical analysis system (the Automated Coagulation Laboratory for Instrumentation Laboratory of Milan that won the *Compasso d'Oro*), what new elements do you introduce? Design Continuum tried to build in the idea of enjoyment and prestige. "You can't have fun with a machine that is in any way threatening you. Individuals who use these machines are used to having to repair them, maintain them, refill them. They can get hurt by them. There's the danger of infection." Once these hazards had been minimized, and function perfected, there were only a few fundamental elements left over—a rotating cuvette receptacle and a pivoting snoutlike pipette. "Those elements can be as much fun as a model railroad," says Zaccai. The prestige for the operator comes with the satisfaction of being able to perform a complex task with apparent effortlessness. "The machine functions the same way a sports car functions for the general consumer." The need to introduce lighter, less mechanistic qualities without compromising the instrument's credibility lies at the heart of this design.

"If the solution is to work at the same time at different levels, it has to address several somewhat conflicting needs at the same time. You have to consider cost in designing elements that will never be seen, because only by doing that will it give you the freedom to put more resources into areas that are seen and touched and felt. You're designing for different motivations—for the salesman who's interested in selling the machine, for the user who's interested in having a trouble-free day, for the passerby, for the patient in the case of medical equipment. A design that only addresses one of those is not enough."

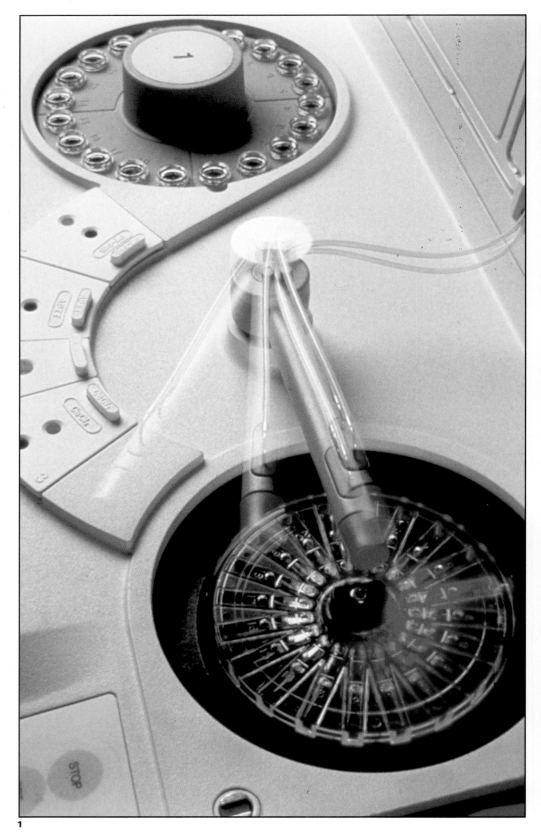

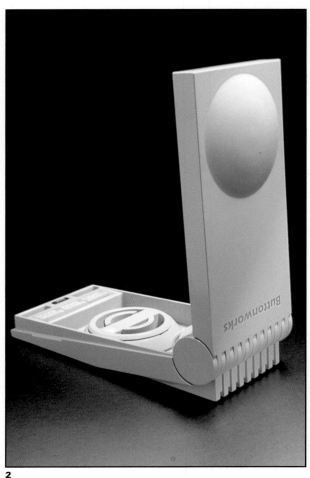

1

2

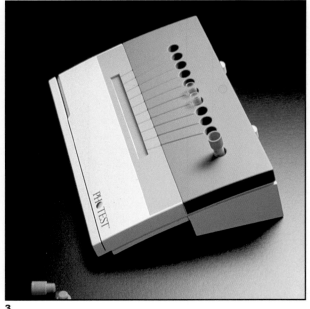

3

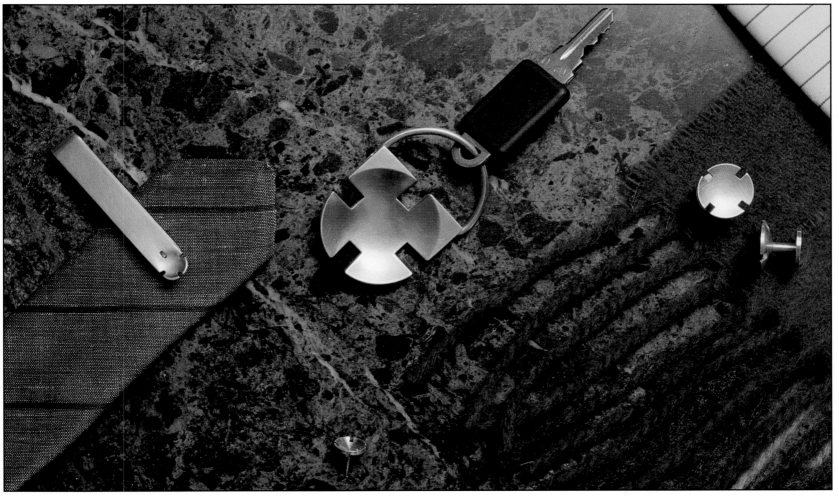

4

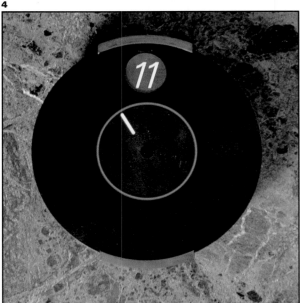

5

Automated Coagulation Laboratory
(1): "As much fun as a model railroad." Other scientific equipment
(2,3) brings similar ease and even enjoyment of use through clean layout
and curving geometries.

Design Continuum's jewelry and clock
(4,5) show that industrial designers
are no longer solely designing industrial products.

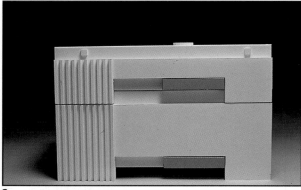

8

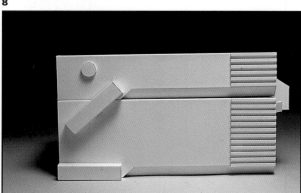

9

7
Computer terminals and peripherals for Symbolics (7–9) adopt a purism more often seen in the best European design. It was deemed appropriate here to make the "intelligent" product appear unthreatening. Reducing the bulk and adopting a highly abstract form achieved this psychological goal, but also threw up a technical one: how to fit all that power into as small a unit as possible. The densely packed terminal occupies roughly the space of a conventional PC, but despite its greater power, requires only natural convective air cooling, making it almost silent in use.

A commission to design booths for Au Bon Pain, a local gourmet bakery (10), led to a job designing an apartment for its president (11).
An in-house project for a personal fan (12) picks up modish colors and elements from post-Modern architecture.

10

11

Doublespace

The action takes place in a cube of a room with flecked grey walls. Minimal music thrums gently somewhere outside the cube. Enter through a corner door that skews the geometry as it hinges aside: David Sterling, diminutive, neat, and nowheresville middle American; and Jane Kosstrin, New York Jewish, larger than life with tumbling red hair.

If this sounds like a promising beginning for a piece of experimental theater, it's not entirely accidental. Sterling and Kosstrin are the principals of the New York graphic design firm, Doublespace, which has made its name working for clients in the avant-garde arts. Their environment serves to get them in the mood for their work.

The key to Doublespace's graphics is in its attempt to capture some of the emotional impact of the original art or performance that it represents. More often than not when a firm tries to convey emotion in graphic design, that emotion will be a positive one—a sense of fun or optimism or humor. This already happens in fashion and cosmetics advertising, where companies such as Esprit and Jordache have made an impact with "real" people and their trivial emotional crises. An equally bland sense of fun comes through in Doublespace's work for a junior fashionwear retailer, Justin Allen.

Where Doublespace differs is in choosing to plumb deeper emotional depths, showing a far richer, denser, and more ambiguous mix of feelings. "Emotion is powerful. It's evocative, it makes you stop. It *is* a sales point in a way," says Sterling. Its most expressive and complex work has been for the Brooklyn Academy of Music, for which it has produced the Next Wave Festival collateral for the past six years. It is graphics to go with the "difficult music" of BAM, such as that playing in the studio today. Kosstrin explains: "We'll play tapes of Steve Reich, Philip Glass or Meredith Monk while we work. We get out our scissors and free-associate."

For it is by old-fashioned cut-and-paste collage that Doublespace chooses to communicate the panoply of human emotion. Human figures and faces—anguished, astonished, ecstatic—sharply juxtaposed at different scales are a favorite vehicle to deliver the required impact, but more abstract contrasts are also collaged to great effect: clashes of black and white, or of primary or printers' colors; a tight control of two-dimensional space and the juxtaposition and layering of ideas within it; a sprinkling of humorous or ironic little icons; all play a part. The 1987 BAM Next Wave Festival material shows the richness that can result. The tabloid brochure is built around the theme of the four elements. Doublespace says, in a moment of forgivable pretension, that it tells a tale of biblical proportions, running from creation (fire), to material existence (earth), to transcendental existence (air), to resurrection and rebirth (water). The decidedly earthbound subject matter for the main draw of the 1987 program, Peter Sellars's opera *Nixon in China*, for example, collages pictures of Cho En-Lai and Mao Tse-Tung with a Nixon silhouette on a background of earth represented both as a globe and as a more material texture of earth surface. Throughout the brochure, secular and pagan motifs—alchemical and zodiacal symbols—are contrasted with more spiritual backgrounds. Rich, dark colors and metallic gold and silver highlights complete a sumptuous effect. A calendar for the magazine *Manhattan Inc.* used similar devices, scattering icons—an Eiffel tower, a fountain pen, an airplane, a key—pertaining to magazine sections on things like travel and business gifts. Perhaps the piece's ironic homage to Mammon—a gold New York skyline was its backdrop—was one reason for its never being printed.

Altogether starker is work from previous years' BAM performances. Vicious cropping of a collage of black-and-white portraits of selected performers makes the 1985 Next Wave poster stand out. Geometric overlays in red and blue draw the composition together and set up a dialogue between the figures. Color changes occur across sharp lines that slice across faces giving a Cubist sense of three-dimensionality. In a 1984 BAM piece featuring the dance theater choreographer Pina Bausch, the images are monochromatic, relieved only by urgent red typewriter type. Without color to bring a sense of dynamism, Doublespace relies on powerful perspective shots and sudden changes of scale.

The work of Max Ernst inspires Doublespace's use of collage, but a range of early 20th century artists who experimented with collage, type, and photographic images also figure as influences, among them Alexander Rodchenko, El Lissitzky, Man Ray, and film director Sergei Eisenstein. "We're image-makers. There's no reason we should be separate from our artist and painter brothers who are also image-makers. There didn't used to be that kind of separation. There's no reason why spirits, guts, life, emotion shouldn't be brought out in this image-making too," says Sterling.

Like Ernst, Doublespace uses found images from contemporary culture as one ingredient. In collage, they take those images and interpret them to create new images. When Kosstrin and Sterling first set out from Cranbrook Academy of Art, however, it was with an impartial eye that they observed and documented their observations through the medium of a magazine called *Fetish*, and subtitled "the magazine of the material world." At first, *Fetish* might appear to be simply the usual crass celebration of consumerism, but it attempted to be something rather more. Deliberately avoiding being curatorial, it was an inclusive rather than an exclusive collection of *things*. And this was in 1980, well before yuppies and Madonna, the original material girl. Now, to cater to our heightened consuming passions, Sterling and Kosstrin want to relaunch *Fetish* as a kind of *People* magazine for objects. "We see it as a year-end catalogue that brings together lots of images and says to people, 'In 1988 the climate was such that x,y, and z were produced.' We want to try to try to make some correlation between what is happening in architecture, art, fashion, music and performance, and begin to see what our culture is really producing," says Kosstrin. Another aim of the magazine would be to push the boundaries of graphic design in its amalgamation with text. *Fetish* promises to offer in print the same sensory overload that MTV offers in video. "Young audiences are used to richness and imagination of visual expression, and I think there's room for that in magazines," says Sterling.

After three issues, the first version of *Fetish* ran out of cash, and Sterling and Kosstrin turned to the potentially more lucrative field of professional design. The fashion and entertainment industry offered an outlet for their art-inspired work, while mainstream business was something to be avoided. Now, however, Sterling detects signs of a change for the better. In the past, corporate America was abetted in its adoption of simple imagery by the Swiss International Typographic Style. What started out as a method for synthesizing one strong central image to express the essence of a company became, in the hands of less skilled designers, simply a recipe for producing anonymous bland logotypes. Later, matters became still more desperate because of the way business was being done in the United States. "Large corporations still want to be more and more abstract because of this new tendency toward mergers. They do so many things that they don't want a specific image. They want a very general image," Sterling observes.

Finally, the conservatism of large corporations is perhaps beginning to wear off. Doublespace discovered this when it was asked to design retail environments for Maybelline Company and Orion Pictures, two sponsors of a "Museum of Unnatural History" exhibition organized by MTV and an entertainment marketing group, MEGA, traveling to malls around the country. Its respective contributions were a walk-through blow-up of a girl's vanity and a space-age deco theater facade. Such special promotions for company divisions serve as a back door for them into less restrictive design, Kosstrin feels, and as younger executives take over that enrichment will continue. "The people who are now attaining positions of power are people who grew up in the television age, in an age when there was that layering of information, with images popping up in front of them all the time. They don't fear that sense of layered meaning."

In the past, BAM has introduced its audience to

JERZY GROTOWSKI,

ROBERT WILSON,

PETER BROOK,

TWYLA THARP. . .

Now BAM introduces. . .

PINA BAUSCH and the WUPPERTALER TANZTHEATER have developed a reputation of legendary proportions in sold-out seasons in London, Paris, and the major European arts festivals. The company will open the Olympic Arts Festival in Los Angeles on June 1, 1 9 8 4. T h e following week they will make their N e w Y o r k debut at t h e Brooklyn Academy of Music in what will be t h e season's major performing arts e v e n t. There will be only 12 perform-ances. O n l y 2500 subscribers can be ac-commodated w i t h the best seats. Please order n o w before the engage-ment is sold out.

"Never

did

"Every t i m e has its fash-i o n s, and every cultural p e r i o d its g u i d i n g personalities. In new theater this person-ality is PINA BAUSCH. I say 'new theater' . . .to desig-n a t e that theater of movement which looks to the future. . . ."

Artforum

PINA BAUSCH. . . .AN EARTHEN RITE, COLE PORTER

1

2

Pina Bausch brochure (1) for the Brooklyn Academy of Music, 1984. The 60-inch long piece achieves the quality of an epic mural.
1985 BAM Next Wave Festival street posters (2–4) can be read separately or together for similar effect.

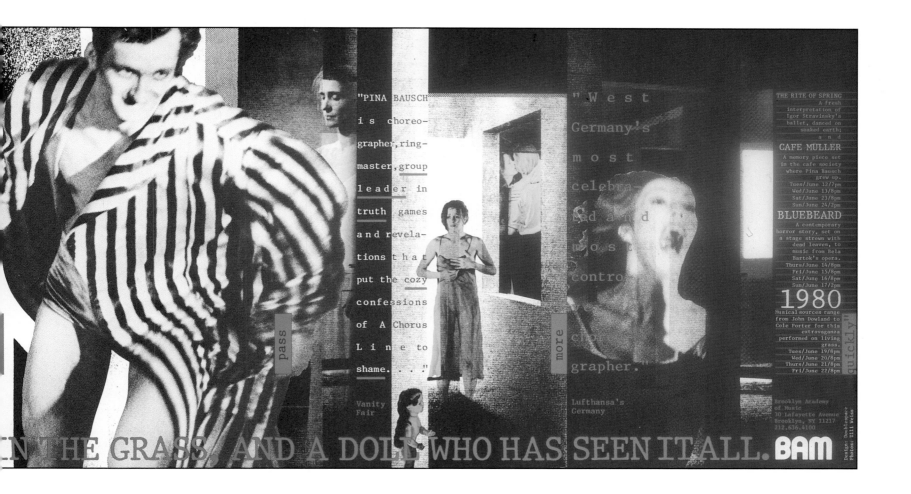

"PINA BAUSCH is choreo-grapher, ring-master, group leader in truth games and revela-tions that put the cozy confessions of A Chorus Line to shame...."

pass

Vanity Fair

"West Germany's most celebra-ted and most contro-ver-sial chor-eo-grapher."

more

Lufthansa's Germany

THE RITE OF SPRING
A fresh interpretation of Igor Stravinsky's ballet, danced on soaked earth; and

CAFÉ MÜLLER
A memory piece set in the cafe society where Pina Bausch grew up.
Tues/June 12/7pm
Wed/June 13/8pm
Sat/June 23/8pm
Sun/June 24/2pm

BLUEBEARD
A contemporary horror story, set on a stage strewn with dead leaves, to music from Bela Bartok's opera.
Thurs/June 14/8pm
Fri/June 15/8pm
Sat/June 16/8pm
Sun/June 17/2pm

1980
Musical sources range from John Dowland to Cole Porter for this extravaganza performed on living grass.
Tues/June 19/8pm
Wed/June 20/8pm
Thurs/June 21/8pm
Fri/June 22/8pm

quickly

Brooklyn Academy of Music
30 Lafayette Avenue
Brooklyn, NY 11217
212.636.4100

IN THE GRASS, AND A DOLL WHO HAS SEEN IT ALL. **BAM**

Design: DoubleSpace
Photos: Ulli Weiss

3

4

85

FE TI SH

The Magazine of the Material World

Premier Issue

T r a v e l

Postmarked Properties

Going Micro

Car Games

$2.00

Car Games

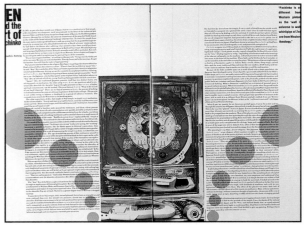

Cover (5) and spreads from *Fetish* on car collection (6) and Japan (7). High-relief graphics for the Modern Mode furniture showroom at the International Design Center, New York (8).

5

6

7

8

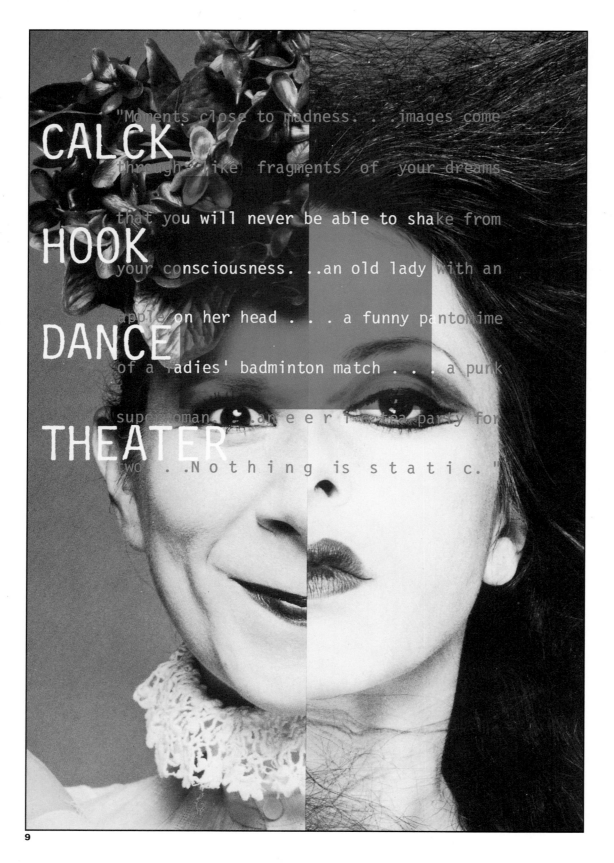

CALCK HOOK DANCE THEATER

"Moments close to madness. . .images come through like fragments of your dreams that you will never be able to shake from your consciousness. . .an old lady with an apple on her head . . . a funny pantomime of a ladies' badminton match . . . a punk superwoman . . . an eerie tea party for two. . .Nothing is static."

Calck Hook Dance Theater brochure, 1985 (9).
1987 BAM Next Wave Festival tabloid format with successive spreads (10–13) relating performances to themes of fire, earth, air, and water.

9

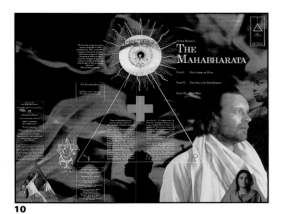

10

11

12

STEVE REICH

"Mr. Reich is enormously skilled . . . a talent of density and substance"
New York Times

THE MESMERIZING MUSIC OF COMPOSER STEVE REICH, THE VIRTUOSO WIZARDRY OF JAZZ GUITARIST PAT METHENY, AND THE SUPERB MUSICIANSHIP OF THE BROOKLYN PHILHARMONIC CONDUCTED BY THE EXTRAORDINARY YOUNG MAESTRO KENT NAGANO, COMBINE TO CREATE AN EVENING OF MEMORABLE MUSIC MAKING. REICH, WHOSE **THE DESERT MUSIC** (ALSO WITH THE BPO) WAS A HIT OF THE 1984 NEXT WAVE FESTIVAL, HAS CREATED THREE NEW WORKS: **THREE MOVEMENTS**, WHICH WAS PREMIERED IN ST. LOUIS IN 1986 AND IS SCORED FOR FULL ORCHESTRA WITH EXPANDED PERCUSSION; **ELECTRIC COUNTERPOINT** WHICH WILL BE GIVEN ITS WORLD PREMIERE IN THE 1987 FESTIVAL AND FEATURES SUPERB JAZZ GUITARIST PAT METHENY LIVE AND ON TAPE; AND **THE FOUR SECTIONS**, ALSO FOR FULL ORCHESTRA AND WHICH WILL RECEIVE ITS NEW YORK PREMIERE.

STEVE REICH
OPERA HOUSE
NOVEMBER 5 – NOVEMBER 8

STEVE REICH

PAT METHENY

KENT NAGANO

THE BROOKLYN PHILHARMONIC

MEREDITH MONK
CAREY PLAYHOUSE
NOVEMBER 20 – NOVEMBER 22

ELLIOTT SHARP AND CARBON

IV
WATER
(SENSITIVE)
THE RETURN

"For vigor, originality, and sheer streets-of-New York excitement (Sharp's music) stand(s) up to anything written today."
Village Voice

ONE OF THE EAST VILLAGE'S REIGNING MUSICAL VISIONARIES ELLIOTT SHARP IMBUES HIS MUSIC WITH EQUAL SHARES OF RAW ENERGY AND MUSICAL INTELLIGENCE. A VIRTUOSO MULTI-INSTRUMENTALIST, SHARP WILL LEAD HIS ENSEMBLE CARBON – EXPANDED TO 13 PIECES – IN THE WORLD PREMIERE OF HIS NEW WORK, **LARYNX**. THE ENSEMBLE WILL INCLUDE FOUR OF DOWNTOWN NEW YORK'S MOST ACCOMPLISHED PERCUSSIONISTS: ROBERT PREVITE, DAVID LINTON, CHARLES K. NOYES AND SAM BENNETT, BRASS AND SLAB PLAYERS DAVID FULTON AND JIM STALEY, AS WELL AS THE SOLDIER STRING QUARTET. WITH INFLUENCES RANGING FROM HENDRIX TO STOCKHAUSEN, FROM CHANTS OF TIBETAN MONKS TO BRASS BANDS OF NEW ORLEANS, SHARP'S COMPOSITIONS ENVELOPE THE LISTENER WITH OVERWHELMING, PRIMITIVE POWER.

MEREDITH MONK
AN ARTIST AND HER MUSIC

DESCRIBED BY GREGORY SANDOW IN KEYNOTE MAGAZINE AS "A SUBSTANTIAL CULTURAL PHENOMENON" MEREDITH MONK IS EQUALLY RENOWNED AS A COMPOSER, CHOREOGRAPHER AND THEATER ARTIST. HER FIRST NEXT WAVE FESTIVAL CONCERT WILL FOCUS ON HER UNIQUE MUSIC, MUSIC DISTILLED FROM HER REMARKABLE VOCAL RANGE AND CHARGED WITH HIGH VOLTAGE EMOTIONS. THESE CONCERTS WILL INCLUDE THE WORLD PREMIERE OF A LARGE SCALE WORK FEATURING HER VOCAL ENSEMBLE: ALLISON EASTER, ROBERT EEN, CHING GONZALEZ, ANDREA GOODMAN, WAYNE HANKIN, NAAZ HOSSEINI, NICKY PARAISO AND NURIT TILLES, PLUS A SERIES OF DUETS WITH PIANIST NURIT TILLES AND ADDITIONAL NEW COMPOSITIONS.

"Remarkable, imaginative artist."
New York Times

THE PETER ZUMMO ORCHESTRAS

"Mr. Zummo's pieces are like watercolors . . . subdued and translucent, their patterns converge and drift apart with an intuitive improvisatory feeling."
New York Times

AS A COMPOSER AND TROMBONIST PETER ZUMMO EMPLOYS A DECEPTIVELY CASUAL APPROACH TO HIS MUSIC, USING HAUNTING REPEATED PHRASES AND GENTLE IMPROVISATION TO CREATE A NEW FORM OF MINIMALISM. THE RESULTS ARE DISARMINGLY MOVING AND BEAUTIFUL. A FORMER MEMBER OF BOTH LOVE OF LIFE ORCHESTRA AND THE LOUNGE LIZARDS, AND WINNER OF A 1986 "BESSIE" AWARD FOR HIS SCORE FOR TRISHA BROWN'S "LATERAL PASS", ZUMMO WILL PRESENT SEVERAL WORKS AT BAM, INCLUDING THE WORLD PREMIERE OF A WORK FOR NINE-PIECE ENSEMBLE MADE UP OF HIS CORE GROUP: MUSTAFA AHMED, GUY KLUCEVSEK, ARTHUR RUSSELL, BILL RUYLE AND HIMSELF, PLUS FOUR ADDITIONAL MUSICIANS.

HENRY THREADGILL AND ORCHESTRA

COMPOSER AND SAXOPHONIST HENRY THREADGILL WILL LEAD 28 HAND-PICKED INSTRUMENTALISTS AND SINGERS IN THE WORLD PREMIERE OF A LARGE WORK TO DATE: **RUN SILENT, RUN DEEP, RUN LOUD, RUN HIGH.** AS LEADER OF THE ACCLAIMED TRIO AIR, AND HIS OWN HOT STOMPING SEXTET, THREADGILL HAS INJECTED A NEW ENTHUSIASM AND REMARKABLE INVENTIVENESS INTO THE JAZZ IDIOM. FOR HIS BAM-COMMISSIONED WORK, THREADGILL WILL MIX ELEMENTS OF WESTERN MUSIC WITH NON-WESTERN PERCUSSION, BALANCING COLLECTIVE IMPROVISATION WITH STANDARD NOTATION TO CREATE A GRAND RITUALISTIC MUSICAL EXPERIENCE.

"Threadgill is redefining the modern jazz ethos . . . interlacing the chamber ensemble, the pit band and the after-hours jam more convincingly than any single figure in music."
Musician

RUN SILENT,

RUN DEEP,

RUN LOUD,

HENRY THREADGILL
CAREY PLAYHOUSE
DECEMBER 11 – DECEMBER 12

ELLIOTT SHARP
PETER ZUMMO
CAREY PLAYHOUSE
NOVEMBER 13 – NOVEMBER 14

13

There are those who refuse to accept frogdesign as a truly American design practice. The name, after all, not only gives the firm its amphibian logotype, but also betrays its origin: frog is an acronym for Federal Republic of Germany. Its office in Campbell, California, was set up five years ago as the German company began to find its base in Altensteig in the Black Forest too parochial for its global ambitions.

Yet frogdesign (this modernist conceit in the use of lower-case letters is preferred) represents the status that many American design firms would like to attain. It is a multinational consultancy with brand-name multinational clients, it charges fees well above the average, and, through the charisma and forcefulness of its founder Hartmut Esslinger, it can push to get good work done and demand those fees. The influence frogdesign exercises over its peer firms, and the respect it has won from them, if grudgingly expressed at times, in the shaping of American design is disproportionately strong for a company just off the boat.

This mythic status was not achieved by chance. Over the past few years frogdesign has run a series of advertisements on the back cover of *Industrial Design*, the profession's principal magazine in the United States. They have served both to stimulate and to intimidate the rest of the design fraternity. The quality of modelmaking and photography for these glossy self-promotions make *Industrial Design's* back covers often more attractive than its front covers.

Another frogdesign intimidation is its internationalism. From the beginning of 1987 when it set up shop in Tokyo, frogdesign has had a base in all three of the free world's important manufacturing centers, the only design firm to do so. Esslinger now talks about the importance of design in the triad, a reference to Kenichi Ohmae's book, *Triad Power*. The way Esslinger tells it, frogdesign's growth came as a result of seeking out new design challenges. "When we wanted to design computers, we had to go to America and work for Apple; when we want to do consumer electronics and cameras,

we have to go to Japan. When you want to do great stuff, you have to go to the great companies." It is an assertion of the designer's supremacy that would have made Raymond Loewy proud. But this is no longer the Loewy era, and the statement raises questions about the nature of the designer-client relationship. How much can and should a design firm choose what it wants to design, and for whom it wants to design it? In evoking the self-assuredness and arrogance of some of the first generation of industrial designers, Esslinger seems to want to return the profession to a simpler time when clients expected of their designers a nothing less than a total esthetic vision. Fortunately, their design is such that clients often oblige.

Equally fortunately, Esslinger has a design philosophy to match that vision. "The biggest cultural task for the designer is to provide a variety, not so much of products, but of emotions, or feelings, or events. You need symbolism and emotional expression to make a product human." The need to bring emotion into products, through what director of design Herbie Pfeifer describes as "female design," is a reaction away from functionalist dogma. "Our tradition is Bauhaus and Ulm. There, emotion was reduced basically to nothing. Design was nothing to do with the individual." An iron for the Helen Hamlyn Foundation, shown at the "Design for the Elderly" exhibition at London's Boilerhouse, for example, has the voluptuous curves that would seem to merit such a sobriquet. Its sensuous form is complemented by the inductive heating technology that allows safe, wireless operation.

Ironically, it is some heavy hardware that helps make designs such as the iron more humanistic. A CAD workstation hooked up to a battery of German-built machine tools speeds the design process. At frogdesign, sketches are quickly translated into rough Styrofoam models. This rapid transfer from paper to three-dimensional solid modeling helps give frogdesigns their great tactility. "We use models from the first," says Pfeifer. "We don't show sketches. People appreciate models. Normally, we present two, three, maybe five concepts, and we always have the feeling that the most

emotional design gets the highest acceptance." Once a few Styrofoam models have been evaluated both for ergonomic and visual appeal, the process is repeated with more accuracy, now involving precise sketching on the CAD system, followed by automated modelmaking from a harder plastic using the milling tools.

Esslinger makes his emotional appeal a global one, assuming that personal expressiveness in a product can be general to all nations and cultures. At a time when many designers are interested in the design of products for so-called niche markets and are reacting against multinational corporate wishes for all their customers around the world to conform to a single taste, it is perhaps surprising to see a company like frogdesign pursuing the global cause. Pfeifer claims that its triad base enriches frogdesign's staff as they move between offices and compete informally with each other on some projects. "We try to be American here, but we have the advantage of looking over borders. We want individuals in frogdesign to be little supermen who understand the world from a higher point. Otherwise you cannot do good design. Maybe that's arrogant, I don't know."

This Nietzschean slip admits that frogdesign's work can only really suit clients, such as Sony in Japan, who achieve quality but at the expense of local cultural values. In America, frogdesign has done cameras for Kodak and Polaroid and children's products for Mattel and Worlds of Wonder, but it is Apple Computer that has been the mainstay of its California office. The personal synergy that grew up between Apple cofounder Steven Jobs and Hartmut Esslinger in some ways parallels that of Eliot Noyes and IBM during the 1950s and 1960s under the aegis of Thomas Watson, then IBM chief executive. Both firms followed a rare pattern of patronage, placing their designers on retainer. But whereas IBM was provoked into improving its design image when it saw the quality of rival Olivetti's product, Apple Computer, to its credit, made design a priority out of sheer belief from the start.

In return, frogdesign created an esthetic that was a significant departure from the established vocabulary of computer design at the time. new design language, dubbed "Snow White" by the two companies, gave Apple computers an appropriately unintimidating look by reducing the bulk of each part of the system so far as was practical and also by reducing the *appearance* of bulk, for example by sculpting away the rear of the monitors. For the first time, it made small, not big, a signal of powerfulness. White was chosen for all Apple products, and their family nature reinforced with a recurring motif of square-cut lines pressed into the molded surfaces. Apple's success has been such that this decorative element has now become a design cliché of the entire personal computer industry. Since Jobs' departure from Apple, the synergetic relationship has evaporated.

Steven Jobs meanwhile acquired Pixar, a manufacturer of animation computers, and launched NeXT to build a new breed of educational computer. NeXT and Pixar both commissioned frogdesign to design graphic computers. Rumors abound concerning the NeXT computer. One says that it will be matt black, a decision that sounds calculated to imbue the product with a saleable cult status among college students weaned on *Star Wars*, more than any higher-minded design thinking.

Esslinger clearly has the ear of America's darling entrepreneur. But he has words of advice for others. Like many other observers from abroad, Esslinger notes America has reserves of talent that are not being put to best use. "There's always been great work done by American designers—in Japan or in Europe. This is still the richest country in the world. Yet it spends nothing on industrial culture. Why should not America teach its managers how to use this very efficient tool to make industrial culture more human?" Esslinger also has a message for designers. "American designers should recognize their abilities and their chances." They must shed their inferiority complex, brag a little more, demand higher fees, promise more and deliver more. "Designers should be more professional in what they ask for, because if you do not ask for more you cannot do a better job."

1

2

3

4

5

Designs for Apple Computer (1–3) and
Worlds of Wonder (4,5) use whiteness
and brightness as well as the rounded
edges of what frogdesign calls "female design" to add emotional appeal
to technological products.

6

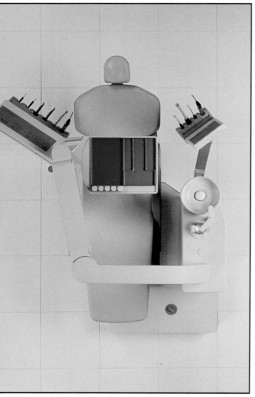

7

Office furniture (6) and dental units (7) for clients in the Federal Republic of Germany. An informal spirit of competition exists in frogdesign's three world offices in Germany, Japan, and California.

An iron design study for an exhibition on design for elderly people (8) shows how computer-aided design and modelmaking leads to sensuous product shapes.

8

9

Roller skates (9) exemplify the soft-edged, colorful approach that frogdesign applies to many of its commissions and that it brought to the United States. In the five years since the firm established its California office, it has become a powerful influence on American designers.

Tom Bonauro

Most magazine travel supplements have dull photographs of sandy beaches and white hotels. Tom Bonauro's ideas about travel, seen in a supplement to *Émigré* magazine, are rather different. The cover and flyleaves show images of the moon. Other spreads have a Michelangelo figure on one page facing a moon of Jupiter, and a detail of Caravaggio's "Saint Mary Magdalene in Ecstasy" opposite a close-up shot of a harpist culled from a book of engravings of musicians. "The idea," says Tom Bonauro, "was to go further than physical travel. I was thinking of emotional and mental travel as well, of being transformed and transfigured without moving physically." The Caravaggio and the harpist, for example, represent religious and secular transports of delight. "Putting them side by side lets the viewer make a comparison."

The luxuriant quality not only of the imagery but also of the paper and printing in this and other Bonauro work belies the fact that he had no formal training as a graphic designer. Working as a one-man operation in San Francisco, he has learned by doing, as he sought to use fine art images remembered from childhood and seen during his art history education at a local community college. "I've just applied my esthetic to the medium, and discovered how to work with the medium through experience and through printers and people who were going to execute my ideas."

Bonauro has turned his lack of a conventional design education to advantage by refusing to acknowledge the restrictions implicit in such an education that draw people into a routine, something he calls "an entrapment of our culture." His methods are different from those of most of the prominent coterie of San Francisco designers, whose work often relies on technical excellence to obscure the banality of the subject matter. "The reason why I stay away from a definite established design community is so that I can keep myself from believing rules that I don't think need to be there," he says.

He divides his own work into two approaches: "I see it as being conceptual, where the graphics are based on an idea behind them. And then there is work that is done strictly for a decorative purpose, design for design's sake. Those are the two styles I find myself interested in—a style that's so visually full that it meets a need on that level, and then work that's more minimal and idea-oriented." Bonauro implies that this sets him apart from some of the local establishment, whose work sometimes lacks both the richness and a conceptual base.

In both sorts of work, Bonauro uses elements drawn from the art of many periods as well as from more industrial sources. His studio shelves are stuffed with all sorts of fine art and copyright-free books, everything from a Diderot encyclopedia to a how-to book on good photography from the 1940s. But it is with Classical and neo-Classical art that Bonauro creates his most distinctive pieces. His hallmark has been the highly personalized cropping of photographs of Hellenistic sculpture and equally assiduously chosen details from the old masters of the Renaissance and the Mannerist periods. Bonauro drew on these periods because they appealed to him at the time of his art history studies and before, so it was something of a disappointment when similar source material, often slickly redrawn and reinterpreted, became the stock-in-trade of glib post-Modern graphic design. "All of a sudden I saw it used just to *represent* a style. I wondered if there was any personal or individual passion for those things. I decided to work in a different way, to get away from the hard-edged, bright pastel graphics and work with more image-oriented pieces."

Bonauro's images are often made up of Classical representations of the human figure, manipulated to capture some of the texture or chiaroscuro of the original, whether it is a mural, an engraving, or a photograph of a sculpture. Cropping of a piece emphasizes perhaps a gesture or a facial expression—features intended, especially by the Mannerist artists, to evoke a certain emotional response. By re-using these details, Bonauro gains a renewed power to evoke the same emotion, or by suitable juxtaposition of images, he can conjure up a different one. Even a fragment of a work as well known as the ceiling of the Sistine Chapel earns renewed attention in this way. "When I use those images," says Bonauro, "what's important is how you isolate them, how you crop them, and in what context you put them. I like to pick out images that, once cropped and taken out of context, you might not know where they are from. I think the issue is dealt with in fine art areas more than in design: it relates to the Marcel Duchamp idea that it's the artist who makes these images important by how they use them."

To the Classical imagery is added a more personal set of symbols that is less easily placed. A planetary sphere recurs in several pieces, and, related to it, the notion of sun and stars, day and night, and the passage of time. This cerebral-cosmic symbolism in everything from champagne promotion pieces to printers' samples to the *Emigré* travel piece serve no real client need, but is simply artistic self-indulgence. The enigmatic quality does not bother Bonauro. "That travel book, though it doesn't really say anything, evokes a feeling at least of question. People ought to start questioning things. That's why I'm not afraid if my work is puzzling or they can't quite define it. If it stirs up something intellectually or emotionally, then it's achieving a goal." Now that other designers have cottoned to the Classical esthetic, Bonauro is broadening his library of images to include scientific and technical drawings that are still more peculiar when reapplied out of context.

The other facet of Bonauro's work, where the graphic seeks to communicate an idea, not just a rich visual esthetic, shows in his own logo, a Works Progress Administration-like symbol of metalworking tools within a wheel that is his sardonic way of saying that although graphic design may look fun, it is really hard work. A more thoroughly worked example is the cover for the 1987 San Francisco Art Directors' Club Show book. Its cover has a Mannerist detail of a figure dancing on a globe depicting the inspirational side of the work contrasted with a starkly industrial magnification of a chemically patinated metal surface of a type used in the printmaking process. On the back cover, a colorful image of nature is made disturbing by its repro-

duction as a blown-up pre-screened image. The whole work is a journey through the alternately emotional and mechanistic process of graphic design.

Such unorthodox graphic and photographic treatments are offset with a richness in the choice of inks, paper stocks, and finishes. It is perhaps strange that it takes a designer without formal training to have such a fascination with the process and materials used in the production of a design. Again, it's an interest that Bonauro credits to his art history training and subsequent work in fine-art and book printing. Contemporary artists are more interested than graphic designers in experimenting with their medium, he finds. But there is a more pragmatic reason to look at unusual techniques and materials. "Some of my clients don't have huge budgets. So my approach is: let me make a $500 budget look like we had $10,000; if we're just printing one color, then let's use a paper that looks unusual, that looks very costly but that might not be."

As he extends his repertoire of motifs and materials and techniques, Bonauro hopes also to expand his business. He plans to set up a firm, initially more of a "school of thought," called Center, that will work as a collective, producing group work as well as pieces by individuals. "I think I've worked long enough by myself and satisfied my own ego," he says. "Now I want more social activity and response from people. As a group you can have a bigger effect. People take notice of you, and it's easier and more fun to work that way." To his roster of local, and some Japanese, clients, mainly in art and fashion, he wants to add national business clients. He says he looks forward to possibly having to fit his singular approach into a more restrictive format. And a recent project designing graphics for a post-Vietnam film, *Dear America*, directed by Bill Couturié, has piqued an interest in doing work that makes a social statement. "Of course, we work to support ourselves, but I would feel really empty if I didn't do a piece once in a while that had some real relevance to people's lives. It is just paper—I don't want to take it too seriously—but people are affected by these things."

1

2

3

4

5

6

7

SUNDANCE INSTITUTE

PRESENTS THE

1987

UNITED STATES

FILM

FESTIVAL

JANUARY 16-25 · PARK CITY · UTAH

CALL: 801-328-FILM

PRESENTED IN COOPERATION WITH THE STATE OF UTAH FILM DEVELOPMENT OFFICE

TICKET OUTLETS: COSMIC AEROPLANE, PARK CITY CHAMBER/BUREAU*
BRIGHAM YOUNG UNIVERSITY*

VOUCHER OUTLETS: UNIVERSITY OF UTAH, INKLEY'S STORES, EC-LEC-TIC

*ADVANCE PURCHASE ONLY. ONCE THE FESTIVAL OPENS TICKETS WILL BE TRANSFERRED
TO THE FESTIVAL BOX OFFICE IN PARK CITY.

8

9

Bonauro's unusual collections and assemblages of found images are put to use in pieces for San Francisco clubs (1), arts events (8), and friends and colleagues in the fashion and design business (2–7, 18). Bonauro's own promotional work (9–12) shows a range from art to industrial and scientific imagery as well as a preoccupation with the use and abuse of printing techniques in the off-registering of colors. The work may be assessed on solely esthetic criteria but the components of each image also invite meanings to be read into them, as with this promotional piece for Prototype Project (13).

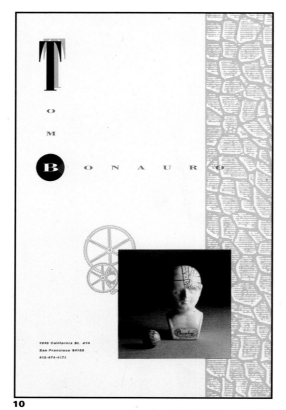

10

11

12

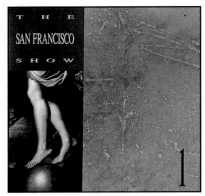

14

15
Scale, texture, and image and the interchange between them play an important part in the covers for the San Francisco Art Directors' Club 1987 "Show" book (14,15).

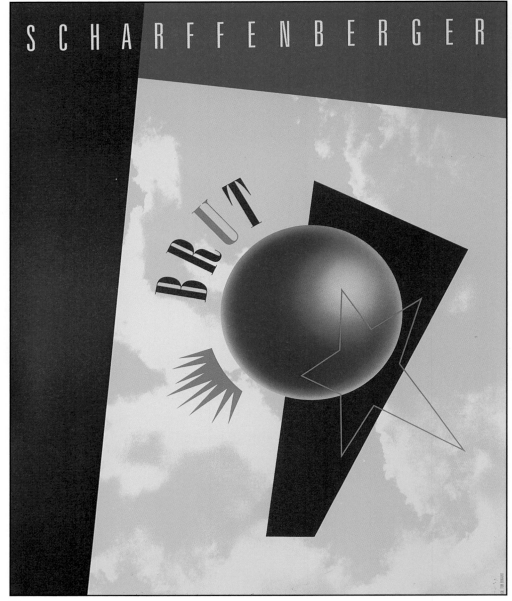

SCHARFFENBERGER

BRUT

17
Stark images from nature assume the enigmatic quality of American Indian petroglyphs on an album cover (16). A promotion for Scharffenberger (17), a champagne vintner, evokes the earth, the sun and the sky, and the passage of time between day and night, all appropriate to the ripening of the noble grape.

16

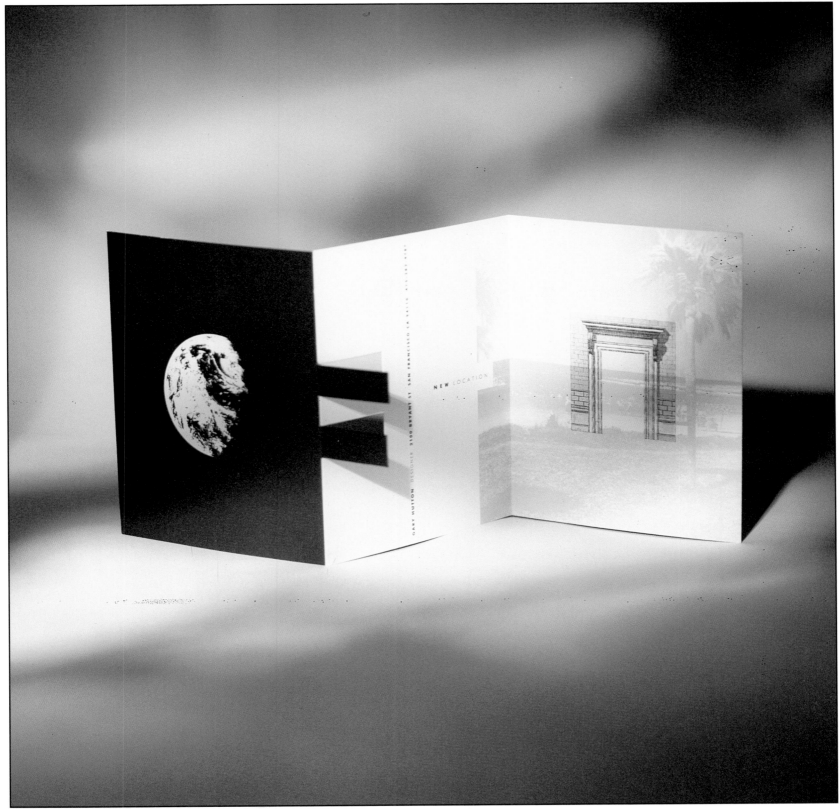

NEW LOCATION

GARY HUTTON DESIGNER 3160 BRYANT ST SAN FRANCISCO CA 94110 415 282 6181

The dynamism of business life in Silicon Valley—companies forever forming, growing, breaking up, and re-forming—is not limited to the computer industry. The design consultants they employ have it too. Consider the family tree of Lunar Design, a four-year old consultancy in Palo Alto. Its principals, Robert Brunner, Jeff Smith, and Gerard Furbershaw, were initially at GVO, a large, established design office in the Valley with a reputation for clean if understated high-tech product design but little in the way of an identifiable style. In 1983 they and colleague Peter Lowe split off to create Interform, a company with a more distinctive design language based on the European formalism of pure geometries, uniform radii, thoughtful detailing, and bold accent colors. GVO gave the Lunar principals a design education, and Interform taught them business. Interform grew to about a dozen strong and was set to expand further. Brunner, Smith and Furbershaw by now knew they wanted to stay small, so they broke away again two years later. What had been their moonlighting projects at Interform became the basis of a new firm, Lunar Design.

Such a frenetic pattern of movement is not unusual in this area. The Silicon Valley opportunity has been, and remains, a special one for a number of reasons. The young entrepreneurs and inventors who typically start their businesses there have nothing but their confidence to persuade venture capitalists to back them and nothing but vague promises to offer prospective vendors. That first product, both in its technological capabilities and its physical form, is all-important. "With small start-up high-tech companies, it's a clean slate. They have no design direction," says Brunner. The more astute start-ups are smart enough to realize they need to present a visible difference and open-minded enough to see that the way to get that is to involve a design consultant from the earliest practicable stage and give a fairly free rein in shaping the product. For the design firm, this often means that a personal working relationship builds up which allows that sort of distinctive work.

As a given technology matures, more companies set up to package it into products, capitalizing on a short-lived novelty. Gradually, the products more and more do the same things and, on the assumption that form follows function, increasingly look the same as well. Companies devise minor technological variations and find new market niches, which is what keeps them multiplying. But in the absence of these specialized new market areas the only way to differentiate is by design. "In the past five years," says Brunner, "practically everything that came out was new and could sell on its own merit. This year, more products are closer together in price and function, so issues of design and quality have become more important. We have some clients coming to us purely saying, 'Make me a beautiful product.'"

This sort of personal liaison worked for Lunar Design with Molecular Dynamics, a manufacturer of desktop microbiology analytical equipment, for which it designed a laser device for scanning gels used in protein analysis, and with the Lucasfilm company Droidworks, for which Lunar designed editing consoles with a joky anthropomorphic droid look with clumping feet and a video monitor like a giant head atop the desk's stocky body. Esprit Systems was the client requesting a beautiful product, and Lunar Design responded with the Opus 2 terminal, a compact, finely detailed terminal intended to look good in a sculptural sort of way from wherever it is viewed.

Requests like this threaten, or promise, to make the designer's role once again that of a "mere stylist," an image the industrial design profession has fought hard to shed. With an amorphous technology such as microelectronics, styling is bound to rear its pretty head. But whereas styling in past decades came to be associated, especially in automobile design, with poor mechanical reliability, there is no reason today why the notion of styling should not lose some of its stigma.

The proliferation of similar products in this very competitive marketplace does not only condition product form, but also determine the very structure of the local design profession. Silicon Valley companies' obsession

with secrecy, the result of many companies in close proximity all manufacturing virtually the same soon-obsolescent goods, often dictates that a given design firm cannot work for two clients on similar products. It is this paranoia that keeps the local design industry buoyant, with firms always fragmenting and reseeding themselves. Brunner credits the resulting confidence of the area's industrial designers not only to general Silicon Valley confidence, which he says is at a five-year high thanks to Apple Computer's recent good figures and to trade tariffs imposed on Japanese chip imports, but also to one design firm in particular, frogdesign, whose polished work for Apple Computer and other local high-tech clients has served to raise the quality of design overall. "They have shown what an aggressive approach can do. Before, designers had a bit of an inferiority complex to architects and other licensed professionals." Jeff Smith amplifies this common envy among designers: "Architects get a foundation that creates a mentality that they can do anything. That goes a long way to helping attack any design problem. A strictly formal product background tends to constrain you."

It is in an attempt to overcome these constraints that many American industrial designers are turning to formal design problems, channeling their spare time and creative juices into making art objects not for clients, but for their own amusement, or in some cases even for their own licensing or manufacture. Architects and many European designers have always indulged their fantasies in this way, but for the conventional American industrial designer of the past generation—a time when industrial design was trying to establish its credibility with business—to confess to such frivolity would have been professional suicide.

The cachet of imported Memphis furniture and Tizio lamps, however, has awakened a sense of competition. Design where pure esthetic concerns predominate is no longer seen as antithetical to more functionally driven work. Lunar Design's desk lamp is a case in point, a purely formal exercise in the manipulation of space and light. Origami was the starting-point to explore the levels of dimensionality possible in product design—from the one-dimensional line of the electrical wire, to the two-dimensional bent plane of the support bracket, to the three-dimensional platonic solid objects that form the lamp's base and halogen light source.

In the real world of product design for clients, Lunar Design manages to overcome the constraints with a use of free-form geometric motifs that are a three-dimensional equivalent of the so-called New Wave graphics coming from nearby San Francisco studios of designers such as Michael Vanderbyl (a friend of Brunner's who designed Interform's logotype). Smith explains: "We began with a very functional approach to design. That's been loosened up a little bit over the last few years. There seems to be a little more freedom to use something just because you like it. We don't try to intellectualize the hell out of what we're designing." Brunner adds that the freedom might be expressed in "a color, a shape, a detail, a triangle, a zigzag, a wave. Maybe we've seen it in a building or a piece of jewelry or another product." A motif might be seen in half-a-dozen projects before being dropped for a new one. Hardline Modernists will revolt at this readiness to submit to such trivial influences, but that will not stop them becoming an important ingredient in post-industrial design.

Keeping a fashion-watcher's eye on trends in product design also gives a sneak preview of less superficial developments. Brunner observes that for any new high-tech product there is a coming emphasis on trying to make it as small as possible. "It's metaphor for efficiency." And because everyone always wants the most efficient product on the market, the smallest assumes a secondary connotation of being the latest. The Japanese realized long ago that this was true for consumer goods, as a glance through the array of calculators and Walkman-like headsets in any electronics store soon reveals. But that realization has been a long time coming to more "serious" products like computers. Says Smith: "Things eventually will get so small that the size will become not a technological issue, but an industrial design issue."

Amtel's direct line printer (1) shows fashionable highlights such as triangular buttons, double-spaced italic graphics, and linear indents molded into plastic casings—the ubiquitous sign of the technology product.
The Opus 2 terminal (2–4) is Lunar Design's response to a request from Esprit Systems to ''make me a beautiful product.'' The flush-mounted switches on the bottom rim of the computer screen show the resulting attention to detail.

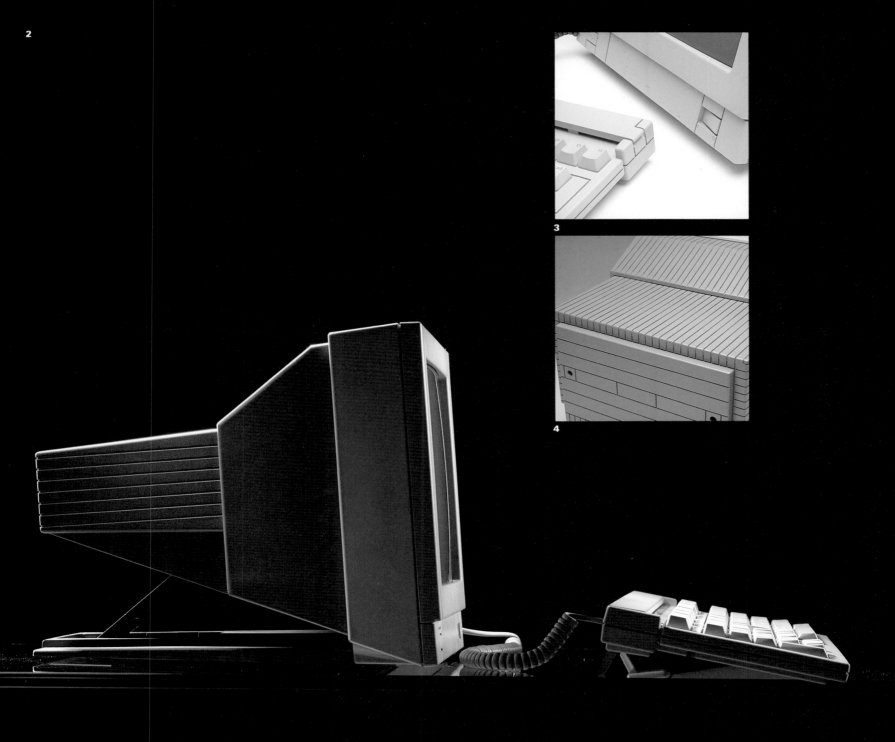

2

3

4

107

5

6

7

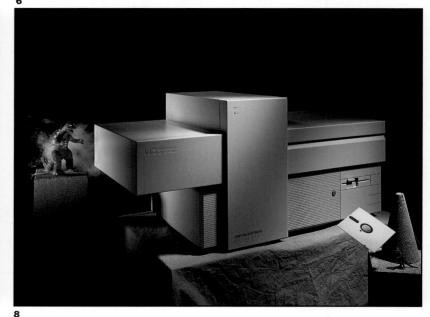

8

A joky anthropomorphism is designed into a video editing console (5) for the Droidworks, a company owned by George Lucas of *Star Wars* fame. "We wanted it to look like a Droid, to capitalize on the *Star Wars* legacy just a bit without killing it," says principal Robert Brunner. Like other Lunar Design electronic equipment—a transportable computer (6), a synthesizer keyboard (7), and a protein-analysis densitometer (8)—it also possesses the clean lines of European Modernist product design.

A halogen desk lamp (9,10) combines one-, two- and three-dimensional elements to create what its designers call an "intertwined form statement." Designers have always had their client work and their experimental portfolio, Brunner notes. Today, however, they no longer feel it will harm their painstakingly acquired reputation for professionalism to show designs that do not suffer the tight constraints of much high-technology product design.

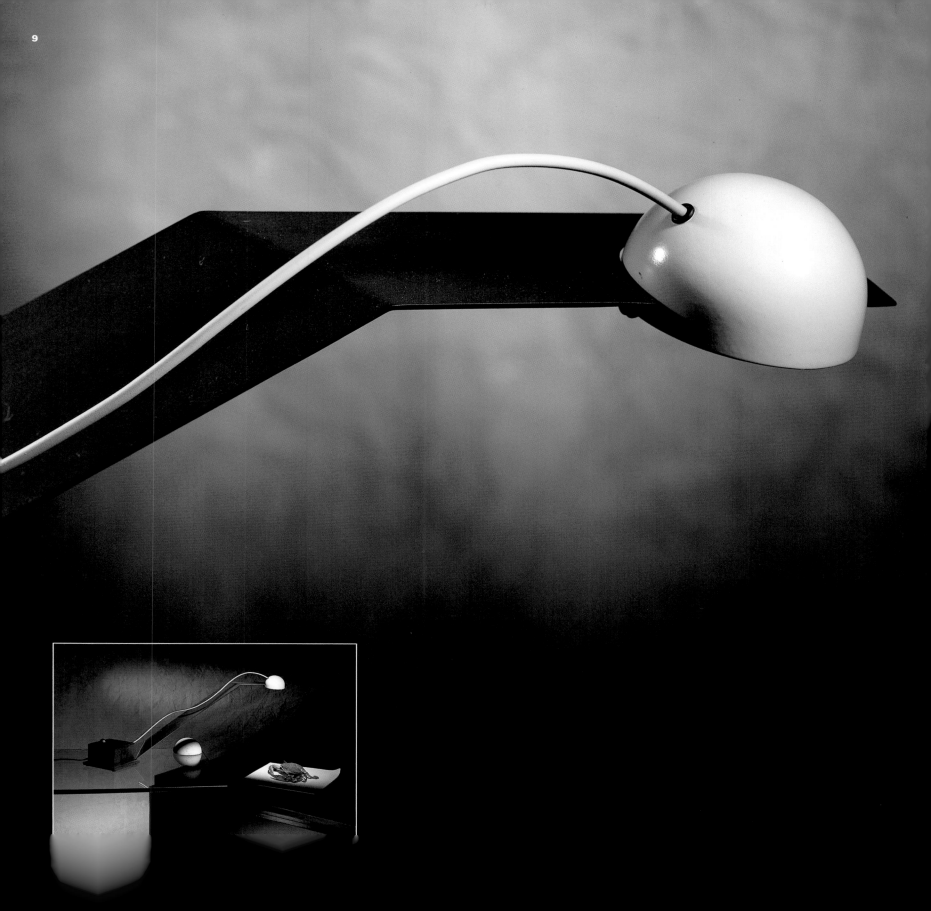

Chapter Three

Reality is allusion

The post-Modern architects started the ball rolling. Mies's "less is more" became Venturi's "less is a bore," and history was no longer bunk. Designers, following their example, have been less headstrong, sensibly maintaining the principles of Modernism, but enriching its vocabulary with their own notions of complexity and contradiction, of reference, allusion, and ambiguity.

Architects have had several millenia from which to whisk up a pot-pourri of historical quotation. Graphic and product designers, on the other hand, have so far been content to look back no farther than the beginnings of their professions in the early years of this century. They look to the fecund decades of Constructivism and Cubism, the Bauhaus and De Stijl.

But with our mounting appetite for instant visual gratification bringing a multiplicity of styles and making design ever more fashion conscious, designers will soon have to open wider their window of reference. They will need to look to styles both ancient and modern, to cultures both indigenous and remote, and to influences from high art to the vernacular. If allusion is to be a new reality in design, then there is certainly much material yet to draw upon.

There is a widespread assumption among the younger industrial design firms in America today that the consultants who espoused the Modernist esthetic in the 1960s and 1970s are spent forces. These giant design institutions are rarely career stepping-stones for ambitious young designers, and so this collective opinion generally is not one that has the benefit of any first-hand experience.

The principals of Design Central are an exception, and can offer a fresh, and presumably less distorted, perspective. Rainer Teufel and Gregg Davis met at RichardsonSmith, one of the country's largest design firms, based in the suburbs of Columbus, Ohio. Teufel had been through the Hamburg Academy for Fine Arts and the Ohio State University graduate program. Davis had come from New York's Pratt Institute by way of Henry Dreyfuss Associates.

Even 16 years after Dreyfuss's death, Henry Dreyfuss Associates remains one of the larger and more revered firms, and it is still doing work in an unadulterated Modernist vein. Often it is good design, but the newcomers feel the sort of work that Dreyfuss does is no longer all that design can be. Davis puts the Dreyfuss contribution in context: "Dreyfuss and the other large offices have had a major influence on design around the world. Now companies, particularly those facing more international trade, have begun to realize that there needs to be an even stronger emphasis on design and more reliance upon its role in the conception of the product." American modern design, in other words, was competent but dull because clients wanted it that way even though "there has always been a design community which has believed in high-quality, exciting, surprising, interesting, provocative design, and not at the expense of human factors."

Where Dreyfuss seems still to be very much a first-generation industrial design firm in the grand manner, RichardsonSmith has realigned itself somewhat to recognize the cross-disciplinary fertilization that can enrich design and go some way toward meeting increased consumer expectations.

Both firms rely on a rational process approach to design, a legacy of Modernist dogma that goes down well with unimaginative clients, but which, for better or worse, rarely produces a truly adventurous product. The thinking that is taking place in design schools now, says Teufel, "has brought an aspect to design that doesn't necessarily need a rationalization."

Design Central, now nine strong, formed three years ago in the chic German Village section of Columbus, a few miles from the suburban sprawl of the RichardsonSmith office, to apply this thinking in a commercial environment. "One of the important things with client companies in America today is for them to be able to appreciate design as an art form, not only as a science or a marketing or engineering discipline," says Davis. Clients, however, have been slow to see the argument. Jenn-Air Company, a major kitchen appliance manufacturer, for example, asked Design Central to redesign one of its cooking tops. With a smooth ceramic top to the unit, the job ended up being more of a graphics project than anything else, and offered no scope to go beyond the harmonious geometric composition. Frustrated, the designers went away and worked up an alternative project. "There is a point where you say: 'Well, I really would like to step out and see what I can do. Maybe I can do something unique with it, using similar technology, but pushing it beyond the barrier that we are being pushed against in some of our day-to-day activities.' We said: 'You're the market leader. Don't behave like the rest. You can be something special.' "

The new design was special too. It escaped from the four-square standard pattern of the burners and the conventional box-like shape. Instead, it made the cooker part of a kitchen counter landscape, integrating form and function with the counter so that it becomes less obvious where one stops and the other begins. Two burners are placed opposite a grill surface in a symmetrical layout of two angled strips that makes the unit wider but less deep, making it easier and safer to use because the cook has less need to reach over the hot areas. Extraction vents run along the back of each strip

flush with the cooker surface rather than towering over the burners as in most designs. The design is intended to be modular, with the grill unit interchangeable with a second pair of burners. The unusual arrangement allows the controls to be placed on the same horizontal surface as the operations they control, and makes a more direct link between the controls and the burners than is often the case on such appliances. Functional innovations are complemented by formal ones. The front rail signals the boundary of the cook's "workstation." The extractor vents have an S-wave shape that helps indicate what their role is.

Admittedly this is not an appliance for small apartments or small pocketbooks. According to Design Central, it caters to a growing interest in customization, both in interiors and in products, among American consumers who can afford it. The firm also feels that good design on a top-of-the-range product can have a healthy knock-on effect, for the client and possibly indirectly for the user. Design Central's Paul Kolada says: "If the company is large enough, and has a product line that spans high- to low-end, it can afford to have a product at that high end that it won't sell as many of perhaps, but that will create a lot more interest, and influence the character of the whole line and create an attitude and expectation for a lot more products."

Design Central received calls from potential European customers asking where they could buy the design, but Jenn-Air responded more coolly. It will not be manufacturing the design, but the process has proven useful in making new ideas more acceptable and in broadening the language for future design work. Work in progress on a full line for Jenn-Air as a consequence is expected to be a little more distinctive. "Such examples," says Davis, "become part of the education and communication process with the client as to what influences their products can take on. Otherwise, you must do it verbally, and designers are not always the best at verbalizing."

The often conflicting set of signs that indicate the "value" of a product is shown in two other Design Central housewares commissions. A series of faucets for Sterling Plumbing Group adopts a typically European look, but, at the client request, it then adds to these sophisticated forms a brass trim that is pure vernacular Americana. Similarly, in the redesign of the kitchen sink for another client, a principal worry is that its intended plastic construction will be perceived as cheap by consumers used to enameled metal units. The potential benefit of the new design—its multi-functional modular design that resulted from the study of videotapes of patterns of sink usage during design development—could be completely canceled by such superficial evaluation based on ill-founded preconceptions about materials and their value associations.

Design Central's approach, especially to the Jenn-Air project and to the wider issue of what it thought Jenn-Air could be, typifies the new arrogance of product designers beginning to rebel against purely functional design and the traditional anonymity that has gone with it. This creative attitude shows too in the minor conceit of small new design companies' going off in search of work that interests *them*. "One of our difficulties," says Teufel, "was that we were coming out of an office that has an incredible spread of involvement. When you are a young organization, you look for markets you have an interest in. We wanted to show our interest in certain areas."

Interest in a given product manufacturing area is indicated, in the absence of a client, by appropriate design studies. In Design Central's case, a calculator succumbs to the voguish colors and forms of post-Modern product design. Nonetheless, it is an elegant exercise, the flow of surface levels guiding the user from on/off switch to numeric buttons to display to function buttons to print-out in a logical sequence. Another exercise uses an assemblage of shapes reminiscent of Constructivist sculpture to create a design for a flat-screen personal computer. So far, it is work such as this that shows Design Central's thinking most clearly. But as the example of Jenn-Air shows, it is also through examples like this that clients come to realize not only what design is, but also what design can be.

1

2

Design Central's project for Jenn-Air
(2) was to come up with comparatively minor refinements to an existing
stove. The firm's putative total solution (1), worked up after the client
work was completed, started from
scratch. It makes ergonomic improvements in the layout of the heating
controls and the positioning of extractor vents along the back edges. The
function of these vents and the front
lip of the cook's territory are indicated in the forms adopted for these
components of the design study.
Compared to the Jenn-Air stove, the
new design would demand non-stan-
dard fitting and greater kitchen space.
Faucets for Sterling Plumbing Group
(3–5) build in a contradictory set of
appeals, seeking to combine purist
form with expressive temperature
controls and a nod to American tradition in the gold-colored trim.

4

5

3

115

6

7

8

Design Central's own projects for a hairdryer (6–9), a calculator (10) and a personal computer (11) predictably reveal a stronger, more unified design language, as well as an awareness of the market drive to give low- to medium-priced electrical commodity products some fashion attributes. Currently seen mainly in the graphics applied to products, this trend is extending to easily exchanged molded parts, such as the grille on the hairdryer. A variety of patterned parts allows a choice of units to be carried in retail stores without greatly increasing manufacturing costs. It permits—or encourages—consumers to replace products that may still function perfectly, for reasons of fashion.

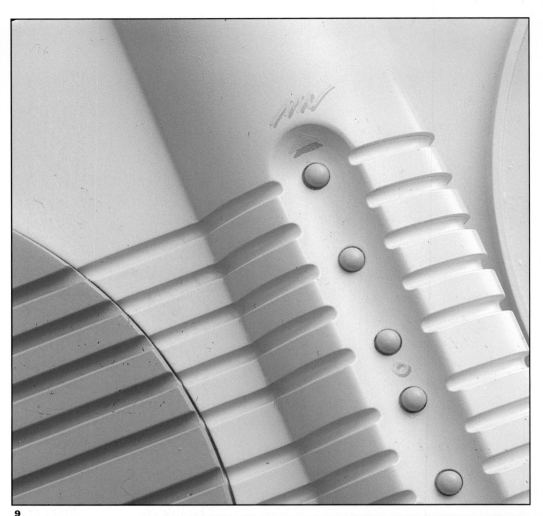

9

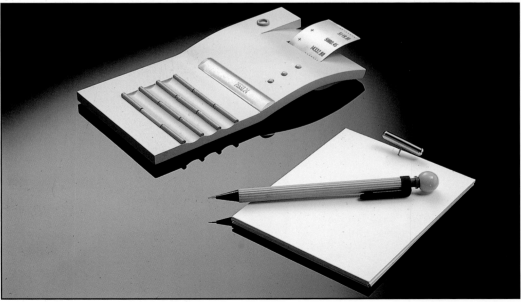

10

11

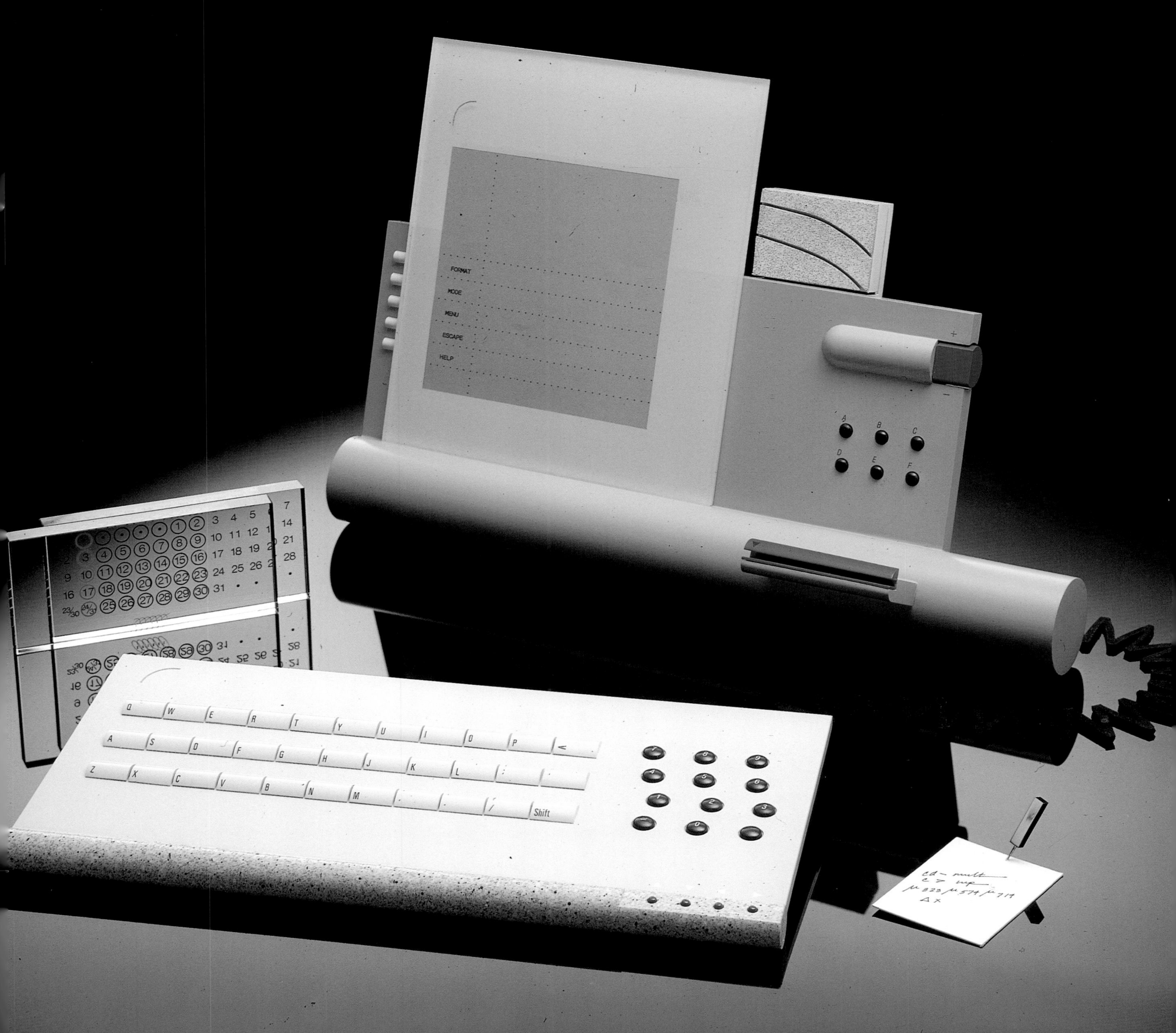

Lucille Tenazas

Lucille Tenazas is a paradigm of California and its design scene. Like many Californians, she is not even from California. She set up her San Francisco office three years ago having come there via graphic design courses at California College of Arts and Crafts and Cranbrook Academy of Art and work experience in New York from her native Philippines. As a consequence, her graphic design, like that of many of her California peers, shows a certain eclecticism.

Also like some of her local peers, she takes pains to distance herself from what some see as the frivolity of the local product. "This whole idea of California design developed while I was in New York," she says. "I was on the outside looking in. When I think of California design, I don't slot in." Tenazas considers herself enriched more by the intellectual and commercial discipline from her time at Cranbrook and in New York.

Initially, however, Tenazas' portfolio, true to Cranbrook type with a concentration on analysis and deconstruction and reconstruction exercises in graphic design, was more of a hindrance than a help. "It was a semantic study that was a very valuable experience. But people in the real world did not see beyond what these experimental projects were supposed to explore in us. I always felt I had to justify what Cranbrook's curriculum was all about, because they had their preconceived ideas and image of what Cranbrook students' portfolios look like." Tenazas justified the Cranbrook curriculum all 65 times when interviewing in New York before finding a position at Harmon Kemp, a corporate communications consultancy. Marshall Harmon, a principal of the firm, had a Basel school background which enabled Tenazas during the four years she worked there to develop an interest in typography that had been instilled at Cranbrook.

Those four years also taught her the difference between the often uninspiring business work that was a staple in Manhattan and the broader possibilities that beckoned on the West Coast. Tenazas had brought a certain color sensibility eastward to New York that was ostensibly a product of her colorful, third-world background, but which dates in fact from her arrival in the United States and first courses at CCAC. The third-world stereotype is one she plays up at times, but its only influence on her work is in a self-conscious use of found imagery and foreign verbiage rather than any more inherent esthetic.

When Tenazas returned to California, she brought her Europeanized sense of typography, a quality some established West Coast designers have noted absent in the new generation of designers. "I realized that what California design lacks is an insistence on typography." Tenazas now spreads the gospel in CCAC courses of her own. Students of graphic design "need to know history, the stellar names in the field" to be able to select type and image combinations appropriate to the design task.

In her own work, Tenazas combines the possibilities for intuitive balance of selected forms of post-Modern graphics with Modernist clarity where it is needed. Her use of the Univers typefaces and white space as background where the New Wave designers tend to use bright color is an inheritance from the 1950s Swiss International Typographic Style that was still a strong influence on the Cranbrook teaching while she was a student there. A promotion brochure for a paper company was an ideal vehicle for showing off these disparate themes. Called "The Third Dimension," it invited Tenazas to explore the parameters of surface, texture and depth in terms of the paper stock and the design elements. Tenazas responded with a stereotypically Cranbrook style of layering of ideas and skewed shapes that appeared three-dimensional. The effect was enhanced by having the book die-cut in a trapezium shape. "It's pure form for me. The way elements are used is the way meaning becomes attached to them. I zero in on something that exemplifies the content. I'm always very conscious of problem-solving in that respect. I'm not bogged down by rationale, but there must always be a reason for an element to be there." For a prospectus of courses at CCAC, therefore, the fun and games went no further than the front cover. Inside, practical good sense prevailed in Garamond and Univers on a strict grid.

Interplay between words and graphics in the Bauhaus tradition serves as a starting point for some of Tenazas' more recent work. A dramatic black-and-white photograph by Richard Barnes of a drive-in theater was adapted by Tenazas for use as a poster by adding letters and words to evoke screen dialogue and those film titles on a cinema marquee in red plastic letters. The white screen became part of a formal symmetrical geometric composition, while the use of letters as a graphic element in this way echoes the work of the Dada and Futurist artists. The poster did not aim to present a social commentary on the dubious merits of going to a drive-in, but became a metaphorical depiction of the medium and message of language placed in a wider cultural context through the use of graphic and typographic association.

A more muted example is provided by a poster for an American Institute of Graphic Arts chapter meeting on Dutch design, in which the inclusion of Dutch postage stamp art provided an excuse to evoke De Stijl and other Dutch themes by up-ending type as on stamps and setting it in arcs resembling postmarks.

Tenazas says she is not excited by much of the work she sees in the United States, but admires in particular the British designer Neville Brody, best known for his type design and layouts in *The Face* and *Arena* magazines, and more mainstream current work for the Dutch post office from Studio Dumbar. "It's raw. There's a certain edge to it," she says, adding that doing such work for an institutional client such as this in America would be nearly impossible.

Tenazas' Dutch homage also included the use of words in Dutch—where they posed no real obstacle to translation. This use of foreign language text is an additional theme in her work, and possibly a reminder of her own offshore origins; it is pursued further in some other poster art where words in other languages (including, of course, Tagalog) and their accompanying symbols appear. Although it is difficult to fathom these messages by trans-lation, they do add nuance to an overall design by their foreign look and from their positioning relative to the type that *is* meant to be read directly. The total effect is of order rather than chaos.

Signing one piece by inverting the word LUCILLE over the word Tenazas produced a further enigmatic foreign flavor as the inverted characters became transformed into letters from other alphabets. In this polyglottal version of Dada, meaning is not lost but actually enhanced. The English words are read for what they say; the foreign ones are there to be translated or guessed at. But the positioning of the two, the foreign-language elements set against parts of the design meant to be comprehended directly, gives its own oblique message. These graphics, like much of Tenazas' work, draw on a range of early Modernist notions, in particular using strings of words used in the manner of the Bauhaus designers to thread together component images of the design. An exercise for the magazine *Photometro* makes the point clearly. Given a number of images to combine into a whole, Tenazas uses collage and layering, and a Paul Rand aphorism to tie them together. Rand's words are sized and arranged rather like a Cranbrook semantic exercise. "When I use words [in a design] I have to make it very involved to engage the reader in another way rather than just as a caption."

Despite the comparatively unstructured program for these poster projects, Tenazas is dissatisfied. Her clients are perhaps *too* receptive to new ideas. "It's not really a challenge to see purely art-related clients—you're not presenting anything totally new to them." Her young business is at the point where she faces the hard decision of choosing whether to stay with clients in the more creative fields who expect everything, but who consequently seem unable to be surprised by anything, or whether to branch out and once again risking doing less exciting work for better-paying clients and experiencing the thrill of pushing for more adventurous content. "I'd like to see clients shaken by some idea that never crossed their minds, where you'd say 'How can this sensibility I have find meaning for them?' "

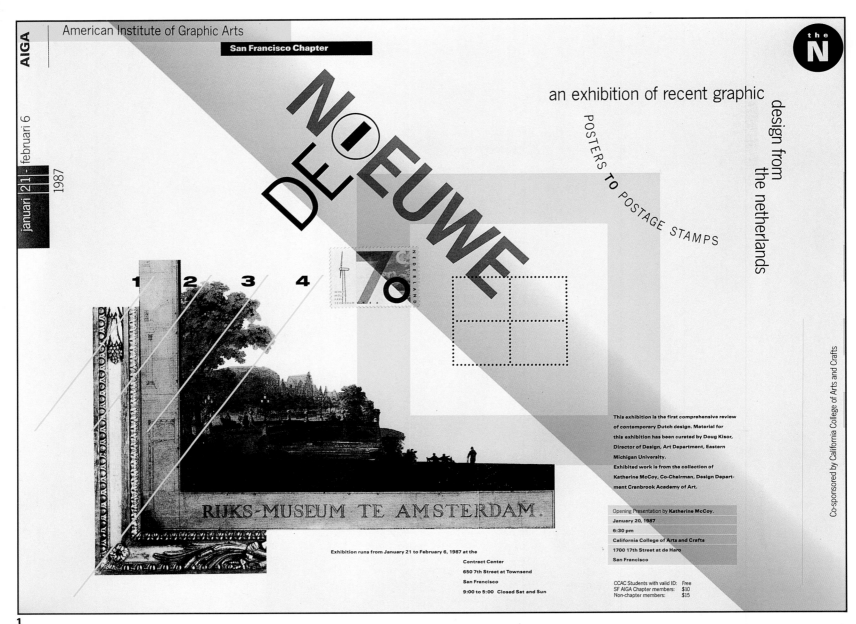

1
Dutch graphic design past and present inspired this AIGA lecture poster (1). When the language used in a design is a foreign one, as in several of Tenazas' pieces, the type serves a dual purpose. It can sometimes be comprehended literally, but also its letterforms are used visually as part of the design. The balance between the two functions depends on the language being employed. Here, for example, ''De Nieuwe'' can be fairly readily deciphered to mean ''The New.'' Another time, Tenazas might use her native tongue, Tagalog, in which case the type as image would predominate over its meaning.

—providing   meaning to a mass of

unrelated

needs,
ideas, words and

**p
i
c
t
u
r
e
s.**

Graphic design is essentially about

visual relationships—

It is the designer's job
to select and fit this

material together—
and make it interesting.
—PAUL RAND

2

San Francisco-based *Photometro* magazine asked 14 local designers to arrange a number of given photographs
and incorporate typography related to
the design. Tenazas' response (2)
shows her fondness for Modernist design techniques. Rules and bars articulate the design, while a quotation
from Paul Rand unites the photographs into a graphic whole. Set in
Univers, each word is sized and positioned according to its meaning. Thus
"unrelated" is set large to remind us
that the images are indeed unrelated,
and "picture" is set vertically to enhance its pictorial value over its literal
one.

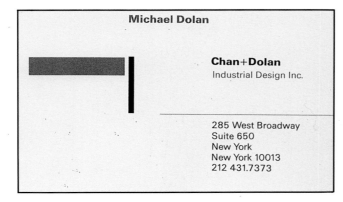

Michael Dolan

Chan+Dolan
Industrial Design Inc.

285 West Broadway
Suite 650
New York
New York 10013
212 431.7373

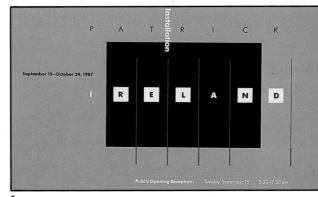

PATRICK

Installation

September 15—October 24, 1987

I R E L A N D

Public Opening Reception: Tuesday, September 15 5:30—7.30 pm

4

Karen Hall

Robin Krauss

Yorkville Station
PO Box 6578
New York
NY 10128
212 348.6575

5

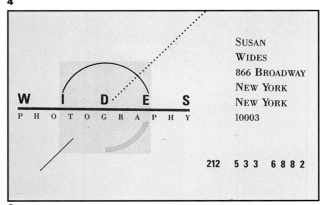

SUSAN
WIDES
866 BROADWAY
NEW YORK
NEW YORK
10003

212 533 6882

6

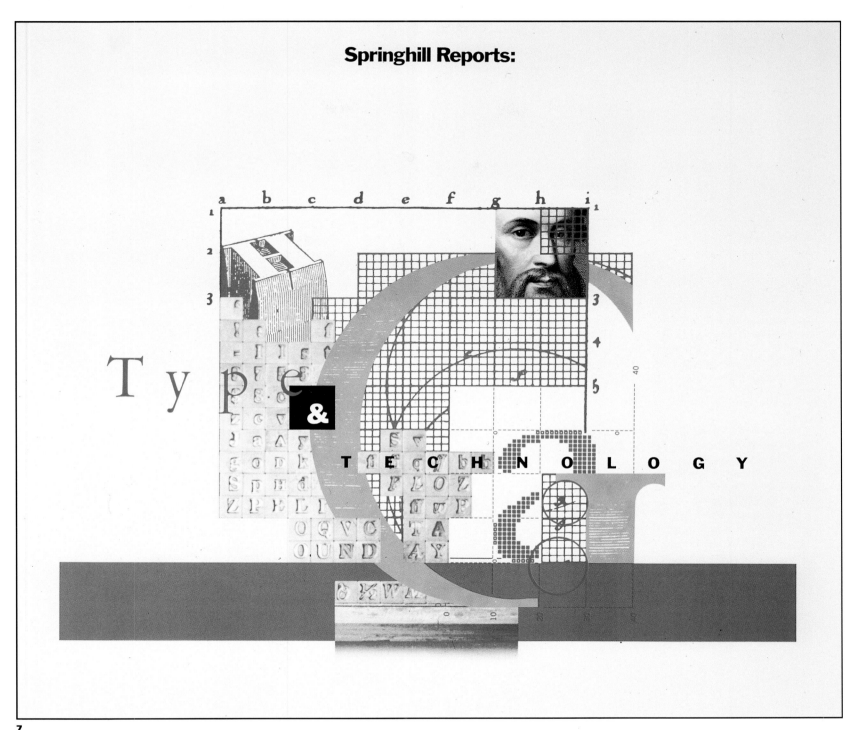

7
Business cards (3–6) continue the use of Modernist typography and geometry, influenced by current Dutch design more than by American work. A brochure cover (7) shows images layered in a more typically post-Modern and American way.

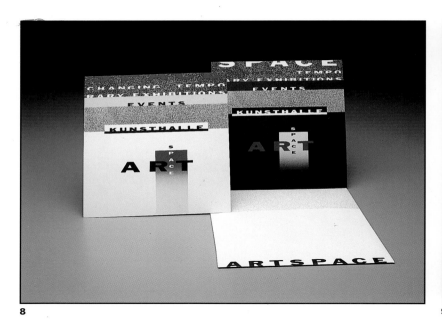

8

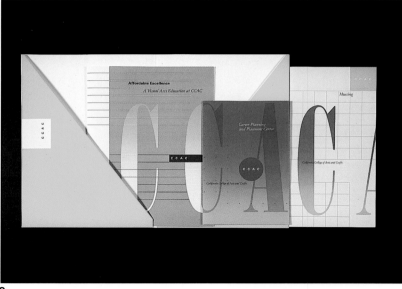

9

Artspace gallery invitation (8);
California College of Arts and Crafts
literature (9).

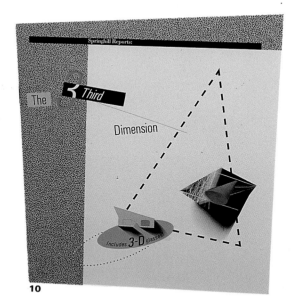

10

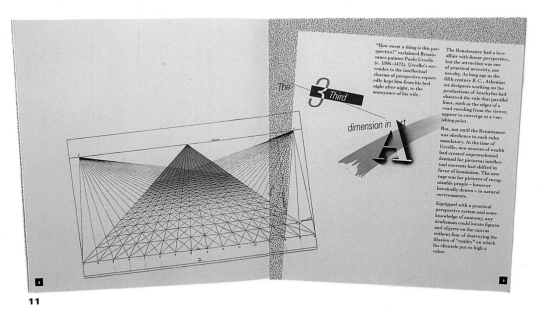

11

A paper company brochure (10,11)
plays the exchange between two and
three dimensions for all its worth with
a hologram on the cover and a 3-D image and glasses inside. The brochure
is irregularly cut for a perspective effect, and generic post-Modern patterns and motifs are used to rare good
effect.

"The image of a stark white screen
looming over a landscape strewn with
letterforms struck me as a metaphor
for language," says Tenazas of this
sequence of studies based on a photograph of a drive-in movie theater
(12–18).

12

13

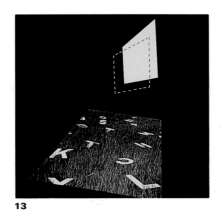

14

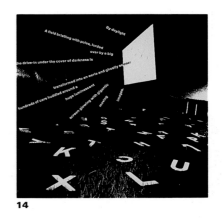

15

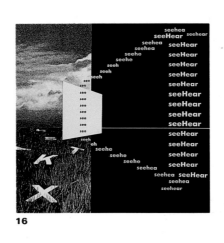

munch

chatter

SEE

come as you
are
No need to dress up

wander

16

seehea
seeHear seehear
seehea
seehea seeHear
seehe seeHear
seeh seeHear
soeh seeHear
seeh seeHear
see seeHear
see seeHear
see seeHear
see seeHear
see seeHear
see seeHear
seeh seeHear
eh seeHear
seehe seeHear
seehe seeHear
seehe seeHear
seehea seeHear
seehea
seehear

17

18

By daylight
A field bristling with poles,

lorded over by a big square, the

drive-in under the cover of

darkness is transformed into

an eerie and ghostly sc n:

Loyd Moore first came to the attention of the design press when an experimental project called the Elaine printer began garnering design awards. The Elaine not only took the now-popular approach to humanizing high-technology equipment of adopting a person's name (Apple Computer was among the first to do this with its Lisa), it also expressed very clearly what it did. Like all computer printers, it has a continuous sheet of paper feeding into it. Unlike all computer printers, however, it spelled out this fact through a molded plastic stand shaped like a scroll of paper. It was the most powerful and direct polemic in favor of a semantic approach to industrial design that the practising American design community had yet permitted itself.

This in mind, it is something of a shock to see the studio of Moore's company, Technology Design. Housed in a converted 1928 church in the Bellevue suburb of Seattle, and overshadowed by the crystalline skyscrapers that symbolize the region's post-industrial growth, it is a soaring clear white space, seemingly a temple to the late-Modernist school of black box minimalism. Clearly, there is something of a contradiction here.

Moore offers a confessional explanation. "There is a certain dichotomy in what we're trying to achieve. We are very much a market-driven company, and we have to respond to our clients' commercial requirements. Late-Modernism is where we position ourselves—Modernism is actually what our clients look for; we try to move them into late-Modernism." Moore is here borrowing terminology of the architecture critic Charles Jencks who distinguishes late-Modern design, which continues the tradition of the Modern movement, from post-Modern design which, to varying degrees, rejects it. The late-Modern precursor of the Elaine is a printer designed for Output Technology Corporation, an elegant rectangular box with crisp edges and the ubiquitous indented line motif that seems to signify computer products. "We then do our own, more modest projects, Elaine being an example, that are driven by our own desires, our visions of where things are. It is a

commercial risk that we were willing to take but that we cannot necessarily foist off on our clients."

Moore's conversion to pluralism came with the suddenness of a religious revelation. Wandering around a discount store, he realized that each display offered not so much a product as a metaphor for living. "They were using the visual clutter and excitement to express something about what this product would bring to your life. It was not necessarily the product itself, it was what it stood for. It became very clear that the issue of what people buy and why they buy is so much broader than the traditional definition."

As a product type, the computer printer provides a clear example of the two approaches. Most printers are conspicuously ugly, or at best, banal. The client's budget and the designer's effort have perhaps been expended on the styling and ergonomics of the terminal itself and its peripherals. The printer, since it is not in continuous use or sight, remains just a box. One of the central questions confronting semantic product design is whether certain products carry so little meaning and have so little symbolic importance that they should just be boxes. Moore underlines that question by thrusting what is traditionally a background product into the limelight. The Elaine also questions the assumption that mundane items like computer printers should be available in only one variety, whatever the intended user environment. Moore suggests the Elaine would be suitable for a computerized executive's office, but not for an institutional bulk buyer. Technology Design states the challenge as being to introduce "differentiation among hi-tech products attaining commodity status." An equally great challenge for designers, however, may be to exercise restraint on products that do not need differentiation. To travesty Loewy's words, is it not possible that there are times when the designer *should* "leave well enough alone"?

Elaine's principal feature is the scrolled base that signals its paper-handling function, but other details are also used to communicate aspects of its role and function. The cooling mechanism, which on another printer would

simply consist of a metal heat-sink hidden behind a vent grille cut into the casing, is made into an expressive feature. It alludes to the convective flow of the cooling air and to heat by being colored orange. Electrical functions, from the control buttons on the front to the motor at the rear, are similarly coded other distinctive colors. The motor itself, housed in a cylindrical plastic molding, is supported by a cupped, hand-shaped molded part in the contrasting color, a strong signal of contact between the hot motor and the heat-dissipating grille.

The Elaine was not commissioned by a client, but designed for Synapse, a product-development company set up within Technology Design. It was widely praised in the design press, but it also made its way into the pages of *Working Woman* magazine. It was that rather unlikely source that produced the pleasant bonus of a client for the idea. A somewhat watered-down version of the original concept was all the client could bring himself to commit to, but that is at least some progress. It is also an illustration that the polemical approach is a legitimate way to raise market expectations.

There is a broader issue that is at the center of designer frustration and client conservatism. Moore explains: "Late-Modern design only addresses a very narrow definition of functionality and functionalism. In everyone's mind, the Modernist ideal and technology are somehow inseparable, and that's why there's a conservatism in [the technology-based product] marketplace. When you sit down and really look at the way people interact with their environment, it's a very complex, multilayered eclectic, confused process. I don't think today's products do that justice."

A second product of this re-examination is the Ischia chair. As a piece of avant-garde formalism, it compares with anything from Milan. It might even be thought that such comparison is invited, but the chair is not named for the Italian island of that name. Technology Design staff had never heard of the place. The eponymous ischia here are the pelvic bones that support the human frame when seated. The project grew from a commission for a client who made birthing beds. Technology Design researched the anatomy of the birthing position preparatory to designing inflatable mattress components that would have ensured the patient a greater degree of comfort during childbirth. The work did not in the end lead to the design of a new product for the client, and Technology Design was left to mull over its now useless figures. "The interesting thing that emerged," says Moore, "was the narrow range of support you really need. That generated this particular approach. What we really did was go back and analyze how we could distribute 80 percent of the weight (the other 20 percent being your feet) in as small as possible an area." The result was the apparent contradiction of a chair that was ergonomically designed yet extremely uncomfortable-looking. It has two tiny and separate buttock supports, an equally diminutive backrest in green, and spindly red legs, behind which looms a shield-like backpiece of positively medieval proportions. "True to our Modernist tradition, the functional elements are completely separate from the more symbolic and decorative backpiece."

A very different Synapse solution in search of a client is simply one piece of molded plastic that serves to store a dozen 3 1/2-inch computer diskettes. Engineering ingenuity here allows the diskettes to be held in place securely, inserted and withdrawn easily when needed, without any moving parts, clips, springs, or anything else. The disk-storage device can be pulled straight from its mold and requires no further cutting, assembly, or finishing. According to Moore, each piece weighs less than five ounces and costs just 48¢ to produce. Synapse is negotiating licensing the design for manufacture at a volume of around one million units a year. It's the sort of economy of materials and value in terms of function-for-weight that would impress any die-hard Modernist. The sculptural elegance with which the diskette-holder casts shadows is an unexpected treat. "This expresses my other interest, in the purely engineering aspect of problem-solving," comments Moore. It is "design in the broadest sense, and every bit as valid."

With its Elaine printer (1–3), Technology Design raises a number of questions confronting product types of generally similar appearance. For example: Is a printer the sort of product where the use of designed signs of its function are necessary or desirable? Or should the design accept only a background role, the conventional solution seen in the actual printer designed for client Output Technology Corp. (6)?

1

2

3

4

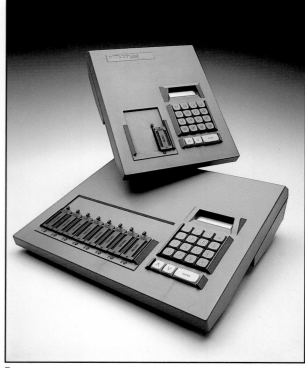

5

6

The stylistic distance that often exists
between designers and their clients is
clear here. The electronic equipment
(5,6) designed for clients is clearly
Modernist, while the furniture pro-
gresses along different avenues into
minimal late-Modernism with the Ta-
boret storage tray (4) and into symbolic post-Modernism with the Ischia
chair (7). Both units were designed as
in-house studies. The Ischia chair
makes use of ergonomic data on the
distribution of body weight while
seated in this revolutionary design.
The pelvic and lumbar supports are
solely functional; the backpiece is
decorative.

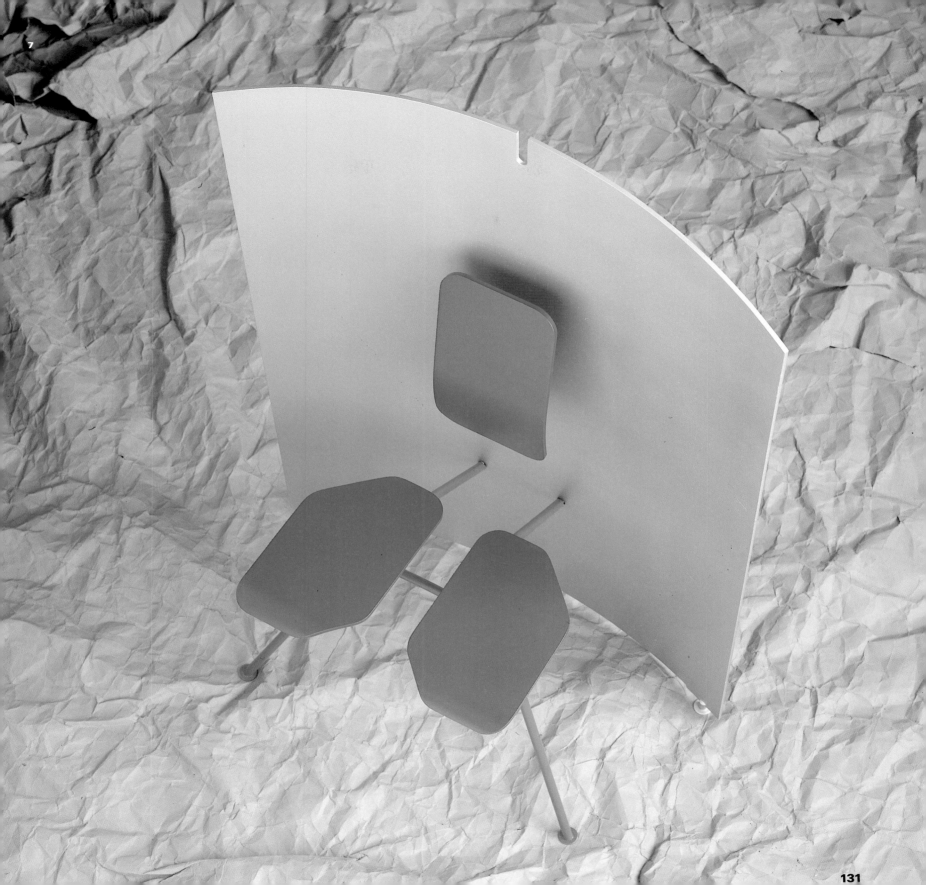

Philip Johnson has a fondness for shocking his fellow architects out of their pretentiousness. He has likened an architect's work for a high-rise developer to that of a whore, yet he revels in such work. Since his transcendence into post-Modernism, he has applied historical styles willy-nilly. He admonishes his peers: "You cannot not know history."

Paula Scher, of the New York partnership Koppel and Scher, is the Philip Johnson of graphic design. At the 1987 Amsterdam design conference—the biennial jamboree of the international professional organizations of graphic, industrial, and interior designers—she stood up and shocked the audience with her frank admissions about working fast, getting the job done, and accepting the commerical client relationship for what it is and no more. No deeper rationale, no higher motivation. She sums up her anti-ideology: "I don't believe it's my responsibility to make the client produce a better product." Her acceding to the remarks of Tom Wolfe at the first national conference of the American Institute of Graphic Arts in 1985 in Boston about history's being a "big closet" for designers to rummage through at will caused similar uproar.

Although Scher condones this pillaging, she is critical of those who do it without first mastering the necessary skills. To succeed, she suggests, the kleptomaniac graphic designer must know what is to be stolen from the closet before committing the break-in. The graphic artist too "cannot not know history." Often when designers try to capture a historical mood, they light upon some derivative element and not the real work from the period they seek. "Most people are just looking for a vague retro look. The problem is that those vague retro looks nine times out of ten are not derived from the original source. It's the designers' finding somebody else's vague retro look made last week and imitating that, as opposed to going back to the real period in history where it came from."

If Scher is as outspoken about graphic design and where it has been and where it is going as Philip Johnson is about architecture, then the work of Koppel and Scher shows similar parallels with Johnson's buildings. Like Johnson's, Koppel and Scher's appropriation of historical themes and motifs is blatant and eclectic. Sometimes the reasoning behind the use of a particular period in graphic design history is immediately apparent, other times a selection seems arbitrary. A series of advertisements for Swatch Watch USA provides a delightful in-joke for graphic designers, adapting Herbert Matter's famous Swissair posters for the new Swiss client. Other Swatch ads take a dig at the 1950s advertising that promised to change people's lives, offering a wry comment on our changing consumer culture.

Turning to fine art for inspiration, a poster for the New York School of Visual Arts confronts the problem of combining a line of text with a compelling image by drawing on ideas of Cassandre and Dadaists who early experimented with type as part of an image, but updates the color scheme for the 1980s. Work for Manhattan Records, on the other hand, looks to Mondrian, whose instantly recognizable art has already been amply reworked. Here, his painting in the Museum of Modern Art, "Broadway Boogie-Woogie," triggered the association with the music business. Despite being something of a cliché, the Mondrian imagery works in Koppel and Scher's implementation because the different applications give play to the geometric variations. The geometric letterforms of Futura bring an appropriate period feel used in conjunction with the color blocks of Mondrian's 1943 painting. The Manhattan Records identity, letterhead, record and cassette labels and sleeves all have slightly different treatments but retain great cohesion because of obviousness of the original source. The relative unimportance of the actual historical allusion used in the work was made clear, however, when EMI America acquired Manhattan Records and the identity was simplified to a cheaper, two-color design using a checkered taxicab theme.

There is a sort of stylelessness to Koppel and Scher's design that makes it hard to place as being from one design studio. Not all their work

comes with an historical reference in tow. For the new monthly *European Travel and Life*, the answer to the design problem was a purely stylistic design that would convey the rich vacuousness of the subject matter. Plenty of white space, initial capital letters on color blocks, and thoughtful picture captions did the job, providing a post-Modern alternative to gridding the pages to death.

The attempt to give graphic design meaning by historical association is sometimes appropriate, but sometimes there is no obvious reference that can be made, as with *European Travel and Life*. In these instances, says Scher, the post-Modernist designer substitutes style for substance. "The post-Modernists use style as a vehicle to make a page look pretty, taking brightly colored shapes and moving them pleasingly around the page." This is being done today with little conceptual basis, whereas the work of Push Pin, the graphics studio of Milton Glaser and Seymour Chwast (Scher's ex-husband) that operated from the 1950s to the 1970s and influenced much American graphic design of those decades, "used style to make a point, to make a parody or create a feeling. That's the difference."

The ignorance of the roots of graphic design is probably strongest in the area of typography. Scher sees eccentric typefaces with specific historical or regional connotations selected from a type catalogue for their pleasingness to the eye and then applied in designs with completely different associations. "In order to use type well, aside from having a basic graphic design sense and an understanding of scale and proportion and the cut of the letterform, you have to have a knowledge of history, of when the face was designed, because it creates a feeling—like it or not—on that page when you use it. Type association has to be taught the way word association can be taught. It's a question of knowing how something exudes a sense of period or feeling." Both Koppel and Scher teach at the School of Visual Arts, and Scher suggests a teaching approach that could be developed for a given typeface: "What is this face appropriate for? List seven things. That can be done."

Scher puts some of the blame for the typographic poverty of most current graphic design work on the International Typeface Corporation. In the 1970s, ITC, worried that the new photographic reproduction techniques would leave typographers unrewarded for their design efforts, commissioned designs for a number of new typefaces as well as "modernized" redrawings of certain other historic faces. "ITC had an enormous impact in this country because it was a national type business. It sold to all the small suppliers, but it destroyed the face of Garamond and it destroyed the face of Bookman," says Scher. Noble old faces such as these had already endured a bout of modernization by the Monotype Corporation near the beginning of the century, but in this less sensitive redrawing they were disfigured at the same time as they were made widely available, and their antecedent letterforms lapsed into obscurity.

Scher suggests the current political environment can also be held accountable for the shaky conceptual foundations of the work of many young graphic designers. "All our movements are affected by the politics and economy as well as the technology of the period. For the past eight years we've lived in a very conservative regime, an era of style over substance, the Reagan presidency. My students, for example, couldn't make a political poster when I assigned one to them because they had nothing to say. It's indicative of our times. My clients would feel uncomfortable with a poster or a series of ads that made a point because it means taking a stand."

Scher illustrates her point with Kit Hinrichs's book *Stars and Stripes* in which a number of prominent American graphic designers offered their reinterpretations of the American flag. "They were the wimpiest flags ever done—either blatantly icky patriotic, or just no comment at all and purely decorative. Fifteen years ago, the same artists doing those flags would have made much more powerful statements." Now Scher predicts a coming enrichment of graphics as designers and other creative professionals begin to reflect a return to greater social consciousness in the wane of Reaganism.

1

THE METAMORPHOSIS 1919

1

As Gregor Samsa awoke one morning from uneasy dreams he found himself transformed in his bed into a gigantic insect.

He was lying on his hard, as it were armor-plated, back and when he lifted his head a little he could see his dome-like brown belly divided into stiff arched segments on top of which the bed quilt. could hardly keep in position and was about to slide off completely. His numerous legs, which were pitifully thin compared to the rest of his bulk, waved helplessly before his eyes.

FRANZ KAFKA

2

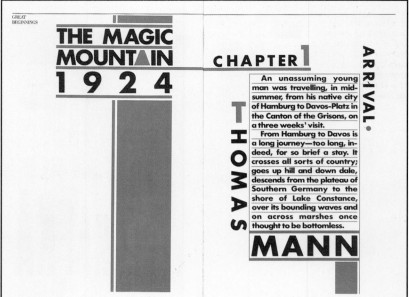

THE MAGIC MOUNTAIN 1924

CHAPTER 1

ARRIVAL.

THOMAS

An unassuming young man was travelling, in midsummer, from his native city of Hamburg to Davos-Platz in the Canton of the Grisons, on a three weeks' visit.

From Hamburg to Davos is a long journey—too long, indeed, for so brief a stay. It crosses all sorts of country; goes up hill and down dale, descends from the plateau of Southern Germany to the shore of Lake Constance, over its bounding waves and on across marshes once thought to be bottomless.

MANN

3

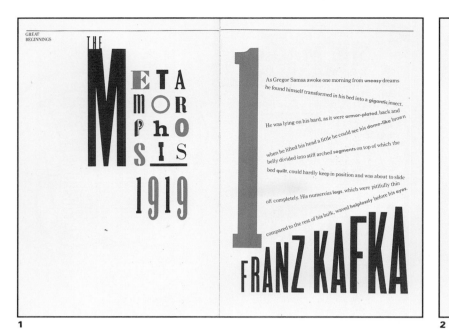

THE C 1947

Catcher in the Rye

If you really want to hear about it, the first thing you'll probably want to know is where I was born, and what my lousy childhood was like, and how my parents were occupied and all before they had me, and all that David Copperfield kind of crap, but I don't feel like going into it, if you want to know the truth. In the first place, that stuff bores me, and in the second place, my parents would have about two hemorrhages apiece if I told anything pretty personal about them. They're quite touchy about anything like that, especially my father. They're *nice* and all—I'm not saying that—but they're also touchy as hell. Besides, I'm not going to tell you my whole goddam autobiography or anything. I'll just tell you about this madman stuff that happened to me around last Christmas just before I got pretty run-down and had to come out here and take it easy. I mean that's all I told D.B. about, and he's my *brother* and all. He's in Hollywood. That isn't too far from this crumby place, and he comes over and visits me practically every week end.

J. D. SALINGER

4

On The Road Nineteen Fifty-five

I first met

Dean not long after my wife and I split up. I had just gotten over a serious illness that I won't bother to talk about, except that it had something to do with the miserably weary split-up and my feeling that everything was dead. With the coming of Dean Moriarty began the part of my life you could call my life on the road. Before that I'd often dreamed of going West to see the country, always vaguely planning and never taking off. Dean is the perfect guy for the road because he actually was born on the road, when his parents were passing through Salt Lake City in 1926, in a jalopy, on their way to Los Angeles. First reports of him came to me through Chad King, who'd shown me a few letters from him written in a New Mexico reform school. I was tremendously interested in the letters because they so naïvely and sweetly asked Chad to teach him all about Nietzsche and all the wonderful intellectual things that Chad knew. At one point Carlo and I talked about the letters and wondered if we would ever meet the strange Dean Moriarty. This is all far back, when Dean was not the way he is today, when he was a young jailkid shrouded in mystery. Then news came that Dean was out of reform school and was coming to New York for the first time; also there was talk that he had just married a girl named Marylou.

by Jack Kerouac

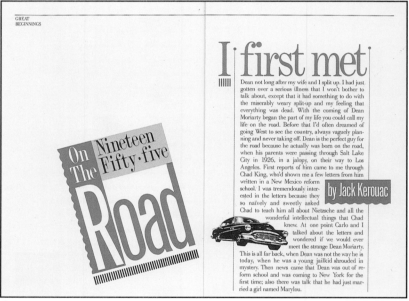

Literal evocation of design styles or works from the past can simply emphasize a period feeling, as in this series of first pages from famous literary works done as an inaugural self-promotional exercise (1–4), or it can gain an added resonance with the present day, as in this reinterpretation of a Herbert Matter Swissair poster for Swatch Watch USA (5).

5

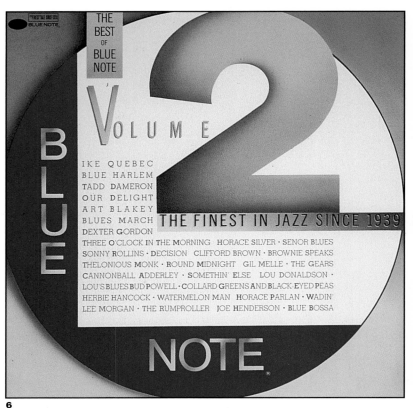

THE BEST OF BLUE NOTE

BLUE NOTE

VOLUME 2

THE FINEST IN JAZZ SINCE 1939

IKE QUEBEC
BLUE HARLEM
TADD DAMERON
OUR DELIGHT
ART BLAKEY
BLUES MARCH
DEXTER GORDON
THREE O'CLOCK IN THE MORNING · HORACE SILVER · SENOR BLUES
SONNY ROLLINS · DECISION · CLIFFORD BROWN · BROWNIE SPEAKS
THELONIOUS MONK · ROUND MIDNIGHT · GIL MELLE · THE GEARS
CANNONBALL ADDERLEY · SOMETHIN' ELSE · LOU DONALDSON ·
LOU'S BLUES BUD POWELL · COLLARD GREENS AND BLACK-EYED PEAS
HERBIE HANCOCK · WATERMELON MAN · HORACE PARLAN · WADIN'
LEE MORGAN · THE RUMPROLLER · JOE HENDERSON · BLUE BOSSA

NOTE

6

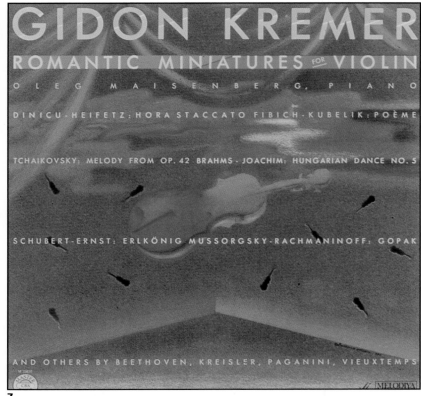

GIDON KREMER
ROMANTIC MINIATURES FOR VIOLIN
OLEG MAISENBERG, PIANO

DINICU-HEIFETZ: HORA STACCATO FIBICH-KUBELIK: POÈME

TCHAIKOVSKY: MELODY FROM OP. 42 BRAHMS · JOACHIM: HUNGARIAN DANCE NO. 5

SCHUBERT-ERNST: ERLKÖNIG MUSSORGSKY-RACHMANINOFF: GOPAK

AND OTHERS BY BEETHOVEN, KREISLER, PAGANINI, VIEUXTEMPS

MELODIYA

7

MUSIC/GRAPHIC DESIGN/ $19.95

From their beginnings in the 1940s, through the psychedelic and surrealistic sixties, and into the more eclectic present, record jackets have played an important role in the music scene. With striking visual imagery, the most inspired designs have reflected the nature of the music as well as prominent trends in American culture.

The Ultimate Album Cover Album is a rich visual history of hundreds of the most outstanding album covers of the last 45 years. It combines the most distinguished examples from the three earlier best-selling books and adds one-third new material in a more comprehensive volume. This is a package irresistible to record fans of all musical persuasions as well as to those who want an unsurpassed collection of the brilliant images that have accompanied and enlivened our musical taste.

P
PRENTICE HALL PRESS · NEW YORK

COVER DESIGN BY PAULA SCHER

ISBN 0-13-935750-5

PRINTED IN SINGAPORE

8

THE ULTIMATE ALBUM COVER ALBUM ◆ DEAN/HOWELLS

PRENTICE HALL PRESS

THE ULTIMATE ALBUM COVER ALBUM

ROGER DEAN & DAVID HOWELLS

9

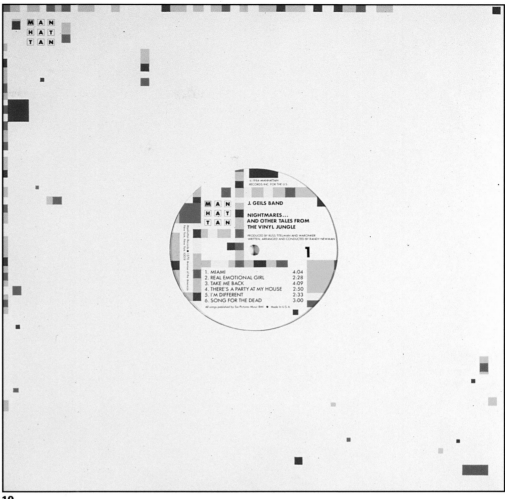

© 1984 MANHATTAN
RECORDS INC. FOR THE U.S.

MAN
HAT
TAN

J. GEILS BAND

NIGHTMARES...
AND OTHER TALES FROM
THE VINYL JUNGLE

PRODUCED BY RUSS TITELMAN AND WARONKER
WRITTEN, ARRANGED AND CONDUCTED BY RANDY NEWMAN

1

1. MIAMI   4:04
2. REAL EMOTIONAL GIRL   2:28
3. TAKE ME BACK   4:09
4. THERE'S A PARTY AT MY HOUSE   2:50
5. I'M DIFFERENT   2:33
6. SONG FOR THE DEAD   3:00

All songs published by Six Pictures Music/BMI ■ Made In U.S.A.

10

Album covers for Blue Note Records
and Columbia Records (6,7) and book
jackets for *The Ultimate Album Cover
Album* and *American Illustration 4*
(8,15) show a less literal application
of historical reference.
Stationery and record sleeves for
Manhattan Records, now EMI Manhattan, part of EMI America (9–11). Mondrian's painting, *Broadway Boogie-
Woogie,* inspired by Manhattan,
served as the source for these graphics. Elements from the painting, which
hangs in the Museum of Modern Art,
were simulated but not reproduced directly. Different groupings of the colored boxes occur on each type of
printed piece. These "variations on a
theme of Mondrian" provide both variety and cohesion for the record company's printed matter.

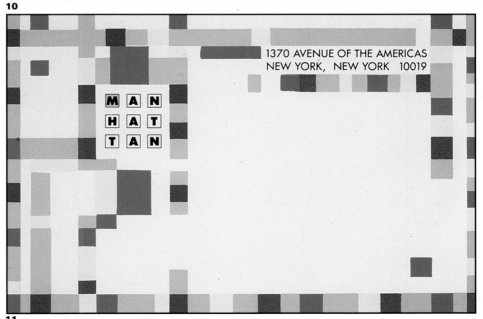

1370 AVENUE OF THE AMERICAS
NEW YORK, NEW YORK   10019

MAN
HAT
TAN

11

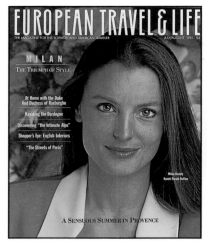

EUROPEAN TRAVEL & LIFE
THE MAGAZINE FOR THE SOPHISTICATED AMERICAN TRAVELER   JULY/AUGUST 1995 $4

MILAN
THE TRIUMPH OF STYLE

At Home with the Duke
And Duchess of Roxburghe

Kayaking the Dordogne

Discovering "the Intimate Alps"

Shopper's Eye: English Interiors

"The Streets of Paris"

Milan Beauty
Benhi Pàroli-Dotton

A SENSUOUS SUMMER IN PROVENCE

12

AMERICANS ABROAD

Friends of French Art

AN ELITE GROUP
GLIMPSES A
PRIVATE,
PATRICIAN
WORLD—HOUSE-
PARTY STYLE.

In

BY LEON HARRIS PHOTOGRAPHS BY HARRY GRUYAERT

the good old days, when rich people traveled, they did so individually; more common clay went in groups organized by Thomas Cook or American Express. "Individually," in those golden times, meant mother with her maid, father with his valet, nanny to look after the children, and the chauffeur as well.

Nowadays, with maids, valets, and chauffeurs harder to find than a bargain-priced Botticelli or Braque, the rich too are traveling in groups. The trips they are taking, often organized by museums, include special visits not only to public galleries but to private houses as well.

The packagers of such posh pilgrimages range from the Museum of Modern Art's International Council and Harvard's Fogg Fellows to the Associates of the Dallas Museum of Art and—what is probably the most expensive organization to join—the Friends of French Art.

Before dinner at the 400-year-old Musée Carnavalet in Paris, the fine Orchestre de Chambre Bernard Thomas entertains a select group of Americans.

Guests gather (opposite) at the base of the sweeping marble staircase of the Musée Carnavalet. The Friends of French Art is one of many new American organizations offering unprecedented access to major art works and private residences in France.

Along the drive to the twelfth-century Château Montmelas, some stretches of landscape are highly groomed.

EUROPEAN TRAVEL & LIFE   NOVEMBER/DECEMBER 1985   175

13

The magic of Elba
is revealed to those who
know where to look,
how to live,
and most of all,
how to get there.

PRIVATE PLEASURES

ONE MAN'S ISLAND

BY PETER J.
ROSENWALD

EVERY TIME I SEE the gentle outlines of Elba's mountains from the plane that makes the half-hour flight from Pisa, I remember the first time—the light, the sounds, the smells, the tastes.

For me, the island means a feeling of contentment and peace with the surroundings, of being part of a society that has more important things to do than worry about the latest world crisis, things like watching the beautiful sunsets reflect on the Mediterranean, or rolling out dough to make fresh pasta for dinner.

My love affair with Elba began in late July, 1967, when I decided to escape for a couple of weeks from a rainy London summer and find some sun in Italy. It was easier said than done.

A few calls to reservation managers at Italian hotels made it charmingly but unquestionably clear that "everything in Italy is completely full for ferragosto," the annual Italian vacation period during the month of August.

Everything may have appeared to be full, but for every rule in Italy there

PETER J. ROSENWALD is a direct marketing consultant who divides his time between London and Elba.

A speck of an island in the Mediterranean, Elba (at left) has been ruled by the Etruscans, the Roman Empire, Barbary pirates, and Napoleon. Today the 86 square miles of beaches, vineyards, and mountainside villages are Italy's domain. Porto Azzurro (opposite), facing the mainland, hosts all kinds of vessels, from fishing boats to pleasure yachts.

14

AMERICAN ILLUSTRATION 4

EDITED BY
EDWARD BOOTH-CLIBBORN

ABRAMS

15

138

Koppel's pages for *European Travel and Life* (12–14) closely parallel his period treatments of the J. D. Salinger and Jack Kerouac beginnings (3,4), but here it is done for stylistic effect rather than for any particular historical association.

Scher's 1987 subway poster for the School of Visual Arts (16) took a week to execute–her "most difficult project," she says. The school requested a typographic design, but Scher wanted to introduce some figurative element. A look to the Bauhaus provided the idea for the necessary compromise.

16

Polivka Logan Designers

Eugene Reshanov, principal of the hitherto largely unremarked Polivka Logan Designers, is having a hard time explaining why one of his recent designs represents such an exciting departure for his firm. After all, the object in question is only a portable lavatory, not the sort of design opportunity that usually produces radical results. Reshanov's answer to the Portosan is revolutionary though. It has a pedimented top, an intricately detailed facade, and attractive fashion-conscious colors. "It is somewhat of a spoof on post-Modern architecture. Things like our toilet were being constructed while we were working on the project," he says, with a gesture to the Minneapolis skyline, visible from a window.

The portable toilet, designed for Synergy III Industries, could be said to mark Reshanov's full conversion to the superficial gloss of American life. It's certainly a long way from his beginnings as a designer in Leningrad. Reshanov emigrated from the Soviet Union in 1977, but the picture he paints of his design education and practice there still provides a salutory reminder for him. It also provides a caricature of the American design world at its traditional worst. Compare, for example, the Leningrad School of Design, with the average here: "My school, at that time the best in the country, tried to model itself on the European experience as much as it could. They lavished us with all the magazines they could afford. So we were pretty much molded by Braun and Olivetti." How many schools and corporations still think "Eurostyle," whatever that is, is the quintessence of good design?

Upon graduation, Reshanov became a quasi-independent designer. "I worked as what comes nearest to a freelancer in the Soviet Union, commissioned projects from government-owned factories done with minimum supervision. It was a complicated concept. Their arrangements for anything are not very conducive to freelancing." Although designers worked without much supervision, the results finally had to go before a judging panel. "It filters out some of the schlockiest things, but also brings everything down to a common denominator. The people on the committee are not necessarily

the brightest and the most pioneering." Again, the worst of the American situation comes through. Large design firms here too undoubtedly stifle exceptional individual expression, both good and bad, and impose a house style on their design output. In the Soviet Union, innovative designs were often just stored away without ever seeing production. "With no market competition, there was no real incentive to produce anything." Here in many fields, American industry has been used to a situation, if not of no competition, at least of a large and easily satisfied home market.

These vignettes offer more than an object lesson in the mismanagement of design. They show what Reshanov and Polivka Logan Designers are reacting against. The faceless machine esthetic that was all that could emerge under Soviet patronage is here supplanted by a directly opposing wry zoomorphism in certain designs. In other products, what could only have been mundane in the Soviet Union here gains the freedom to adopt elements from art and architecture.

On his arrival in the United States, Reshanov spent an unsatisfactory two years working on beer promotion signage, before landing an industrial design job at Polivka Logan. After a spell at a local NCR subsidiary, which was spent implementing its RichardsonSmith-designed long-term identity program, Reshanov in 1984 got called back to Polivka Logan as principal on the retirement of its principal Logan Johnson. He was able to take advantage of 20 years' name recognition for the studio and to give full rein to his unfettered esthetic, to which he adds a thoroughly capitalist outlook on the design process that stems from the frustration of doing designs that simply ended up stored in some Soviet bureaucrat's office. For Reshanov, a design is only complete when it is manufactured, distributed and sold.

Expertise in the mechanical engineering that lies behind most industrial design is a key component in the service offered by Polivka Logan Designers. "For me, mechanical engineering was the greasing of the road to our success. It's like passing a fragile object through a bunch of hands: It would be very little consolation if it were smashed just when the next to last person was passing it to the last. When we have [in-house] engineering, we assure that almost all hands are our hands, and the chance of smashing the thing is significantly decreased. An uncontrolled engineering group can, with all good intentions, nothing malicious, demolish a design without knowing it." Polivka Logan's engineering is supported by the opportunity to use the computer-aided design equipment of the consultancy with which it shares office space. CAD, says Reshanov, is not so much a tool to originate designs, but more a valuable way to verify that a design would actually be in three dimensions what the designer envisions it to be from engineering drawings and after having gone through the modifications of human factors engineering and design development. In the case of drawings leading to a prototype model sometimes, he says: "what you see isn't at all what you get." But with CAD, "it cannot be that something only looks correct without also being dimensioned correctly. It is impossible."

An example of a design project where a high level of engineering expertise is called for came when Polivka Logan looked into designing a device that would allow handicapped people to drive a car. "Here is the problem. Cars are mass-produced, but handicapped people are relatively small in number. Apparently no automotive company produces any device that would enable a person with no legs or no arms to drive a vehicle." It therefore falls to a small company to come up with a universal converter that would allow paraplegics and perhaps even some quadriplegics to drive a range of automobiles. Polivka Logan is evaluating existing ergonomic data and collecting its own, having built an engineering model of a prototype wheel to be able to conduct tests in order to devise a design to meet this huge range of conditions of usage. This sort of highly specialized design relies for a successful outcome on the designer having the humility to admit when the requirements of the project surpass his own technical knowledge and call in a more specialist consultant.

On the other hand, most projects are carried out solely by such specialist engineering teams with little time for formal or cultural values. Polivka Logan does not accept that its sort of heavy industrial and scientific niche products need forgo these sophistications. "They require intricate understanding of each new process of a small but concentrated niche in the market. We accept that their technology makes sense, so we only have to re-engineer the human interface, the esthetics, the environment of use."

The controls for a surgical laser for Minnesota Laser Corporation, for example, are neatly laid out on an angled surface that appears more like a tablet of stone from the way the colored molded plastic sections are joined. The emergency cut-off is a melodramatic, giant red pushbutton. The whole unit is supported on a tall trolley that in side view shares the outline of a classical column. A device called the Fluxatron, used to treat cutting tools for wear resistance, designed for Innovex, recalls Russian Constructivism when viewed from certain angles, signifying its awesome magnetic flux function with a dangerous looking red disc that is the centerpiece of a formal composition that would please El Lissitzky. The product stands on cast-aluminum feet that are stylized versions of the cast-iron feet used on Victorian chairs and bathtubs.

More humorous is an appropriately zoomorphic design for a clinical audiometer for Maico Hearing Instruments that has its left and right ear controls arranged left and right on the unit with a central control in the position of the mouth giving an animated look to the overall unit. The animal feet reappear here to emphasize the effect. Despite this designerly joking in these products, and at the expense of post-Modernist architects in the toilet, Reshanov believes such powerful tools must be handled with care. He warns: "Semantics should be used sparingly, on things that have genuine symbolic value. If you start decorating all the world's widgets with symbols, that's too much. I think it's going to happen though. I think the semantics thing will be blown out of proportion. We will be back to the black box very soon."

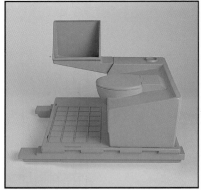

Polivka Logan mocks post-Modern architecture with its temple-like portable lavatory (1,2). The design is serious as well as frivolous, however, in its choice of innovative blow-molded plastic panel construction over the more usual fiberglass.

A clinical audiometer, a device used to measure hearing ability (3), has an appropriately zoomorphic appearance with controls located as "ears" and feet for supports.

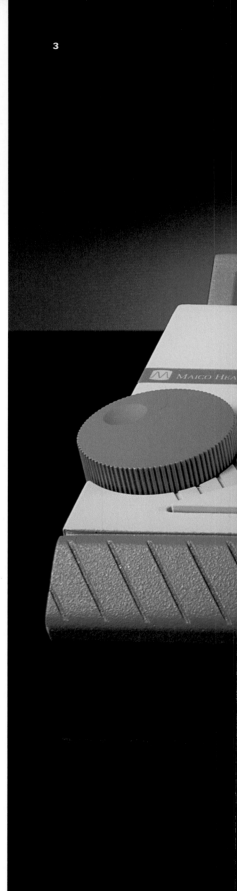

1

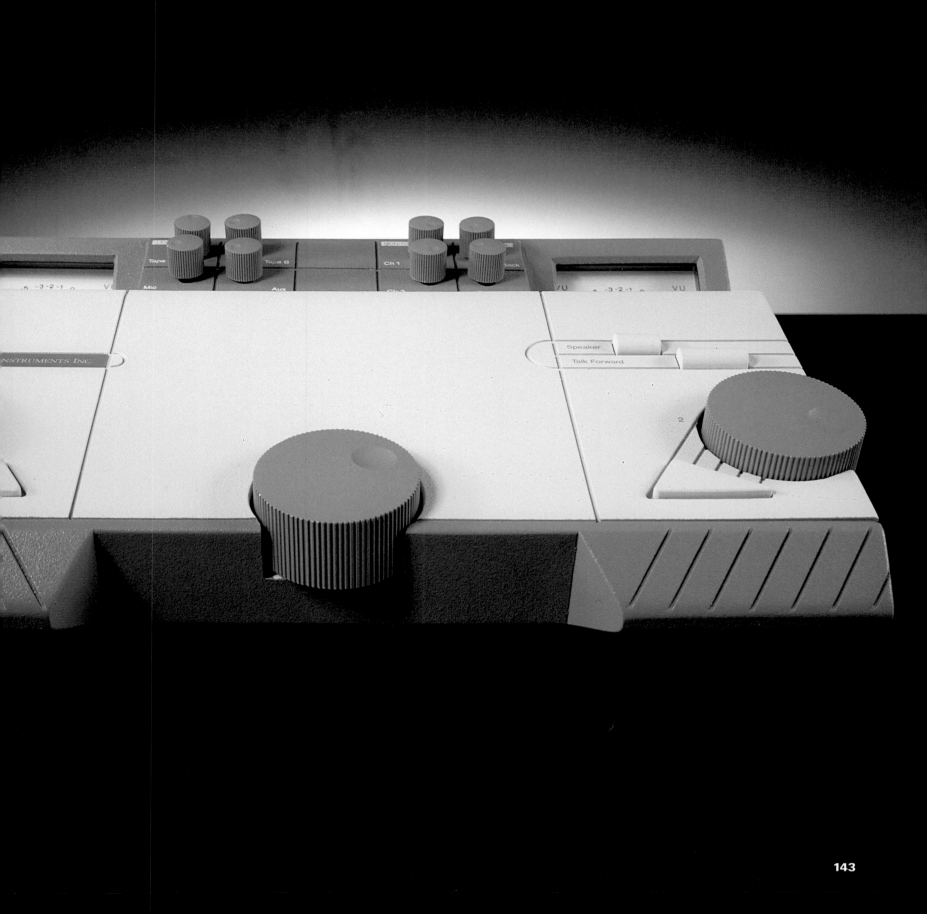

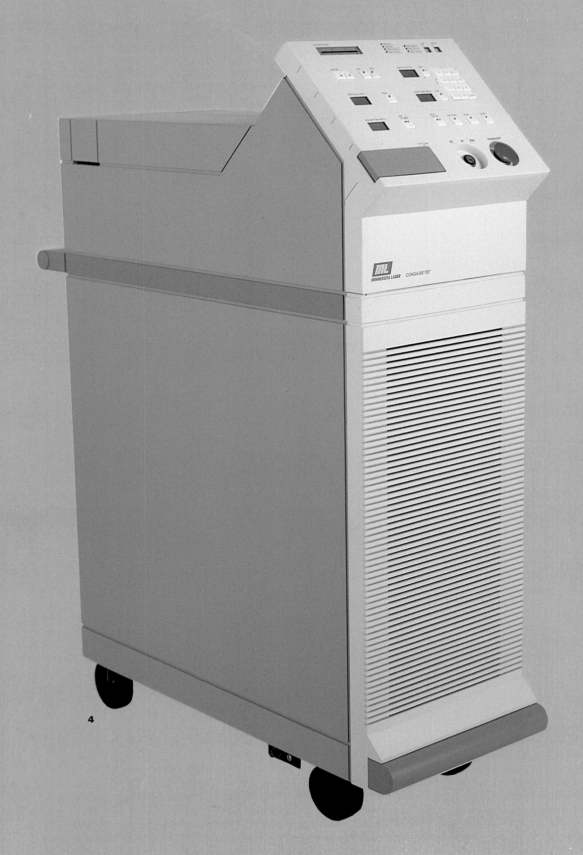

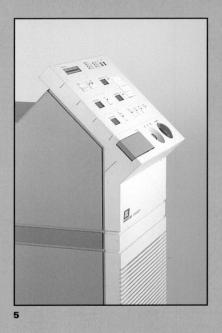

5

144

Working for clients with complex scientific equipment, says Polivka Logan principal Eugene Reshanov, the designer "must accept that their technology makes sense." Such was the case with a medical laser (4,5) and the Fluxatron (6,7), a device for improving the wear resistance of cutting tools using a magnetic field. The design task is to engineer the human interface and appearance of the unit.

6

7

When photography and graphic design meet, it is usually as vague acquaintances rather than close friends. They keep their distance, maybe exchanging pleasantries. A photograph is cropped to fit a layout with type surrounding it or overlaying it. In extreme cases, a photographic detail might be cut out to become part of a collage, but any more integrated treatment of the two techniques is rare.

At Skolos Wedell and Raynor, in Charlestown near Boston, it's all very different however. Nancy Skolos was on an undergraduate graphic design course at Cranbrook Academy of Art when she met Tom Wedell and his childhood friend Kenneth Raynor, who were both pursuing graduate degrees in photography. In the experimental spirit that Cranbrook encourages, they began to play with combinations of the two disciplines.

Those combinations have become the distinguishing mark of the practise they set up in 1980 in Boston, a city they chose, they say, because as midwesterners they were captivated by its old world charm, although the opportunity provided by the area's rapidly expanding industry during the past decade was not unwelcome. Skolos Wedell and Raynor can cope with the conservative corporation, often working like many other photographic studios, for example doing shoots for annual reports. For smaller clients it might be solely a graphic design office. But the best work is done when both techniques are evident in the same finished work.

It takes a certain restraint and unspoken understanding to be able to work together like this, and it seems likely that their marriage in 1979, after Cranbrook but before Boston, is a key to their success. Says Wedell: "One of the things I was always excited about was that the photograph wasn't finished after the shutter clicked, which is usually the perception. It could be reworked, almost like Polaroids by mushing the emulsion around. It became a starting point rather than an endpoint. When Nancy and I started to work together, I only took half a photo in a sense, and then it was worked and reworked." Adds Skolos: "It couldn't look too finished; it had to have

something left out to be completed by the graphic artist." Wedell sums up: "I think one of the keys to our work is that we do unfinished works and combine them." The combination of the two techniques in this way can be seen as an extension of the techniques of graphic collage and its analogue in photography, multiple exposure, that Skolos Wedell and Raynor use individually. Thus, the images produced are not only layered in the way that much contemporary graphic design is layered, with multiple images and type, but also layered in terms of the techniques used, with graphic design and photography used alternately to build up artwork.

The result of this collusion is that the work possesses an ambiguity. Although obviously two-dimensional, a poster will frequently use simple solid objects, laid over an incomplete graphic and cleverly spotlit to make clear their three-dimensionality. The ambiguity is further compounded when the penumbra that falls from a spotlit solid object lying on top of a graphic is echoed in two dimensions by Skolos's use of gradated papers. "We're trying to incorporate a sense of life through light in the photography. That's one of the things photography brings to graphics, and then the graphics responds ·with its own methods, in the gradations of the papers," says Wedell.

Skolos Wedell and Raynor's own stationery as well as that for a Boston architecture firm, Archetype, and a New York retailer of architect-designed tableware, Swid-Powell, exemplifies the dramatic sensuousness achieved with gradated papers in rich shades of unusual colors. Designs where the paper is used in conjunction with objects has the appearance of being two-and-a-bit dimensional, leaping up from the paper to capture the viewer's attention, as with a poster for Berkeley Typographers that uses two- and three-dimensional rules, arcs, and cones to show the classical construction of a letter B. Such examples provide a happier resolution to the apparent frustration with their medium felt by some graphic designers who resort to axonometric layouts, trivial solid motifs, and poorly handled exaggerated perspective in the attempt to escape the flatness of the printed page.

Skolos Wedell and Raynor's confusion of dimensionality is deliberate, and would be hard to achieve with any but the simple Platonic solid shapes used. It has been done before by Bauhaus artists such as Laszlo Moholy-Nagy who experimented with photograms and multiple exposures. A clear precursor is seen with Herbert Bayer's 1928 cover for the Bauhaus magazine that was a photographic compilation of printed graphics and typography with sharply lit platonic solids arranged over them. What's improved since then is the photographic and printing technology that allows sharper, more colorful compositions to be created.

Ironically, one problem with Skolos Wedell and Raynor's geometric surrealism is that it now shares it inspiration with the computer graphics buffs putting their expensive hardware through its paces to simulate, say, the reflective and refractive properties of glass and chrome. When Skolos Wedell and Raynor use chrome, however, it may look computer-generated, but in fact it turns out to be simply photographed rolled cones of mirror-finished Mylar.

Skolos Wedell and Raynor look back to the artists and great graphic designers of the early part of the century, but their Cranbrook education and Skolos's industrial design schooling has led them also to look at developments in current product design as well as in architecture. In common with many of their peers, they look at the early-Modern artists. Like many post-Modern architects, they find the work of De Chirico an inspiration. His illusory spaces have much in common with their work, but a recent project for the Mead annual report design competition paid him more direct and amusing homage. A painting called "Recompense" was recreated using models and local lighting to simulate the artist's imaginary creation, and the key detail of a soothsayer in the foreground was replaced by an unfolded annual report fluttering down from the heavens. The clock that recurs as a symbolic element in many De Chirico compositions has here had the time altered to the relevant midnight hour, alluding to the submissions deadline.

Wedell explains his ulterior motive for looking at this art: "We have to become more personalized in our symbolism. We can no longer rely on the graphic solids to represent thoughts and ideas. In that sense, the surrealists become a great influence with their ability to translate personalized symbols into paintings. It's a vantage point that we haven't fully utilized yet."

One reason to use geometric models is because they allow Skolos Wedell and Raynor to control how much illusion they want through design, lighting, and photography. But looking at the work of the surrealists offers clues as to what new directions might be taken. "One of our biggest blind spots is our lack of use of people in our photography and design," confesses Wedell. "We tend to avoid the portrait and figures. We feel that a figure is so readily identifiable in scale and form that it becomes too real." The potential for creating a memorable image is there however, in the work of Magritte, and to a degree in the work of the Swiss designer Herbert Matter, who used collaged, overscaled figures to enhance a startling photographic perspective.

Control is important to Skolos Wedell and Raynor. They keep control of both the substance of an image and the process of creating it by doing their own graphic design, shooting, photographic processing, and directing their modelmaking. Unlike many design firms, says Wedell, "we like to handle the technical aspects. We like to control the entire continuum from start to finish." But there is always a tension between this high level of technical control and a need to capture the moment. Skolos outlines her method: "I work really intuitively on the level of a thumbnail sketch and try to keep it from losing its magic as much as I can." From there, she'll make a comp in no more than an hour or two. Skolos helps assure that spontaneity by using a graphics computer and an enlarging photocopying machine to generate and manipulate graphics as fast as she can.

Now, with a growing business attracting ever larger, but slower clients, the problem is to keep up that pace. Says Skolos: "That's getting harder for us, keeping that energy alive, that out-of-control feeling."

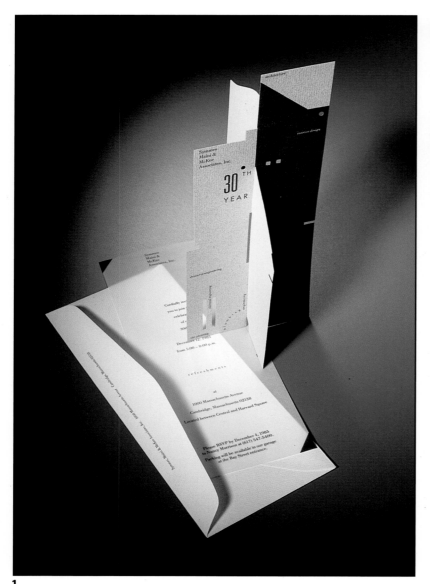

1

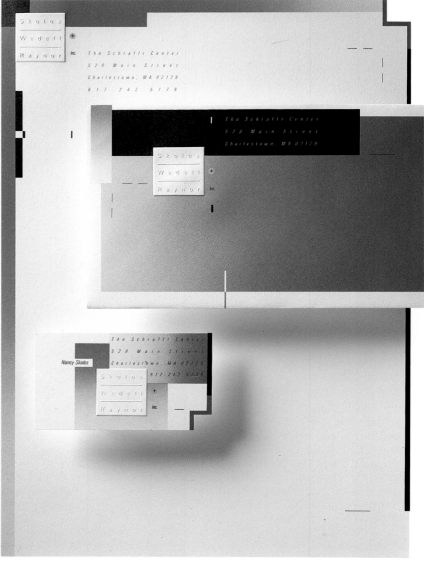

2

Stationery by Skolos Wedell and Raynor for a firm of architects (1) and for themselves (2) uses die-cuts, clever folding, and gradated papers to escape the Flatland of two dimensions. Work for print and type companies (3–6) takes the confusion of dimensionality further with textured surfaces and solid objects photographed to become part of the layout.

The influence of European Modern art is seen in different guises in much contemporary American graphic design. In a poster for SBK Entertainment (7), it is hinted at. There is a direct quotation in artwork for the Mead annual report design competition (12), where the De Chirico painting *Recompense* (see page 34) is reassembled with a few key changes in a process of design, modelmaking, and photography (8–11).
Poster for a video company (13) layers technological motifs.

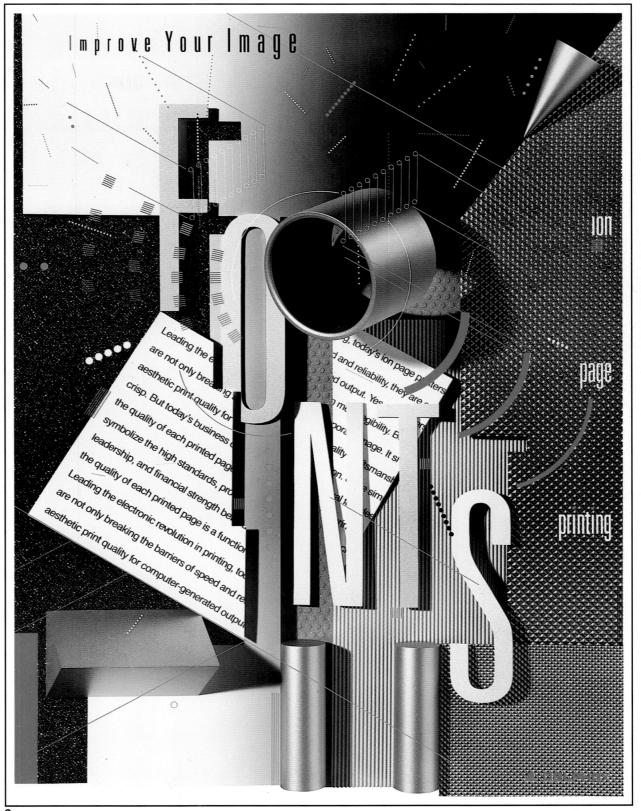

Improve Your Image

FONTS

ion

page

printing

Leading the electronic revolution in printing, today's ion page printers are not only breaking the barriers of speed and reliability, they are aesthetic print quality for computer-generated output. Yes crisp. But today's business the quality of each printed page symbolize the high standards, leadership, and financial strength the quality of each printed page Leading the electronic revolution in printing, are not only breaking the barriers of speed and aesthetic print quality for computer-generated output

3

149

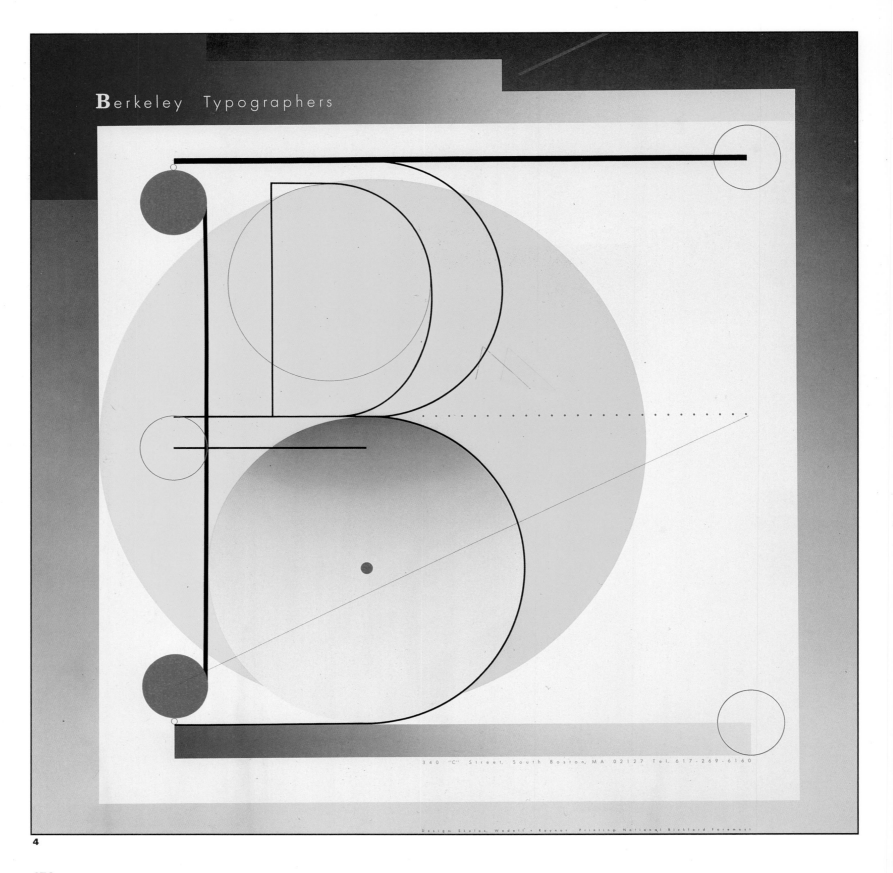

Berkeley Typographers

340 "C" Street, South Boston, MA 02127 Tel. 617-269-6160

Design Skolos, Wedell + Raynor Printing National Bickford Foremost

4

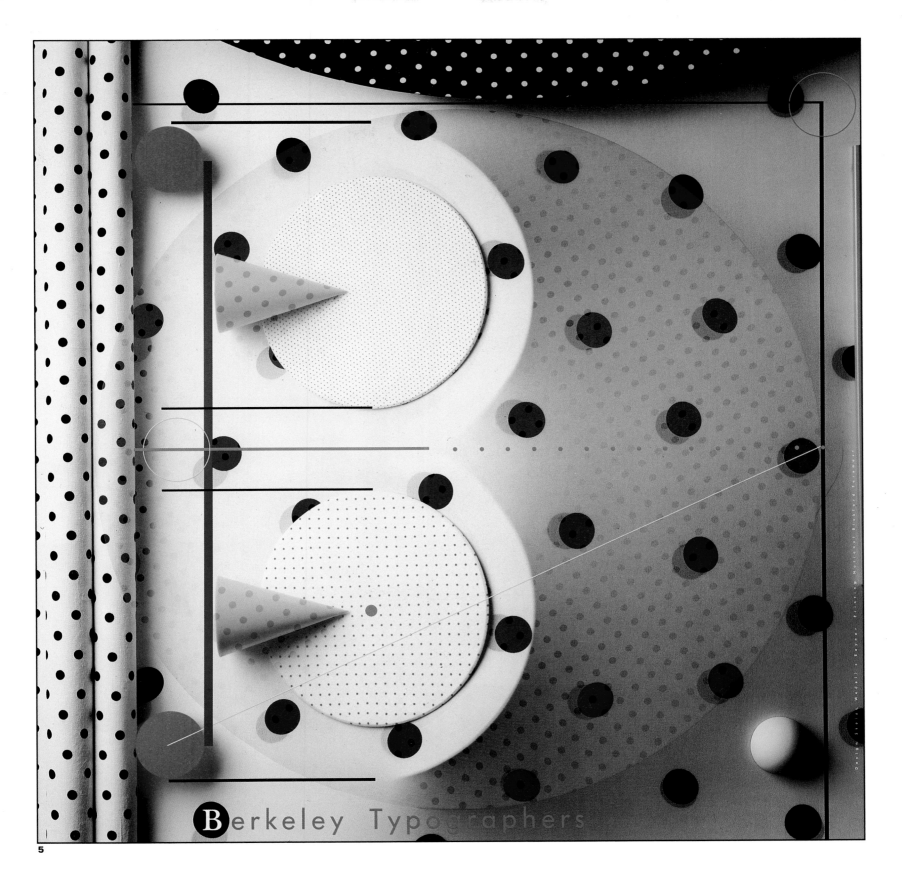

Berkeley Typographers

5

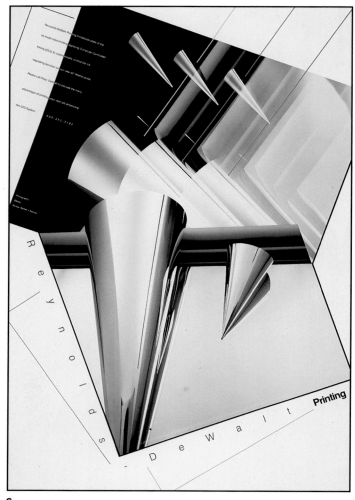

6

7

8

10

9

11

12

The microelectronic age is changing both the style and the substance of design. Products now function at the command of tiny

semiconductor components. Often, they have no moving parts. Shape becomes determined no longer by the interior workings to

be hidden, but by a subtler set of physiological and psychological concerns. Parts that come into human contact must be

designed ergonomically to meet the physical demands of the user. But equally important, the rest of the design must respond to

the human need for cultural and social symbols.

    Because technology no longer expresses itself clearly, as it did in the days of moving mechanical parts, designers have

adopted a new language of technological expression. Ornament, once a crime, is now a sign. Styling is back.

    In electronic products and computer-generated graphics, dots, grids and grilles have come to signify hidden electronic

power. As our capacity to be awed by electronic technology diminishes, so will these transient indicators of its presence. The

designer's mission is to find deeper relationships that associate technological products and images no longer only with them-

selves and their technology, but with a broader frame of historical and cultural reference.

The dismal science of ergonomics is going through a painful adolescence. Through the 1960s and 1970s, making things ergonomic was a prime concern of designers striving to have their still comparatively new profession recognized and valued by industry. Now that this has to some extent been achieved, ergonomics has become just another buzzword to unscrupulous advertising copywriters, and even many designers find it something of a chore. There is a feeling that its importance has been exaggerated over broader cultural issues. Tanaka Kapec Design Group is well positioned to pass comment. Its work is strong in its ergonomic foundations, but rarely lapses into the prosaic appearance that concern for such details often seems to dictate.

"In a home environment, the human factors questions are ones of safety and common sense," says Jeffrey Kapec. Designers have sufficient reserves of common sense to design simple products to an acceptable level of comfort and ease of use. The potential for trouble arises when the product has a complex interaction with its user. A designer's sense of "intuitive ergonomics" will suffice in shaping a hairdryer grip, for example. But for some precision tool, for example, the situation is different. Designers need the humility to know when a problem begins to require specialist information. In other areas, it is the human factors engineer who must concede to the designer. At work on a computer interface, the designer, with a reasonable awareness of human factors, may still make a suggestion based on intuition. "Human factors scientists will never come up with a new idea based on an insight or intuition. Scientists must prove whatever result they come up with. If you come up with a concept that just has an intuitive sense that it may be right, they could not support that. That's always been the contention between designers and scientists. Designers are trained *not* to be scientific about their work, up to a point."

When Tanaka Kapec was asked by Johnson and Johnson to redesign a dispenser used by dentists to squeeze filling material into cavities, the designers wanted to minimize the threatening bulk of the tool. In its existing version with the squeeze action controlled by a power grip in the fist, the tool bore an uncomfortable resemblance to a brass knuckle wielded in front of a patient's face. It was intuition, not any fundamental human factors study, that led them to reshape the device like a pen and use a small lever operated by the dentist's forefinger to control the flow of composite. Consensus said that a finger could not produce the pressure to push the composite along, but Johnson and Johnson encouraged Tanaka Kapec's innovative approach, and tests finally proved its feasibility.

A similar-looking implement for use under even more stringent conditions required careful attention to ergonomic details as well as to psychological aspects of the product in its context. The problem was to design a disposable microsurgery tool for Ethicon, a Johnson and Johnson company, to replace an existing titanium device that could be sterilized and used over. The new tool had to signal its disposability, but not look so cheap that a surgeon wouldn't touch it. The starting point was something that looked like a ball-point pen that would have been functional but little else. Tanaka Kapec modified the design, moving the logo from the middle to the end of the tool barrel, and positioning it so that when it faced the surgeon he would know that the business end of the instrument was also oriented a certain way without having to look under the microscope. Molded matt-black ribbing gave the tool grip in the slippery conditions of surgery as well as a suitable "high-tech" status association.

Even with comparatively simple products, the volumes of published human factors research are often insufficient for the designer's needs. Designing a garden hose end sprayer for Melnor Industries, for example, Tanaka Kapec found data on hand and arm positioning, but nothing on the dynamics of muscle grip and action, and nothing on how to use general information for a specific design problem faced with other constraints on dimensions owing to material costs and tooling requirements. "Each problem sets up new and

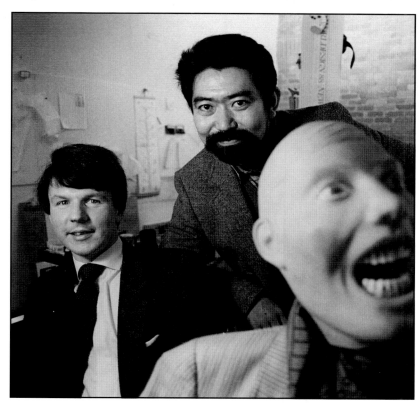

unique parameters. You can't just apply the information to it. We have to compromise. Where do we make the adjustments? The literature never tells you that. You have to back up and interpret." Ergonomics is not, as some would have it, an exact science. "It's like a lawyer interpreting the law."

Both designers and ergonomists believe that form follows function. But whereas ergonomists often think that just one form follows from a set of requirements, most designers would hold that there are many possible forms. Any role played by a product other than its purely functional one is open to the designer's speculation. "A product has to have a personality because it is part of your environment. Even though it may be a serious product, it still has a certain psychological, physical, and visual connection with your life." The Melnor equipment is given its personality with the choice of a crazy 1950s fluorescent green color. Design here and in other products that claim "personality" is, however, not so much in the service of the user as of the manufacturer.

The Melnor design evolved from a series of modelmaking exercises, a stage in design development that Tanaka Kapec feels firms are too ready to omit as product lead times shrink. The advantage of using models is illustrated in designs for sterilization trays for De Puy. Typically, these would be the province of an engineering firm that would simply do layout drawings before building a sheet-metal box. Tanaka Kapec went to a hospital, observed the use of trays, then went away and made some models, and returned and asked the nurses to comment. Useful feedback was obtained because it was the potential users who had seen a design in a form they could comprehend. Clients were impressed too. "They suddenly saw that the model was an invaluable tool. It could give you much more information about the product."

Tanaka Kapec's most detailed ergonomic design study was for a product type that is notoriously well researched—a typewriter keyboard. Japanese manufacturer Brother Industries had already conducted its own research at home, but came to an American consultancy for an independent viewpoint from its major export market. Tanaka Kapec did the usual videotaping of typists, comparison of existing designs, and human factors literature research, all of which confirmed Brother's findings. Using new flexible circuit-board technology under the electronic keyboard, they came up with a dished surface unlike other keyboards that place the keys in stepped rows, an arrangement that is not harmonious with the arc of a typist's finger motion. The keys themselves were also altered. Three sides of each key were defined with sharper than usual edges, while the top edge curved away. The crisp shaping is intended to create a better "home sensation" as each key is struck.

"The Japanese are very much more aware of design these days," says Kazuna Tanaka. Japan's historical homogeneity dictates today that if one product reaches a certain level of stylistic or technological merit, its competitors must follow suit. All this keeping up with the Kobayashis makes product design more like the fashion industry every day. With a product life of, say, two years, and perhaps a couple of dozen manufacturers in each market, the pace of superficial change is very fast. "For Japanese products selling in Japan, the visual elements change monthly now," says Tanaka. Manufacturers have it down to a fine art where they are prepared to change a color or a pattern or even modify the tooling to put some extraneous adornment on a basic product to satisfy some short-lived consumer whim, and still wring a small profit from the process. American industry will doubtless soon find itself adopting similar methods.

Even if this isn't about to happen tomorrow for all types of products, the value of the observation is that some companies are already planning for it. The Japanese are forecasting the technologies that will be around at the end of the century, and also working on the design languages that will appeal to the markets at that time. Says Kapec: "The Japanese tend to look down the road. Brother will begin talking about design now for a product that may not exist for another ten years. I have never seen an American corporation do that. They want to know, 'What are we doing six months from now?'"

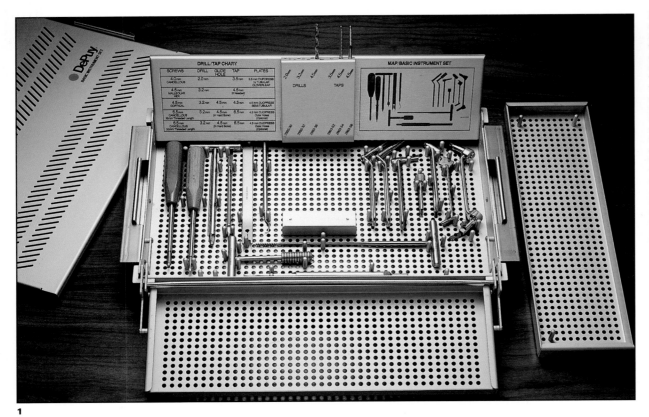

1

In-depth ergonomics study is a necessary forerunner for successful design in many fields. Tanaka Kapec's design for a sterilization tray for De Puy (1) evolved after hospital visits. On the strength of informal nursing staff surveys, the designers were able to return with models of potential designs and gain valuable feedback from the people who would be using the trays, rather than relying on data from the client or non-user buyers. In the case of a dental dispenser for Johnson and Johnson (2), it was the designers' intuition, however, that gave the idea for an improvement that would allow dentists to operate the tool using only a finger control in place of the clumsy hand-grip that is standard on such equipment. A keyboard for Brother Industries in Japan (3,4) required a similar blend of methodical and intuitive human factors attention.

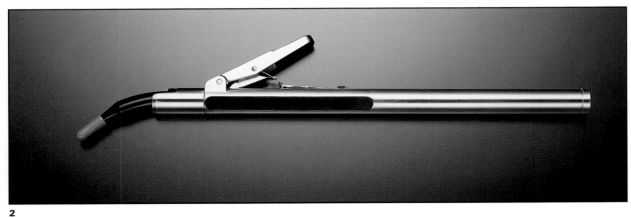

2

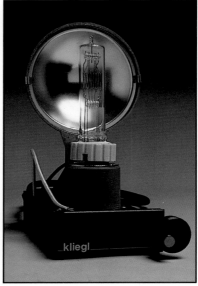

6

7

These theater lights (5–7) and this garden equipment (8,9) show that an expressive feeling for color and form need not be ruled out by ergonomic concerns.

5

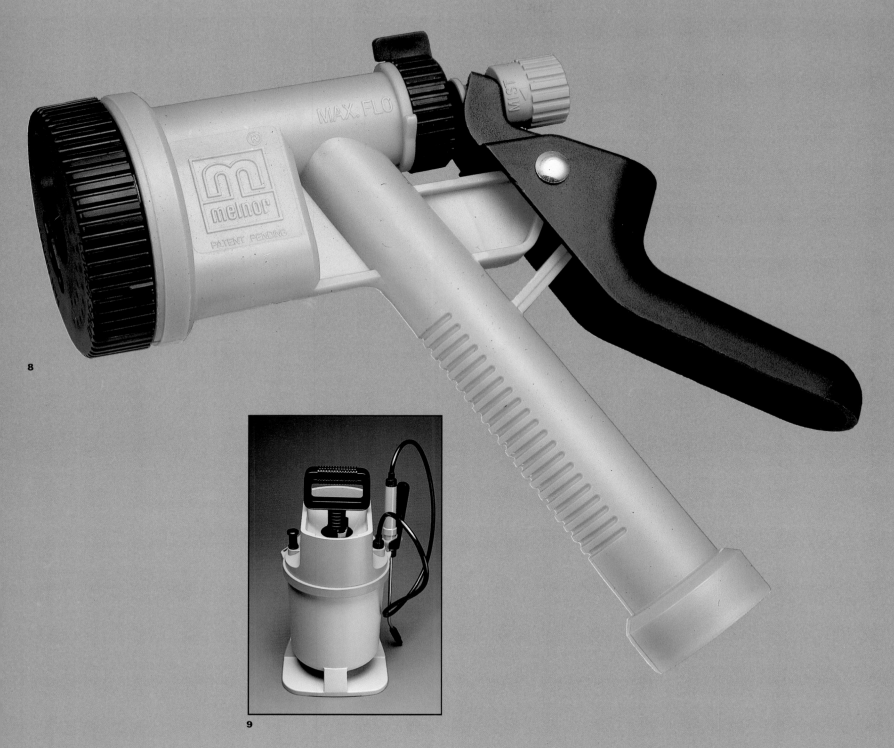

8

9

161

Émigré Graphics

My dictionary defines as an émigré "a person forced to emigrate for political reasons." Rudy VanderLans became an émigré under rather different circumstances. Odd as it may sound, he left his job in the Netherlands, a country that is currently producing some of the world's most original graphics, because he was bored by the corporate-identity work he was doing there. Graphic design, he says, "can be a very expressive profession. I didn't feel it was expressive doing identities." After graduate work at Berkeley and a stint on the *San Francisco Chronicle* as a designer and illustrator, he finally found a greater freedom of expression by launching his own magazine, called, naturally, *Émigré*.

Émigré, subtitled "the magazine that ignores boundaries," is published roughly twice a year in Berkeley. With a print run of only 3000, and a price that varies according to the unpredictable excesses of various artistic inserts, it is a modest concern by most publishing standards. Nonetheless, *Émigré* broke even on production costs last year, the third year of publication, about the same time more conventional magazines often take to prove themselves.

Great play is made of the title, with a number of logo variants that add layers of association. The principal title drops the acute accents of the word *Émigré* onto the crossbars of the Es, creating a foreign-looking graphic of a foreign word. Another makes judicious use of lexicographic pronunciation symbols to remind us of the word's full meaning. The device also offers a further clue to the magazine's coverage—language and art that addresses the barriers, boundaries and overlaps between our various cultures. On each *Émigré* the subtitle is translated into a different language.

More important than *Émigré*'s occasionally vapid and self-indulgent articles are its graphics. One of its ignored boundaries is the one that often exists between the editor and the art director of a magazine. The feeling is that editors rarely care for inventive graphic treatments of their text, and that art directors seldom read the copy they are responsible for laying out and illustrating. "Editors look at type and text very differently from graphic designers," observes VanderLans. "I think a lot of designers look first of all at text in terms of gray blocks. At art school, you do nothing but squint at text and see how gray it looks. They should first teach us how to read, and then how to be designers."

Émigré has no editor, only an art director, VanderLans. "I'm proud of that fact. It's obviously put together by visually oriented people." He hastens to add: "I like reading a lot. But I have a hard time getting into reading, for example, poetry—400 or 500 pages of poems [that are presented] visually all the same. If a collection of poems—discrete expressions of pure art—cannot be relieved by varied graphic and typographic treatment, then what hope for a novel or a daily newspaper?"

VanderLans explains his approach to *Émigré*: "I try to look at the magazine as a three-dimensional object, something that people go through. There's a sequence from page to page. When there are pages that are very dense and intricately designed, the next page would be very white."

Another boundary ignored is the one between tradition and technology, represented by *Émigré*'s use of the Macintosh for much of its typography and layout. This came about by lucky accident. Zuzana Licko, VanderLans's wife, is the typographer of the *Émigré* duo. She says: "For the first two issues we had used typewriter or Xeroxed type. We started with the Macintosh when it first came out because it was cost-efficient." They bought it as an illustration tool, but quickly made other discoveries. *Émigré* could not afford to set a lot of alternative type treatments. "If you don't need a cheap typesetting tool, if you can just as well send out for typesetting, then send out," says Licko. But for the budget operation that is *Émigré*'s desktop publishing, the Macintosh *is* that cheap typesetting tool.

VanderLans and Licko set out to prove that cheap Macintosh typography did not necessarily also mean nasty. They rejected the proprietary Apple Computer faces, which they found to be poor imitations of classic faces at best. They also rejected the notion held by some type specialists that

designing for the limitations of today's computers is a waste of time, since the technology is bound to evolve to represent classic faces as well as or better than other techniques. Instead, Licko designed her own faces, achieving a distinguished legibility despite the real constraints imposed by the hard-copy machines at that time. "If you start putting Helvetica or Times Roman into digital typefaces, the coarser the resolution, the worse they're going to look. If you print them out, they look really bad. So I designed typefaces that would look good on a coarse resolution printer. I'm not inventing faces for the sake of decoration." Several low-resolution faces were created on the computer's Font Editor program and set using MacWrite or MacPaint and the ImageWriter printer. "When you do your own typesetting as a designer, it changes the way you use type," Licko observes. For example, it prompts experiments and allows variations to be tried that would be expensive and impractical to request from a typesetter.

Writing in what amounts to a manifesto for her designs, she adds: "Designing our own fonts and doing our own typesetting on the Macintosh has given us endless possibilities that with traditional production methods would be impossible to execute or finance. We believe that as personal computer publishing gains momentum, it should not continue to result in the degradation of graphic standards."

VanderLans and Licko show that it need not. They still use the low-resolution alphabet because they still like its look. But they have also designed higher-resolution versions that take advantage of the greater capabilities of Apple's LaserWriter and its smoothing algorithm. They began with two basic Licko faces, Emperor 8 (so-called for its letter height in pixels) and a condensed version, Emperor 14. Smoothed on the LaserWriter, Emperor 14 became Modula, so called because the algorithm changed each letter from pixel components to modular components—horizontal, vertical, and 45-degree diagonal lines, and quarter- and semi-circles of a certain radius.

But the design did not stop there. Licko put distinctive 45-degree serifs onto letters where a sharp corner on the low-resolution face had been smoothed away. Another human touch was a slight resizing of the letters for optical correction of their x height. The key to the success of this type design is in the designer's knowing when to use the computer and when to take over manually. The end result is that Modula is a highly mannerist typeface. Here the serifs serve no purpose as they once did in the days of hot metal, but simply act as a historical link.

Knowing when not to use the computer is also important in the layout of VanderLans's work. He prefers to arrange the computer-set type by hand and not to use the layout capability of the Macintosh. The small screen of the computer does not allow enough room to shuffle images and text. It would also decrease the likelihood of bringing about those chance collages that are a large part of his page designs. These combine dramatic black-and-white illustrations and swirling soft-focus photography layered with bold blocks of color and the fresh look of the computer-generated type.

Now Licko and VanderLans are designing a number of other publications. A new quarterly, *Shift*, that aims to assuage San Francisco's inferiority complex about its art scene (the shift in question is of attention away from New York and Los Angeles), gave VanderLans his first opportunity to lay out entire pages solely on the Macintosh. Another arts magazine, *Glashaus*, VanderLans describes as a more commercial version of *Émigré*, intended to make money on advertisement sales. The challenge here is to retain a cohesive design despite, or possibly even because of, the advertisements. Some *Glashaus* advertisers have allowed their ads to be designed for them, but others are sceptical that their message can be made to fit in, yet still stand out.

Émigré meanwhile has attracted the admiration of more convention-bound magazine art directors. If they would emulate what they see, VanderLans's wish may yet come true: "I would like to see all the things that I am doing now be applied to commercial magazines."

EMIGRE MAGAZINE

(em′ə grā′)

SUBSCRIBE

5

Edizione Italo-Francese

4

EMIGRE

The Magazine that Ignores Boundaries

1

2

3

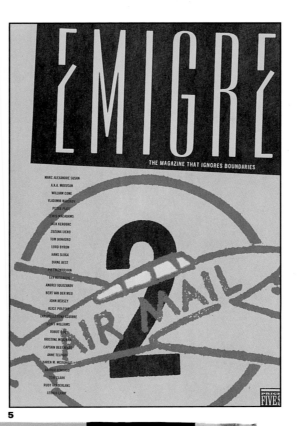

4

5

melon on was giving herself away. the wind was beginning to hurt. when i got up from the chair once marco said i moved like an american. the blue truck could go off the road because he was the water. we all take our wind collecting. she's a marine girl and should be careful picking cherries.

yellow chairs on top of town. they tile their patios like swimming pools. they tile the roof. they tile something so you can see it. round corals took a swim. i look up thru the nose and there is the sun. her eyes invite themselves places. muscles out longing. i have a villa. when i stand up in the morning the world smells of calamari. so hot the sweat was in the pebbles, thought i couldn't move. got to the water and as i swam was cooled by the movements. luci, luci, putting lots of sugar in the espresso. sitting on the cove of the rocks lushing. the night fastens diamonds. once i had warm fish on toast. pulling the pieces from my eyes as i used to do for shag. the edges of eyes accumulating. tile is a cool place to breath. yesterday in the cove reckless, barely the stones slip you in. plunge. later in the fish bath black stones came out the size of a question. they float birthmarks over skin, given to fate. somebody asks if i want something and i do. cactus on the sky baby. on top of a boat all the way to capri. lived some pink rocks. nothing hesitates to be beautiful. more protective the smell. cement with a seat of green tile. blue until plunge. lizards everywhere. large pebbles moon size. on an island. leaving is hard. mozzerella pommedore basilica grisini tornesi acqua della madonna. sprayed talk to rocks. really to ask questions and to see the grotto. capri sapphires glinting. white sand on the bottom and sun light underneath. the blue grotto. heads under. acqua, acqua. on the water sitting high up the hull. i was moving by rocks. pink grains. the longer i watched the more alive they became. looking should have an idea. the air continually cleans the rocks. these men the sees as iguanas, skinny to the water's edge. flitting stones it takes practice to walk on descending beauty. laps a bit of green or turquoise fills in. aqua, aqua. in now recommended to suffer the heat and be reduced. relaxing under a cover for her head. black flint. took the curves not the steps to get here. some of the stones are of places. some of the stones are of time. the moon steps further. gathering the stones you threw off your body when you were wet. plagued.

6

Covers, pages, and details from *Émigré* magazine (1–11). Bold illustrative, graphic, and photographic treatments combine with digital and conventional typography. Although much of the type is computer-generated, the layouts and picture treatments are clearly the product of human intuition.

THE MAGAZINE THAT IGNORES BOUNDARIES

EMIGRE MAGAZINE

é·mi·gré (em'ə grā')

SUBSCRIBE

Subscription rate for the U.S. and Canada is $10. for 3 issues (individual), $12. for 3 issues (institutional). Foreign subscriptions by surface mail cost $12.60, by airmail, $21.90. Make check, money order (U.S.) or international money order (outside U.S.)

7

166

8

WOODCUT BY CARLOS LLERENA AGUIRRE

9

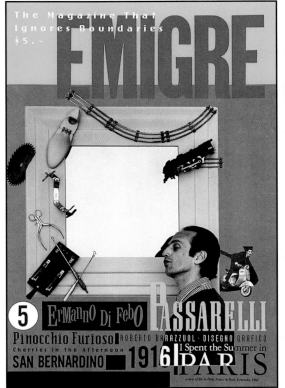

10

11

DIGITAL FONTS

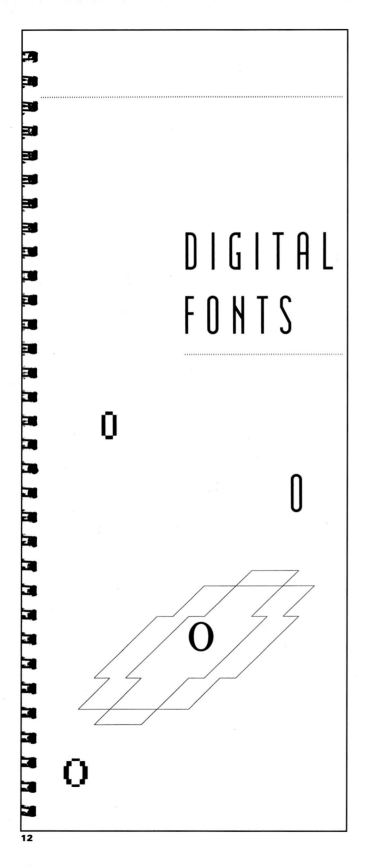

12

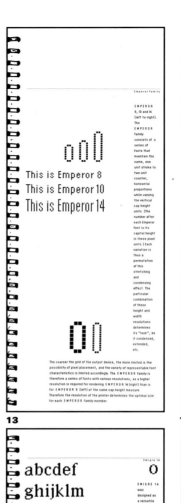

EMPEROR 8, 10 and 14 (left to right). The EMPEROR family consists of a series of fonts that maintain the same, one unit stroke to two unit counter, horizontal proportions while varying the vertical cap height units. (The number after each Emperor font is its capital height in these pixel units.) Each variation is thus a permutation of this stretching and condensing effect. The particular combination of these height and width resolutions determines its "look", be it condensed, extended, etc.

This is Emperor 8
This is Emperor 10
This is Emperor 14

The coarser the grid of the output device, the more limited is the possibility of pixel placement, and the variety of representable font characteristics is limited accordingly. The EMPEROR family is therefore a series of fonts with various resolutions, as a higher resolution is required for rendering EMPEROR 14 (right) than is for EMPEROR 8 (left) at the same cap height measure.
Therefore the resolution of the printer determines the optimal size for each EMPEROR family member.

13

abcdef
ghijklm
nopqrst
uvwxyz

EMPEROR 8 uses the minimum number of pixels required to define a complete alphabet, while maintaining the characteristics of its family.

abcdefg
hijklmn
opqrstu
vwxyz

The high resolution MODULA typeface was derived from the low resolution EMPEROR 14 bitmap font. Unlike most PostScript fonts which have separate outlines for their inside and outside boundaries, MODULA is a stroked font, meaning that each character is defined by a single line of a uniform width which may be varied to generate different weights of the font.

This is Smooth Emperor 10
This is Smooth Emperor 14

With certain Macintosh applications, such as MacPaint's "Print final" command and MacDraw's "smoothen" option, the LaserWriter prints smooth versions of the EMPEROR bitmap fonts and essentially creates a new font. MODULA is based on this smoothened Emperor font.

14

abcdef
ghijklm
nopqrst
uvwxyz

EMIGRE 14 was designed as a versatile text font for the coarse printing methods of the dot matrix printer, originally the only printer available for the Macintosh.

This durable bitmap font is optimized for legibility at virtually any point size.

abcdef
ghijklm
nopqrst
uvwxyz

The MATRIX font is derived from EMIGRE 14. It retains the modularity of EMIGRE keeping it very much in harmony with the digital grid. MATRIX thus consumes relatively little memory space to store in the printer and generates printouts very quickly.

MATRIX was designed to be an economical font and thus the points required to define it were limited to the essentials. As a result several changes were made in the font characteristics in its derivation from EMIGRE. One example is the treatment of serifs shown here. EMIGRE's serifs (left) are square, the exact size and shape of one pixel, while the serifs of MATRIX (right) were reduced to triangular wedges, thus eliminating one of the points that would otherwise be required to render a square serif. The 45 degree angle of the serif wedge was employed as this is the smoothest-looking diagonal that a digital printer is capable of generating.

15

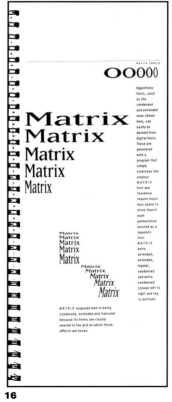

Matrix
Matrix
Matrix
Matrix
Matrix

Matrix
Matrix
Matrix
Matrix
Matrix
Matrix
Matrix
Matrix

Algorithmic fonts, such as the condensed and extended ones shown here, can easily be derived from digital fonts. These are generated with a program that simply stretches the original MATRIX font and therefore require much less space to store than if each permutation existed as a separate font. MATRIX extra extended, extended, regular, condensed and extra condensed (shown left to right and top to bottom).

MATRIX responds well to being condensed, extended and italicized because its forms are closely related to the grid on which these effects are based.

16

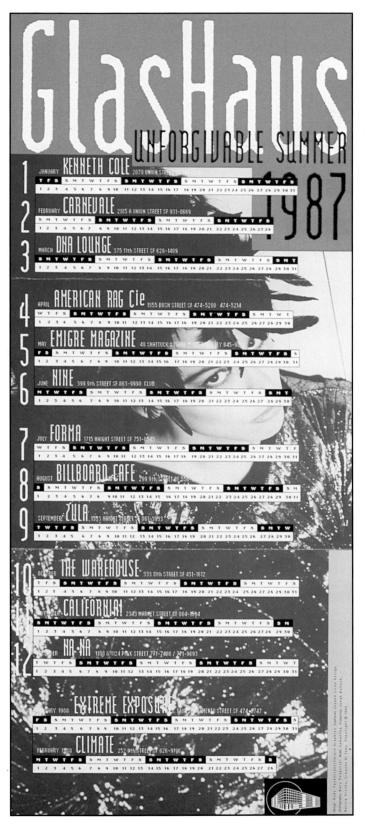

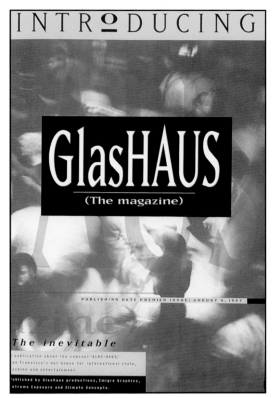

Digital fonts designed by Zuzana Licko (12–16). A variety of low- and high-resolution typefaces are used in Émigré Graphics' design for a number of San Francisco arts publications, such and *Glashaus* (17, 18) and *Shift*. Rudy VanderLans and Licko are trying to overcome what they regard as a stigma that attaches to obviously computer-displayed type. There will always be the need for low-resolution bit-mapped alphabets, for example on cheap or portable computers, they say. "It is essential to address graphic design specifically to these devices."

ID Two

When America's founding fathers of industrial design came together to form their new profession, they had been practising a variety of trades. They were illustrators and commercial artists and stage designers before they were industrial designers. Nearly sixty years on, Bill Moggridge thinks that history is due to repeat itself. A similar coalescence of disciplines is needed to tackle the problems confronting today's designers and their clients.

The realization grew out of work Moggridge's San Francisco consultancy, ID Two, has been doing for its Silicon Valley clients with their ever more capable, ever smaller inventions. "Once you make machines more intelligent, then you have to design for their intelligence. The approach is always just to ask the simple questions—what does the user do? Does he like it? What matters? But as times change and technology changes, that drives you to come up with answers which embrace other disciplines."

Moggridge coined the term "interaction design" to describe this pursuit, which aims to combine the talents of human factors scientists, mechanical engineers, psychologists, and writers with those of software, graphic and industrial designers. In trying to build a new discipline around a name, ID Two is consciously echoing the approach taken by Raymond Loewy, Walter Dorwin Teague and Henry Dreyfuss in the late 1920s to give their work credibility and visibility when they christened industrial design as a legitimate profession.

Up to a point, these skills are already routinely brought to bear on high-technology design problems. Often, however, each specialist is only called in on an "as needed" basis to work on what is perceived by the client as the pertinent stage of a design development. Moggridge wants to give ID Two the ability to provide all these services as a consultancy, and bypass the sort of thinking that perpetuates this harmful compartmentalization of disciplines.

ID Two also has global ambitions. Its parent company, Design De-velopments, already comprises the London consultancy Moggridge Associates and a modelmaking group, IDM. It recently added a West German office, Design Drei. In the United States, a loose association with the large design consultancy RichardsonSmith in Worthington, Ohio, gives both firms an infrastructure that can be drawn upon to address almost any problem a client might throw at them.

Interaction design is the responsibility of Bill Verplank, a human factors engineer formerly with Xerox Corporation. Xerox, especially its Palo Alto Research Center, has long taken a pioneering role in the business of making computers "user-friendly." Its particular contribution was the perfection of the bit-mapped display that made screen graphics a reality. The job of the interaction designer now, says Verplank, is to "forget the barriers and think about all the things the computer does to present itself to the user and all the things the user has to do to sense and control the computer." In too many cases, according to Verplank, barriers are erected where there need be none. He objects violently to the jargon word "dialogue" because it implies that a computer can somehow talk back. "A lot of people call themselves 'dialogue designers'—it's another anthropocentric view of what computers are that is mostly misleading. It's an interesting academic exercise to make machines like people, because then you learn more—about the people!" But trying to make computers that think like people, and designing the interface to signify that this is how they "think," could be decidedly premature when scientists still know so little about how people do actually think.

Nevertheless, the first step in interaction design is to mimic what is current practice today, adopting readily understood similes or metaphors to make equipment easier to use. Consider, for a simple example, the wristwatch. The analogue watch with mechanically driven hands is what we all recognize and understand. Electronics made possible watches with a digital display replacing the moving parts, and the compulsion of novelty dictated that manufacturers make their watches digital, despite the fact that it then

took longer to get an approximate idea of the time, and setting the time became a nightmare. Interaction design would recognize, as some manufacturers now do, that the analogue presentation had always been preferable, and use an approach of "naive realism" to create digital-analogue watches with hands that moved around the face by a changing display. Deeper consideration of interaction design might find a way to use an electronically displayed representation of the traditional winder to adjust the "hands" in place of today's pencil-point pushbuttons, which are practically impossible to use. Ultimately, the many disciplines of interaction design might devise a more appropriate but as yet unforeseen way of showing the passage of time.

Any everyday notion can suffice as a metaphor to simplify working with a powerful computer. Even apparently conflicting metaphors can be used together. "A lot of people say you have to decide on a metaphor: it's going to be a desktop, or a workbench, or a factory, and you have to stick with that metaphor," says Verplank. "That's ridiculous. People are quite happy to mix metaphors. Successful user interfaces have strange mixed metaphors." Witness the Macintosh computer with its clockface icon appearing in a "window" in surrealistic fashion to mean "please wait."

As computers become artificially intelligent, the problem of creating an unobtrusive interface will become greater. Both suitable software and an appropriate physical form will assume greater importance. ID Two designer Neil Taylor asks: "What should a box look like? There's a lot of stuff inside it, but you don't have to know anything about it. Is there anything that needs to be expressed? Probably not. It could just take on a nice shape."

The possibilities inherent in the design of intelligent computers present an intriguing parallel with a past challenge facing designers. A plastic, by definition, is a substance capable of adopting any shape. But when designers first started using plastics, they mimicked the shapes of the wooden cabinets and metal cases that had preceded them. "It wasn't until a few years after plastics had been brought in that the people started designing in a *plastic*

sense. That could happen with the computer. It is anything it can be imagined to present itself as: hysterically funny or comical or intriguing or standoffish. It might even present itself differently to different people."

The excitement in ID Two's futuristic thinking is often not shared in its products. A minimal restraint is more likely to prevail, although the sense of giving a product a character was a particularly strong consideration in one of ID Two's most successful designs, the Grid Compass, a portable computer for "mobile professionals," and one of the first with a flat-screen display. Using the latest technology and putting it all in a diecast magnesium case made the computer ludicrously expensive but gave its owner the reassurance that if, say, he were accidentally to drop it from his executive jet, it would probably survive the mishap. The precision detailing, sleek lines, and compulsory matt black finish completed the image, and ensured that the Compass made its way into the collection of the Museum of Modern Art. Here was the computer as status symbol to the max.

Another flat screen unit, the Touchware PC Translator for Newex, achieves a jaunty friendliness with bright yellow corner accents and distinctive waffle-iron motifs. A Z-form hinge allows the translator to be variably positioned between the keyboards and screens of different personal computers, adding new functions through its touch-screen keys. Still more expressive of its adjustability is a terminal designed for Lynk Corporation. The intricate mechanism to raise and tilt the monitor recalls the working of an old steam train.

These designs are firmly rooted in the present. The qualities of personality that Verplank talks about introducing are not present here. As Taylor points out, designers, however creatively they may be thinking about the future of design and technology, are still at the behest of their clients and the technology *they* are using. "I'm sorry to say I think industrial designers are following rather than leading in things like computers, because they are not the people working on the technology that makes it all happen."

2

3

ID Two employs a variety of design languages in its computer terminals. For Grid (1–3), it designed sleek black portables for executives. The first model came out when flat screens were still prohibitively expensive for most consumers, and was unashamedly styled primarily for status consciousness with a virtually indestructible magnesium housing—a technocrat's answer to the attaché case. The second version (1) is more practical and affordable with plastic construction, but its smooth lines retain the power image. A terminal for Lynk Corp. (4–6) appeals to a more playful sense, with an articulated pop-up mechanism for the monitor. Simlinc's computer (7–9), on the other hand, appears powerful with a dark plastic housing and exaggerated features such as the coiled cable. The screen mounted almost flush with its surround seems ready to burst from the terminal body.

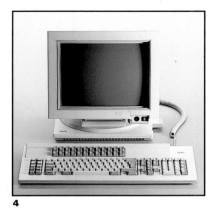

4

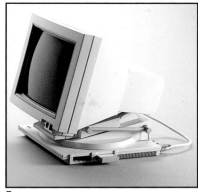

5

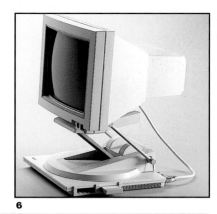

6

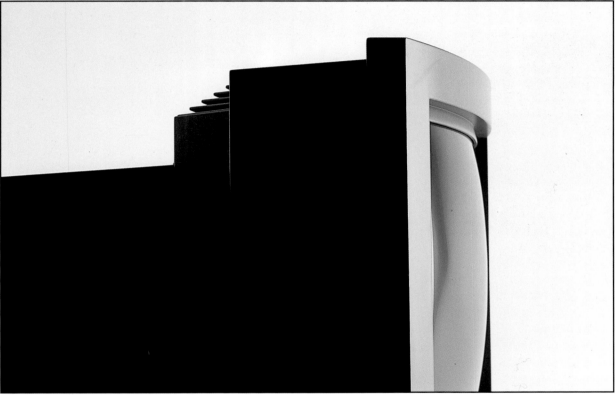

7

8

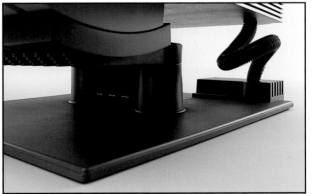

9

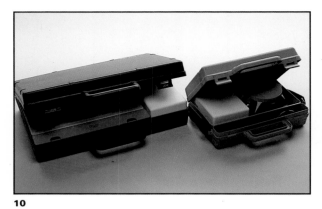

10

11

Modular design of lunchboxes for a company called Joe (10–13).
How or whether to make historical reference in products has proved problematic for many designers. ID Two's ventures into this area, seen in the ornamentation on a set of clip-together photograph frames (14–16) and in a PC Translator for Newex (17,18), defy precise categorization. Elements are present from post-Modern architecture, from Memphis, and from product and crafts design at the turn of the century.

12

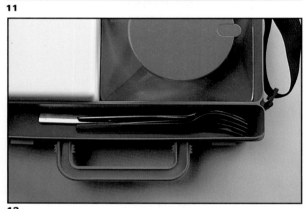

13

14

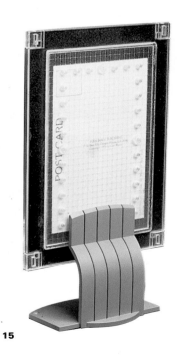

15

16

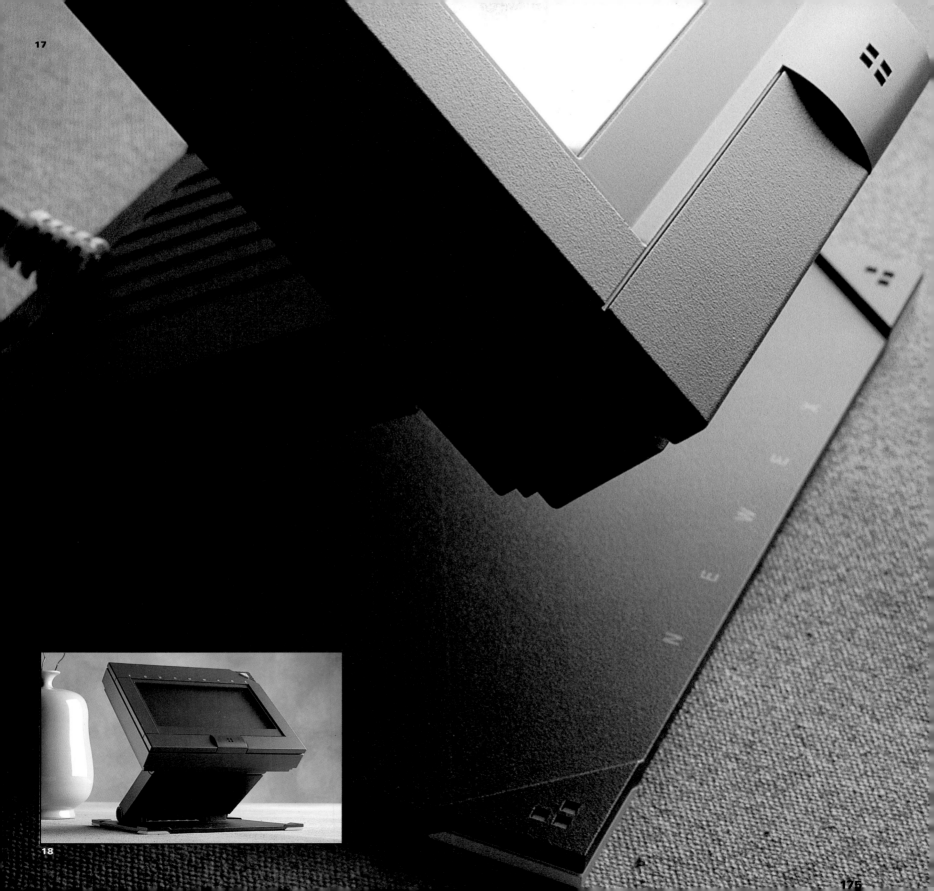

18

Mike Nuttall is not much of a fan of the current trend toward semantically understandable products. Design school in his day was about more than who could get the nicest details, he says bluntly in his North of England accent. Nuttall studied design at London's Royal College of Art before coming from Moggridge Associates in London to help set up its California office in 1979. Nuttall split off to form his own consultancy, Matrix Product Design, six years ago as ID Two accumulated more and more like-minded clients and problems of conflicts of interest—always a sensitive issue in Silicon Valley—began to arise.

The RCA today is producing some visually exciting sculptural design, if sometimes at the expense of practical considerations. In Nuttall's day, priorities were very different. Under the aegis of Bruce Archer, the school then was taking a severe methodological approach, analyzing design step by step from the statement of a problem to the devising of a solution.

Nuttall's work shows that this indoctrination is not incompatible with the creation of design that is occasionally sensuous and symbolic. Nuttall looks back for an ideal: "Look back toward the calculators that were coming out of Olivetti 20 years ago. In terms of the quality of the plastic parts, and their not having to worry about plastic getting in the way—as designers able to be in full control of the visual characteristics and the human factors characteristics of small electronic products—that was happening then."

Like other Silicon Valley designers, Nuttall senses something of a renaissance in American industrial design. "In the next five to ten years, the media will start treating design on a much more glamorous level. The electronics industry has been central to that revival. It's done two things: it's given designers a new challenge, a new kind of problem; and it's attracted a lot of designers from Europe, and that's given a different perspective.

"Until seven or eight years ago, when this industry started becoming a fertile ground, designers in America weren't doing anything. There'd been this tremendous growth of the design profession in the 1950s and maybe the 1960s, and then during the 1970s there was nothing to do. Industry slowed down. All the refrigerators and mixers had been designed. I think it was shortsighted of American designers, working mainly in the midwest and on the East coast, not to see the opportunities that were here before they did.

"One of the reasons that industrial designers were suddenly welcomed by the computer industry is that to some degree computers got to the point where they were the same." Design became one of the few ways to differentiate a product in a crowded market.

Matrix achieved a spectacular differentiation in the case of a workstation for Metaphor Computer Systems, a new company with its first product. Analysis of the problem began with the fact that the terminal was intended as a managerial tool. It might spend long periods idle on a manager's desk, or have to cope with short but frequent bursts of activity. So it had to be unusually easy to use and to store away. A keyboard, for example, would take up too much room when not being used. This led to the idea of multiple input devices, not just a keyboard, but also a mouse and a keypad, only one of which would be used at a time and all of which would be stored away. The cables these devices usually need would soon have made any desk look a mess. The Matrix designers worked with David Kelley Design, a local mechanical engineering consultancy that prides itself on meeting technical constraints and the esthetic whims of designers, to overcome this obstacle by perfecting wireless infra-red links between them.

The technical innovation of this solution was matched by a tightly controlled design language. Each component of the Metaphor system has a slot for it in the L-shaped monitor support; even the main keyboard slips under the front of the screen. The sense of belonging is emphasized in the design elements shared by all the parts, the principal one being an enigmatic vitreous black segment on an edge of each component that hides, yet still signifies, the infra-red connection between them. The color scheme of the plastic casings and keys and the detailing of the molding joints provide further

unity to the separate components of the Metaphor.

A similarly minimal approach was adopted in Nuttall's designs for voice-activated telephones for Innovative Devices. Some designers might add physical details to signal this unexpected way of using the phone, but Nuttall plays down the importance of the voice activation. "Blatant use of metaphors becomes boring very quickly. There's no subtlety."

In technological products with complex and subtle actions, such as the Voice Dialer or the Metaphor workstation, the designer's problem remains one of traditional ergonomics, not of formal gesture, Nuttall suggests. He finds the general concern for ergonomics is still at a pitifully low level. "If you're designing a telephone, it's well respected by most people who would like to manufacture a nice telephone that you spend a lot of trouble getting the feel really nice. But what does that mean if you're designing a powerful floor-standing computer? The level there is currently pathetic, almost non-existent. For most people developing electronic products, the main focus is still in superior hardware."

Nuttall expects this situation to improve gradually, as each company begins to pursue its own software and hardware development more in harmony with each other. Apple Computer has been an influential trendsetter in this area. Already, Silicon Valley manufacturers look to designers to give them differentiation between hardware that all does similar work. As more computer manufacturers imitate Apple's advances, and bring an equivalent level of sameness to their software, a demand will grow for designers with "soft" skills as well as the ability to style a box.

One area where this move is already being felt is in the design of the "mouse," that tactile means of interaction between human and machine. Matrix Product Design called up David Kelley Design for engineering expertise and Bill Verplank of ID Two for human factors studies. It was a long and detailed project, despite the modest size of the end product, because the interaction was critical. But Nuttall dispels an illusion about how scientific

such design gets. Reams of ergonomic data were not the starting point, as might be expected. Instead, he says "it came from a gut feel of what's nice to hold. Then you make one and play with it and change it." Then, with Verplank and the help of design students at nearby Stanford University, the designers tested the mouse "to validate the design decisions. Ergonomics helps, but really only to validate. It doesn't tell you what you should be doing," Nuttall cautions.

A still more daunting project than any computer was a potentially characterless box used to produce slides. Designed for Presentation Technologies, the Image Maker digitally captures images from a computer screen to make high-resolution slides. "It was an electro-optical mechanical nightmare. For a while, you thought: what can you do with a shoebox?" In the end, Matrix and Kelley did design a box, a basic black cube with notches cut into it. The notches help explain the working of the machine, not in any literal semantic sense, but by indicating a hierarchy. The deepest Vs, cut into the top, are where an operator interacts most physically with the machine, inserting and retrieving type wheels. A smaller set of Vs signifies a lesser degree of contact where the user simply operates a switch, while a third size of Vs indicates the machine's "voluntary" response of lights showing operational status. The smallest Vs of all signify the Image Maker's "involuntary" action of circulating air to cool the device. The vents cut at an angle in place of the usual square-cut slots also disguises their presence from most angles at which the slide-maker is seen.

The Image Maker illustrates clearly the peculiar nature of design in Silicon Valley, where the miniaturized electronic content of many products is pulling form and function further than ever apart. "With most of the things that we design here, there are actually problems to be solved and improvements to be made, and the styling aspect is definitely secondary," says Nuttall. He adds, with mischievious ingenuousness: "The idea is to make the form look almost accidental, as though it really did follow the function."

3

180

5

6

7

An executive terminal for Metaphor Computer Systems (1,2) uses a tightly controlled design language of common elements to make the various peripherals appear as members of a family. The unity was more than usually desirable because here, in contrast to most computer systems, there is no physical link between the components, which communicate by infra-red. Equal restraint is exercised in the design of other high-tech products—a voice-activated telephone (5), a mouse (6), and the Workslate for Convergent Technologies (7).

Halogen floor lamp (3) displays both formal severity and technical ingenuity with each bulb unit held in place by friction and with the two support rods doubling as the electrical conductors.

Matrix principal Mike Nuttall dismisses obvious references in product design: "Blatant use of metaphors becomes boring very quickly." But he does find time for more formal coding of function. The Image Maker (4) uses a hierarchy of V-cut notches molded into its case as redundant signs. The largest notches signify points of greatest man-machine interaction—the insertion and extraction of type wheels for labeling slides. Smaller notches successively indicate lesser physical interaction with switches, followed by visual interaction with status indicators.

The popular stereotype of Los Angeles is, or was, of a cultural wasteland. That sentiment was shared by New York-born graphic designer April Greiman until she visited the city on a job and saw that its apparent disadvantage was also an opportunity. "Because of the lack of tradition, it was a little more open. I realized that the climate was better for educating clients."

Today, the artistic awakening of Los Angeles is the envy of other modern American cities. April Greiman was both a leader and a beneficiary of that awakening. One of Los Angeles' leading graphic designers almost since her arrival, she soon was dubbed the Queen of the New Wave, a 1970s Southern California graphics style.

Hers is an unlikely synthesis: West coast sensory overload of information, color, and fun; but also a Swiss Modernist sense of control and knowledge of typography. The result shows. "There's a certain refinedness or even elegance that I would attribute to my European experience."

Greiman acknowledges the importance of history, clarity, and typography learned directly or indirectly from the Basel Kunstgewerbeschule, but she rejects some of its more condescending dogmas. "The Swiss school says that you reduce, you keep taking away until you get down to the essence. I did that for a while. Then I came out here, and because of the culture, which is a media culture really more than any other place in the United States, I just started saying, 'Okay, I've got all this stuff. Am I making a more meaningful message by reducing and simplifying it, or am I making a more meaningful message by throwing it all in?' I prefer to assume that the viewer is more sophisticated and can handle more, because that's where our culture is. Why am I the judge of what's the most important part of a message as long as I have many things that are contributing? Why should *I* eliminate certain things?" What Greiman seems to be saying is that the Swiss dictum of selecting one image for the sake of clarity is just as arbitrary a process as the selection of many images for the complex layered graphics she favors.

"I think I've been philosophically in line with Wolfgang Weingart," the Basel design teacher who was an early challenger of the inflexibility of the Swiss International Typographic Style. "In researching and getting information and getting into the problem, you gather lots of different things," she explains. Greiman has been able to layer images and ideas to a greater extent than most other designers for a number of reasons. The most important of these is the Swiss-influenced education that gives an underlying discipline that helps ensure that visual excess does not degenerate into simple mess. Other reasons stem from Greiman's eclectic sources and varied working methods.

Greiman's knowledge of design and typography came from the masters, but, in true California style, her color theory was gained from a dream therapist. Her palette draws not only from the sun-drenched California landscape, but from other Pacific Rim countries such as Mexico and Japan. "The Mexican influence is in the whole color sense," she says. "I started using Day-Glo colors out here—now they're called classic southern California graphics colors. They're also associated with the 1950s—turquoise and peach, celadon and chartreuse.

"The Japanese influence is in a subtler range, some of the darker colors, the Japanese printers' ink books—the range when you get into the darker colors! There are, like, 75 of each of them. In our PMS books there's nothing."

The questioning of the Swiss tradition and this search for new colors a decade ago was the beginning of this New Wave that rejected the reductive motif, severe typography, white space, and rigid grids in favor of an inclusive approach that used a dense layering of ideas, images, and type at different scales and in a lurid new color palette. Today the New Wave is positively geriatric, yet still shows no sign of breaking. It is now widely imitated, both well and badly; it has spread far from the Pacific shores; and it represents the single most significant and identifiable occurrence in American graphic design since the European influence.

Another particularly Californian factor is its high-tech industry. This not only provides Greiman with many of her clients (about 40 per cent of her work is for computer corporations), but also now with new tools of her trade. "I'm easily bored," she says. "If I was going to stay in graphic design, I had to find more tools."

Macintosh terminals now litter Greiman's studio, looking incongruously businesslike amid the fluorescent furniture. Greiman also rents time—at $500 an hour—on a Quantel Paintbox. All this apparatus she sees as a logical armory in helping her execute her designs. The Mac is the day-to-day tool. "It's less expensive, it's easy to use, it can involve a lot of people, and it can bring together in one document things that would otherwise take a lot more effort."

Another area where the computer has proven advantageous is in layering and scaling the various images that go to make up a finished work. Colors, textures, grids, and different sizes and faces of type can be overlaid and interleaved almost endlessly in pursuit of the right effect. The manual chore thus avoided, the Mac then allows a designer to indulge in more experimentation and still get quicker results. "The computer's the ultimate tool for layering," affirms Greiman.

Her use of video grew from certain ideas that Greiman found recurring in her conventional work. "What I was doing looked like it had time in it—things with drop shadows, or something repeated, or made into a sequence even though it was still, or trying to create three-dimensional spaces on a two-dimensional surface. That led me into video."

Then there is the element of surprise a computer brings. "It opens up the idea of chance," says Greiman. "You hit the wrong button and all of a sudden you've got dots all over your logo. Accidents are usually the best things to happen to my work." The logo with superimposed dots is an exaggerated example, but such serendipities do often serve as the germs of new ideas.

Greiman uses computer technology not only to help generate ideas, but also to assist in transferring ideas from medium to medium. In the past, Greiman has licensed the use of video or computer-generated graphic designs for reproduction onto textiles by Japanese clients. Three-dimensional design also springs fully formed from the computer. A sculpture for a 1987 Venice exhibition of the work of California designers was conceived as a series of two-dimensional sketches on the Macintosh. The sketches were sent by facsimile transmission to Italy and the sculpture was constructed directly from them. The only thematic link between the sculpture and Greiman's graphic material for the same show—T-shirts and a poster—was the common technology by which they were created.

Greiman uses computer technology in two more or less separate ways: as a tool simply to give rapid but professional results, and in a consciously mannered fashion. "There are times when I'm really pushing for that computer look," she says. Such work offers an ironic commentary on the heavy-handed ugliness of most computer imagery. For a Los Angeles architecture magazine called *Main*, for example, Greiman designed a cover logo in a low-resolution Mac rendition of a serif typeface. She then enlarged the logo, but did not, as she sometimes does, "clean up" or smooth the result. "I wanted it to look desktop-published. The letters were very fuzzy, but I liked them. They looked like glyphs."

Taking computer hard-copy out of context in this way fascinates Greiman precisely because it produces these unexpected allusions—here coarse futuristic lettering evoking mysterious symbols from ancient cultures. It is a discovery that could greatly extend and enlarge the role of computers within the graphic design profession. Says Greiman: "On the one hand it's very sophisticated; on the other it's very primitive. These combinations bring out a very interesting emotional response. I don't know if we're going forward or back, if we're expanding or collapsing. I don't know which way we're going, but we're going *fast!*"

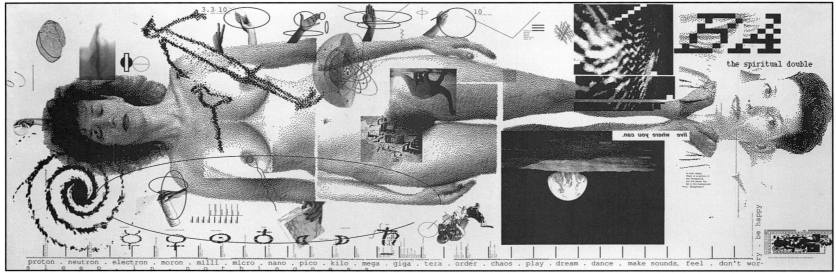

1

2

Design Quarterly issue designed by April Greiman (1,2,8 detail). Only Paul Rand, Armin Hoffman, and Wolfgang Weingart, the designer who has been a great influence in Greiman's work, have had full issues of this prestigious journal devoted to their work. Greiman was accorded the honor for her exemplary use of computer technology in graphic design.

Greiman created this sculpture (3) for the "Pacific Wave: California Graphic Design" exhibition in Venice by simply faxing elevation drawings created on a Macintosh along with dimensions and color instructions to Italy for on-site construction. A poster for the show (13) also used digitized imagery and different scales.

3

4

9

pearlsoft

5

6

8

Great Design Co

10

gyrosphere

11

MAIN

7

12

186

Logotypes (4–7, 9–12) based on a single central idea and variously using
clean sans serif or classic typefaces,
mixed type, and digital type reveal
Greiman's Swiss-inspired style.
Greiman's posters (13–18), on the other hand, show a more complex esthetic with type and imagery in multiple
layers yielding graphics that contain
an overload of written and visual
data.

13

14

15

16

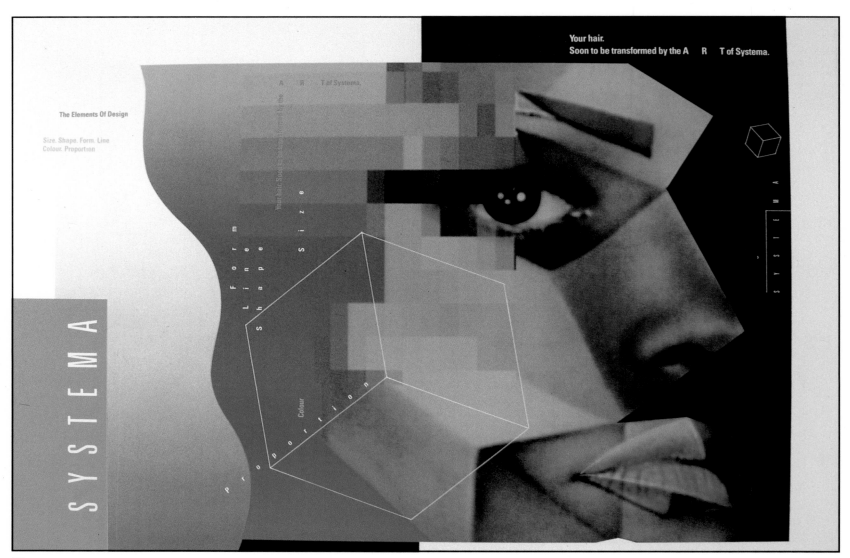

The Elements Of Design

Size. Shape. Form. Line
Colour. Proportion

S Y S T E M A

17

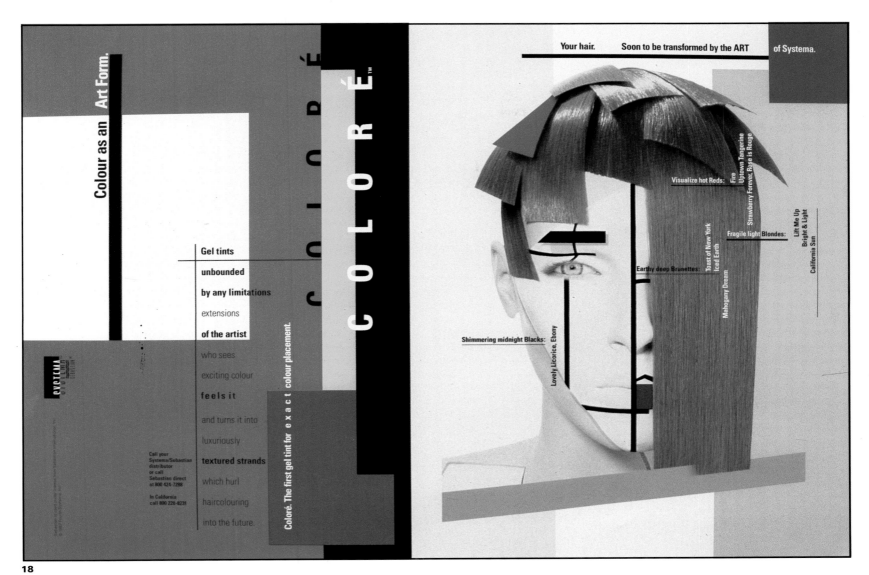

Colour as an Art Form.

COLORÉ

COLORÉ™

Coloré. The first gel tint for e x a c t colour placement.

Gel tints

unbounded

by any limitations

extensions

of the artist

who sees

exciting colour

feels it

and turns it into

luxuriously

textured strands

which hurl

haircolouring

into the future.

Call your
Systema/Sebastian
distributor
or call
Sebastian direct
at 800 424-7288

In California
call 800 226-8231

Your hair.   Soon to be transformed by the ART   of Systema.

Visualize hot Reds: Fire
Uptown Tangerine
Strawberry Forever, Rose is Rouge

Fragile light Blondes: Lift Me Up
Bright & Light
California Sun

Earthy deep Brunettes: Toast of New York
Iced Earth
Mahogany Dream

Shimmering midnight Blacks: Lovely Licorice, Ebony